Microsoft® Office Word® 2016 Manual

to accompany

Gregg College Keyboarding & Document Processing

11e

Scot Ober

Jack E. Johnson

Arlene Zimmerly

Mc Graw Hill Education

Microsoft Office Word 2016 Manual to accompany
GREGG COLLEGE KEYBOARDING & DOCUMENT PROCESSING, ELEVENTH EDITION
Scot Ober, Jack E. Johnson, and Arlene Zimmerly

This book is printed on acid-free paper.

1 2 3 4 5 6 7 8 9 0 DOC 21 20 19 18 17 16

ISBN 978-1-259-90793-7
MHID 1-259-90793-7

All screenshots are from Microsoft Office Word 2016.

Photo credits for design elements: Pixabay.com and © McGraw-Hill Education.

Cover credit: © *Robert Adrian Hillman/Shutterstock*

mheducation.com/highered

Contents

Reference Manual

COMPUTER SYSTEM

CORRESPONDENCE

EMPLOYMENT DOCUMENTS

FORMS

LANGUAGE ARTS

PROOFREADERS' MARKS

REPORTS

TABLES

U.S. POSTAL SERVICE STATE ABBREVIATIONS

Reference Manual

A. MAJOR PARTS OF A COMPUTER SYSTEM

© Tetra Images/Alamy RF

B. THE COMPUTER KEYBOARD

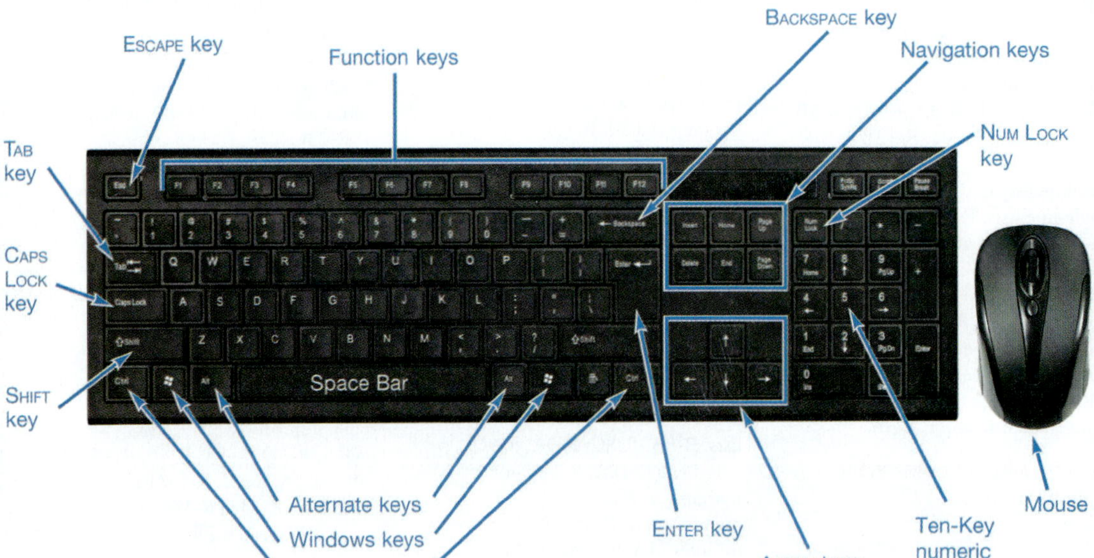

© Eastphoto/inmagine.com

A. BUSINESS LETTER IN BLOCK STYLE

(with standard punctuation and indented display)

↓5X

Date line September 5, 20-- ↓4X

Inside address Ms. Joan R. Hunter
Bolwater Associates
One Parklands Drive
Darien, CT 06820 ↓2X

Salutation Dear Ms. Hunter: ↓2X *Standard punctuation*

Body You will soon receive the signed contract to have your organization conduct a one-day workshop for our employees on eliminating repetitive-motion injuries in the workplace. As we agreed, this workshop will apply to both our office and factory workers and you will conduct separate sessions for each group. ↓2X

We revised Paragraph 4-b shown below to require the instructor of this workshop to be a full-time employee of Bolwater Associates: ↓2X

→indent 0.5″ Paragraph 4-b of the Bolwater Associates agreement is hereby amended as follows: The instructor of the one-day workshop on eliminating repetitive-motion injuries at the workplace must be a full-time employee of Bolwater Associates. ↓2X ←indent 0.5″ *Indented display*

If this revision is satisfactory, please sign and return one copy of the contract for our files. We look forward to this opportunity to enhance the health of our employees. I know that all of us will enjoy this workshop. ↓2X

Complimentary closing Sincerely, ↓4X *Standard punctuation*

Signature *Jeffrey Olszewski*

Writer's identification Jeffrey Olszewski
Vice President for Operations ↓2X

Reference initials jc

B. BUSINESS LETTER IN MODIFIED-BLOCK STYLE

(with multiline list and enclosure notation)

left tab: 3.25″ (centerpoint)

↓5X

→ tab 3.25″ (centerpoint) May 15, 20-- ↓4X

Mr. Ichiro Xie
Bolwater Associates
One Parklands Drive
Darien, CT 06820 ↓2X

Dear Mr. Xie: ↓2X

I am returning a signed contract to have your organization conduct a one-day workshop for our employees on eliminating repetitive-motion injuries in the workplace. We have made the following changes to the contract: ↓2X

Multiline list

1. We revised Paragraph 4-b to require the instructor of this workshop to be a full-time employee of Bolwater Associates.
2. We made changes to Paragraph 10-c to require our prior approval of the agenda for the workshop. ↓2X

If these revisions are satisfactory, please sign and return one copy of the contract for our files. We look forward to this opportunity to enhance the health of our employees. I know that all of us will enjoy this workshop. ↓2X

→ tab 3.25″ (centerpoint) Sincerely, ↓4X

Jeffrey Olszewski

Jeffrey Olszewski
Vice President for Operations ↓2X

pec

Enclosure notation Enclosure

C. BUSINESS LETTER IN SIMPLIFIED STYLE

(with subject line, single-line list; enclosure, delivery, and copy notations)

↓5X

October 5, 20-- ↓4X

Mr. Dale P. Griffin
Bolwater Associates
One Parklands Drive
Darien, CT 06820 ↓3X

Subject line WORKSHOP CONTRACT ↓3X

I am returning the signed contract, Mr. Griffin, to have your organization conduct a one-day workshop for our employees on eliminating repetitive-motion injuries in the workplace. We have amended the following sections of the contract: ↓2X

Single-line list

- Paragraph 4-b
- Table 3
- Attachment 2 ↓2X

If these revisions are satisfactory, please sign and return one copy of the contract for our files. We look forward to this opportunity to enhance the health of our employees. I know that all of us will enjoy this workshop. ↓4X

Rogena Kyles

ROGENA KYLES, DIRECTOR ↓2X

iww

Enclosure notation Enclosure
Delivery notation By e-mail
Copy notation c: Legal Department

D. PERSONAL-BUSINESS LETTER IN MODIFIED-BLOCK STYLE

(with international address and return address)

left tab: 3.25″ (centerpoint)

↓5X

→ tab 3.25″ (centerpoint) July 15, 20-- ↓4X

Mr. Luis Fernandez
Vice President
Arvon Industries, Inc.
21 St. Claire Avenue East
International address Toronto, ON M4T IL9
CANADA ↓2X

Dear Mr. Fernandez: ↓2X

As a former employee and present stockholder of Arvon Industries, I wish to protest the planned sale of the Consumer Products Division. ↓2X

According to published reports, consumer products accounted for 19 percent of last year's corporate profits, and they are expected to account for even more this year. In addition, Dun & Bradstreet predicts that consumer products nationwide will outpace the general economy for the next five years.

I am concerned about the effect that this planned sale might have on overall corporate profits, on our cash dividends for investors, and on the economy of Melbourne, where the two consumer-products plants are located. Please ask your board of directors to reconsider this matter. ↓2X

→ tab 3.25″ (centerpoint) Sincerely, ↓4X

Jeanine Ford

Jeanine Ford
Return address 901 East Benson, Apt. 3
Fort Lauderdale, FL 33301
U.S.A.

A. BUSINESS LETTER ON EXECUTIVE STATIONERY

(7.25" x 10.5"; 1" side margins; with delivery notation)

↓5X
July 18, 20-- ↓4X

Mr. Rodney Eastwood
BBL Resources
523 Northern Ridge
Fayetteville, PA 17222 ↓2X

Dear Rodney: ↓2X

I see no reason why we should continue to consider the locality around Geraldton for our new plant. Even though the desirability of this site from an economic view is undeniable, there is not sufficient housing readily available for our workers. ↓2X

In trying to control urban growth, the city has been turning down the building permits for much new housing or placing so many restrictions on foreign investment as to make it too expensive.

Please continue to seek out other areas of exploration where we might form a joint partnership. ↓2X

Sincerely, ↓4X

Jennifer Gwatkin

Jennifer Gwatkin, Director ↓2X

mme
Delivery notation By fax

B. BUSINESS LETTER ON HALF-PAGE STATIONERY

(5.5" x 8.5"; 0.75" side margins)

↓4 X
July 18, 20-- ↓4X

Mr. Aristeo Olivas
BBL Resources
52A Northern Ridge
Fayetteville, PA 17222 ↓2X

Dear Aristeo: ↓2X

We should discontinue considering Geraldton for our new plant. Housing is not readily available.

Please seek out other areas of exploration where we might someday form a joint partnership. ↓2X

Sincerely, ↓4X

Chimere Jones

Chimere Jones, Director ↓2X

adk

C. BUSINESS LETTER FORMATTED FOR A WINDOW ENVELOPE

(with open punctuation)

↓5X
July 18, 20-- ↓3X

Ms. Reinalda Guerrero
BBL Resources
52A Northern Ridge
Fayetteville, PA 17222 ↓3X

Dear Ms. Guerrero ↓2X **Open punctuation**

I see no reason why we should even continue to consider the locality around Geraldton for our new plant. Even though the desirability of this site from an economic view is undeniable, there is insufficient housing readily available for our workers. ↓2X

In trying to control urban growth, the city has been turning down the building permits for new housing or placing so many restrictions on foreign investment as to make it too expensive.

Please continue to seek out other areas of exploration where we might form a joint partnership. ↓2X

Sincerely ↓4X **Open punctuation**

Augustus Mays

Augustus Mays
Vice President for Operations ↓2X

woc

D. MEMO

(with ruled table, left- and right-aligned columns, and attachment notation)

↓5X →tab
MEMO TO: Nancy Price, Executive Vice President ↓2X

FROM: Arlyn J. Bunch, Operations *ajb*

DATE: July 18, 20--

SUBJECT: New Plant Site ↓2X

As you can see from the attached letter, I've informed BBL Resources that I see no reason why we should continue to consider the locality around Geraldton for our new plant. Even though the desirability of this site from an economic standpoint is undeniable, there is insufficient housing available. In fact, as of June 25, the number of appropriate single-family houses listed for sale within a 25-mile radius of Geraldton was as follows: ↓2X

Ruled table

Agent	Units
Belle Real Estate	123
Castleton Homes	11
Red Carpet	9
Geraldton Homes	5

↓1X
In addition, in trying to control urban growth, Geraldton has been either turning down building permits for new housing or placing excessive restrictions on them. Because of this deficiency of housing for our employees, we have no choice but to look elsewhere. ↓2X

woc
Attachment notation Attachment

A. MULTIPAGE BUSINESS LETTER

(page 1; with on-arrival notation, international address, subject line, and boxed table)

↓5X

May 13, 20-- ↓2X

On-arrival notation CONFIDENTIAL ↓2X

Mr. Lester Thompson
Associate Director
British Mutual Broadcasting
24 Portland Place
International address London WIN 4BB
ENGLAND ↓2X

Dear Mr. Thompson: ↓2X

Subject line Subject: International Study Tour ↓2X

I have been invited by the Federal Communications Commission to participate in a study of television news programming in six European countries. The enclosed report explains the purpose of the study in detail. ↓2X

I have been assigned to lead a study group through six European countries to gather firsthand information on this topic. In addition to me, our group will consist of the following members: ↓2X

Boxed table

14 pt **INTERNATIONAL STUDY TOUR GROUP** ↓1X

12 pt↓

Name	Organization	Location
Mrs. Katherine Grant	WPQR-TV	Los Angeles, CA
Dr. Manuél Cruz	Miami Herald	Miami, FL
Mr. Richard Logan	Cable News Network	Atlanta, GA
Ms. Barbara Brooks	Associated Press	Chicago, IL

↓1X

Our initial plans are for the team to spend at least one full day in each of these countries. That, of course, could change. Many different events have been planned. I will be organizing and facilitating meeting with the news programming

B. MULTIPAGE BUSINESS LETTER

(page 2; with page number; multiline list; company name; and enclosure, delivery, copy, postscript, and blind copy notations)

2 *Page number*

staff of one or two of the major networks, touring their facilities, viewing recent broadcasts, and, in general, getting a firsthand view of actual news operations.

Our tentative itinerary calls for a departure date of Monday, July 26. Our arrival city is London. We will spend at least two days there to be sure that all meeting participants have arrived safely.

We should arrive at Heathrow Airport at 7:10 a.m. on Tuesday, July 27. We will immediately go to our hotel and begin our tours the next morning. Would it be possible for us to do the following: ↓2X

Multiline list

1. Meet with various members of your staff sometime on July 28. We would be available from 8:30 a.m. until 1:30 p.m.
2. Receive a copy of your programming log for the week of July 26-30 and especially a minute-by-minute listing of the programming segments for your national news reporting. ↓2X

I would appreciate your contacting Barbara Jones, our liaison, at 202.555.3943 to let us know whether we may study your operations on July 28. ↓2X

Sincerely, ↓2X

Company name METRO BROADCASTING COMPANY ↓4X

Denise J. Watterson

Denise J. Watterson
General Manager ↓2X

rcp
Enclosure notation Enclosures: FCC Report, Biographical Sketches
Delivery notation By FedEx
Copy notation c: Barbara Jones, Manuél Cruz ↓2X

Postscript PS: The Federal Communications Commission will reimburse your organization for any expenses associated with our visit. ↓2X

Blind copy notation bc: Public Relations Office, FCC

C. E-MAIL MESSAGE IN MICROSOFT OUTLOOK

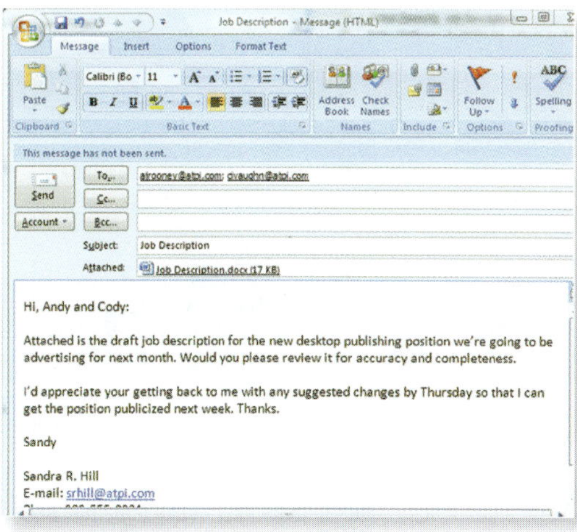

D. E-MAIL MESSAGE IN MSN HOTMAIL

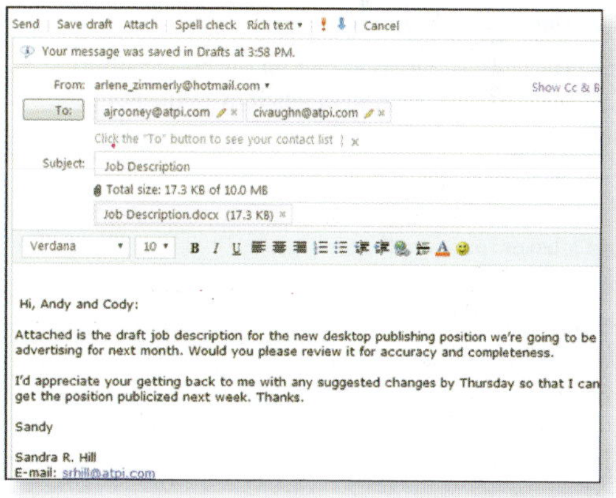

A. FORMATTING ENVELOPES

A standard large (No. 10) envelope is 9.5 by 4.125". A standard small (No. 6¾) envelope is 6.5 by 3.625".

A window envelope requires no formatting because the letter is formatted and folded so that the inside address is visible through the window.

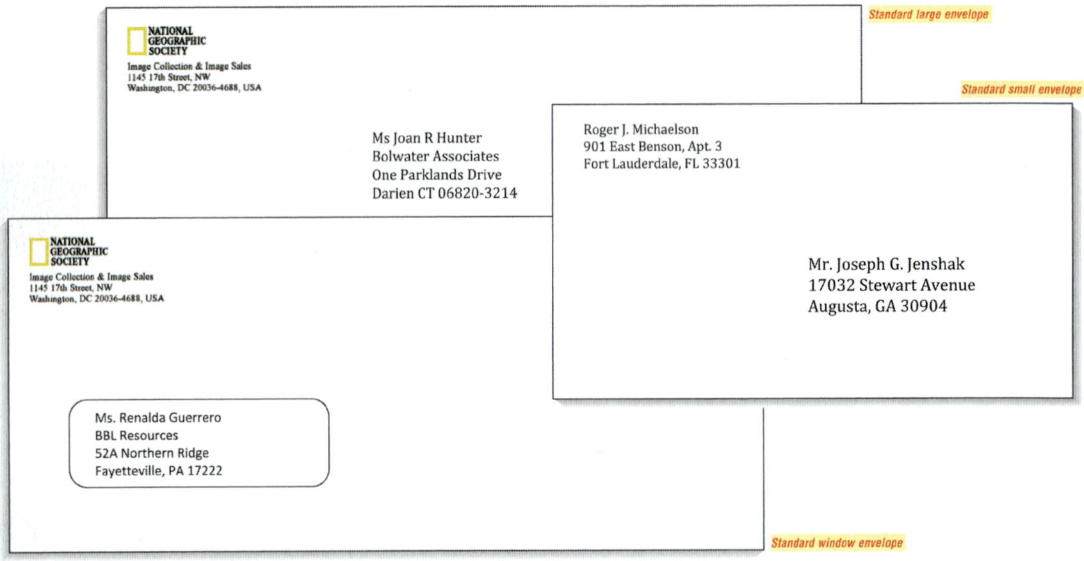

B. FOLDING LETTERS

To fold a letter for a large envelope:

1. Place the letter *face up,* and fold up the bottom third.
2. Fold the top third down to 0.5 inch from the bottom edge.
3. Insert the last crease into the envelope first, with the flap facing up.

To fold a letter for a small envelope:

1. Place the letter *face up,* and fold up the bottom half to 0.5 inch from the top.
2. Fold the right third over to the left.
3. Fold the left third over to 0.5 inch from the right edge.
4. Insert the last crease into the envelope first, with the flap facing up.

To fold a letter for a window envelope:

1. Place the letter *face down* with the letterhead at the top, and fold the bottom third of the letter up.
2. Fold the top third down so that the address shows.
3. Insert the letter into the envelope so that the address shows through the window.

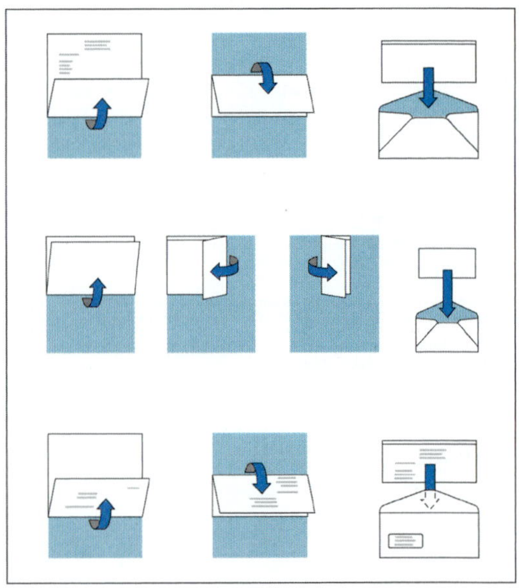

A. OUTLINE

(with 2-line title)

right tab: 0.3"
left tabs: 0.4", 0.7"

↓5X

2-line title 14 pt **AN ANALYSIS OF THE SCOPE AND EFFECTIVENESS OF ONLINE ADVERTISING** ↓2X

12 pt ↓ **The Status of Point-and-Click Selling** ↓2X

Jonathan R. Evans ↓

January 19, 20-- ↓2X

I. INTRODUCTION ↓2X

II. SCOPE AND TRENDS IN INTERNET ADVERTISING
   A. Internet Advertising
   B. Major Online Advertisers
   C. Positioning and Pricing
   D. Types of Advertising ↓2X

III. ADVERTISING EFFECTIVENESS
   A. The Banner Debate
   B. Increasing Advertising Effectiveness
   C. Measuring ROI

IV. CONCLUSION

→ tab 0.3"
→ tab 0.4"
→ tab 0.7"

B. TITLE PAGE

(with 2-line title)

center page ↓

2-line title 14 pt **AN ANALYSIS OF THE SCOPE AND EFFECTIVENESS OF ONLINE ADVERTISING** ↓2X

12 pt ↓ **The Status of Point-and-Click Selling** ↓12X

Submitted to ↓2X

Luis Torres
General Manager
ViaWorld, International ↓12X

Prepared by ↓2X

Jonathan R. Evans
Assistant Marketing Manager
ViaWorld, International ↓2X

January 19, 20--

C. TRANSMITTAL MEMO

(with 2-line subject line and attachment notation)

↓5X →tab

MEMO TO: Luis Torres, General Manager ↓2X

FROM: Jonathan R. Evans, Assistant Marketing Manager *jre*

DATE: January 19, 20--

2-line subject line **SUBJECT:** An Analysis of the Scope and Effectiveness of Current Online ↓1X
→tab Advertising in Today's Marketplace ↓2X

Here is the final report analyzing the scope and effectiveness of Internet advertising that you requested on January 5. ↓2X

The report predicts that the total value of the business-to-business e-commerce market will continue to increase by geometric proportions. New technologies aimed at increasing Internet ad interactivity and the adoption of standards for advertising response measurement and tracking will contribute to this increase. Unfortunately, as discussed in this report, the use of "rich media" and interactivity in Web advertising will create its own set of problems.

I enjoyed working on this assignment, Luis, and learned quite a bit from my analysis of the situation. Please let me know if you have any questions about the report. ↓2X

plw
Attachment notation Attachment

D. TABLE OF CONTENTS

left tab: 0.5"
right dot-leader tab: 6.5"

↓5X

14 pt **CONTENTS** ↓2X

A. MULTIPAGE BUSINESS REPORT

(page 1; with side and paragraph headings, multiline list, footnote references, and footnotes)

↓5X

2-line title — 14 pt **AN ANALYSIS OF THE SCOPE AND EFFECTIVENESS OF ONLINE ADVERTISING** ↓2X

Subtitle — 12 pt ↓ **The Status of Point-and-Click Selling** ↓2X

Byline — **Jonathan R. Evans** ↓2X

Date — **January 19, 20--** ↓2X

Online advertising uses the Internet for the sole purpose of delivering marketing messages to customers. Some examples of online advertising are ads on search engine results pages, banner ads, interactive media ads, and online classified advertising. One major benefit of online advertising is the immediate publishing of content that is not limited by geography or time. Interactive advertising presents fresh challenges for advertisers.[1] ↓2X Footnote reference

Side heading — **GROWTH FACTORS** ↓2X

Online business has grown in tandem with the expanding number of Internet users. That trend will only increase as time goes on. ↓2X

Paragraph heading — **Uncertainty.** The uncertainties surrounding advertising on the Internet remain one of the major impediments to the expansion. ↓2X

Reasons for Not Advertising Online. A recent survey found two main reasons cited for not advertising online:[2] ↓2X

Multiline list

1. The difficulty of determining return on investment, especially in terms of repeat business and first-time shoppers.
2. The lack of reliable tracking and measurement data.

Footnotes

[1] Shannon Newsome, "Effective Online Advertising," *E-Mail Marketing Daily*, August 12, 2010, p. R6.

[2] "eWebStats: Online Trends in the United States," *eWebStats Home page*, August 11, 2010, <http://www.ewebstats.com/trends/ad>, accessed on September 7, 2010.

B. MULTIPAGE BUSINESS REPORT

(last page; with page number, indented display, side heading, boxed table with table number and note, and footnote)

3 Page number

who argue that banners have a strong potential for advertising effectiveness point out that it is not the banner format itself that presents a problem to advertising effectiveness, but rather the quality of the banner and the attention to its placement. According to Steven Mocha, president of Web Ads International: ↓2X

Indented display — →indent 0.5" A banner ad notifies visitors of the product or service and presents reasons why the consumer should choose the product in question. If the reasons are not compelling, then the banner ad has failed to achieve its purpose. If the banner ad is unattractive and obtrusive, it will alienate the consumer. When written and designed well, the banner ad is extremely effective in garnering business.[4] ←indent 0.5" ↓2X

Thus, while some analysts continue to argue that the banner advertisement is passé, there is little evidence of its abandonment. Instead, ad agencies are focusing on increasing the banner's effectiveness. ↓2X

SCOPE AND TRENDS IN ONLINE ADVERTISING ↓2X

Starting from zero in 1994, analysts agree that the volume of Internet advertising spending has risen rapidly. However, as indicated in Table 3, analysts provide a wide range of the exact amount of such advertising. ↓2X

Table number title — 14 pt **Table 3. INTERNET ADVERTISING**

12 pt ↓ **Current Year Estimates** ↓1X

Source	Estimate
Internet Advertising Conference	$3.92 billion
Forecaster	3.30 billion
IPC International	3.20 billion
Brown Media	980 million
Note: This information is subject to change.	

Table note ↓1X

The differences in estimates of total Web advertising spending is generally attributed to the different methodologies used by the research agencies to gather the data. Further research is pending and will be reported next month.

[4] Steven Mocha, "Banner Ads That Really Work," *The Online Advertising Journal*, June 17, 2010, p. D1.

C. MULTIPAGE ACADEMIC REPORT

(page 1; with 2-line title, endnote references, and multiline list)

↓5SS

2-line title — 14 pt **AN ANALYSIS OF THE SCOPE AND EFFECTIVENESS** ↓1DS

OF ONLINE ADVERTISING ↓1DS

12 pt ↓ **The Status of Point-and-Click Selling** ↓1DS

Jonathan R. Evans ↓1DS

January 19, 20-- ↓1DS

→tab One major benefit of online advertising is the immediate publishing of content that is not limited by geography or time.[i] ↓1DS

GROWTH FACTORS ↓1DS

Online business has grown in tandem with the expanding number of Internet users, which is growing exponentially each year.[i] ↓1DS Endnote reference

Reasons for Not Advertising Online. A recent survey conducted by TAIR found two main reasons cited for not advertising online:[ii]

Multiline list

1. The difficulty of determining return on investment, especially in terms of repeat business and first-time shoppers.
2. The lack of reliable tracking and measurement data.

Obviously, there are many other reasons in addition to these two for not advertising online. However, with the growing number of Internet users, these

D. MULTIPAGE ACADEMIC REPORT

(last page; with page number, indented display, and endnotes)

14 Page number

advertising effectiveness, but rather the quality of the banner and the attention to the banner placement. According to Mike Windsor, president of Ogilvy Interactive: ↓1DS

Indented display — →indent 0.5" It's more a case of bad banner ads, just like there are bad TV ads. The space itself has huge potential. As important as using the space within the banner creatively is to aim it effectively. Unlike broadcast media, the Web offers advertisers the opportunity to reach a specific audience based on data gathered about who is surfing at a site and what their interests are.[vii] ←indent 0.5" ↓2SS

→tab From an advertiser's perspective, most effective Internet ads do more than just deliver information to the consumer and grab the consumer's attention—they also gather information about consumers (e.g., through "cookies" and other methodologies). From the consumer's perspective, this type of interactivity may represent an intrusion and an invasion of privacy.

Endnotes

[i] Shannon Newsome, "Effective Online Advertising," *E-Mail Marketing Daily*, July 12, 2010, p. R6.

[ii] "eWebStats: Online Trends in the United States," *eWebStats*, August 11, 2010, <http://www.ewebstats.com/trends/ad>, accessed on September 7, 2010.

[iii] Barbara Fisher, "Net Ratings Index Predicts Rise in Web Ads," *Advertising Today*, July 19, 2010, p. 10.

[iv] Ron Heisman, "Internet Banner Ads Growth Trends," *Internet Associates Conference* November 13, 2010, <http://www.iac.net/conference>, accessed on December 8, 2010.

[v] Alexis Dirkson, "Point-and-Click Bargains for Internet Ad Surfers," *Internet Age*, March 8, 2010, p. 12.

[vi] Andrew Romero, "Gathering Statistics to Grow Your Internet Business," *The Wall Street Journal*, March 2, 2010, p. C20.

[vii] Lisa Gunderson, "Banner Banter" *The London Financial Times*, June 17, 2010, p. D1.

A. LEFT-BOUND BUSINESS REPORT

(page 1; with 2-line title, single-line list, and footnotes)

left margin: 1.5″
right margin: *default* 1″

↓5X

2-line title 14 pt **AN ANALYSIS OF THE SCOPE AND EFFECTIVENESS OF ONLINE ADVERTISING** ↓2X

12 pt ↓ **The Status of Point-and-Click Selling** ↓2X

Jonathan R. Evans ↓2X

January 19, 20-- ↓2X

Online advertising uses the Internet for the sole purpose of delivering marketing messages to customers. Some examples of online advertising are as follows: ads on search engine results pages, banner ads, interactive media ads, and e-mail marketing. One major benefit of online advertising is the immediate publishing of content that is not limited by geography or time. Interactive advertising presents new challenges for advertisers.[1] ↓2X

GROWTH FACTORS ↓2X

Online business has grown in tandem with the expanding number of Internet users. That trend will only increase as time goes on. ↓2X

Uncertainty. The uncertainties surrounding advertising on the Internet remain one of the major impediments to the expansion. All of the Internet advertising industry is today in a state of flux. ↓2X

Reasons for Not Advertising Online. A recent survey found two main reasons cited for not advertising online:[2] ↓2X

Single-line list

1. The difficulty of determining return on investment.
2. The lack of reliable tracking and measurement data.

Footnotes

[1] Shannon Newsome, "Effective Online Advertising," *E-Mail Marketing Daily*, July 12, 2010, p. R6.

[2] "eWebStats: Online Trends in the United States," *eWebStats*, August11, 2010, <http://www.ewebstats.com/trends/ad>, accessed on September 7, 2010.

B. BIBLIOGRAPHY

(for business or academic style using either endnotes or footnotes)

hanging indent ↓ ↓5X

12 pt ↓ 14 pt **BIBLIOGRAPHY** ↓2X

Book—one author: Adams, Ana B., *Internet Advertising*, Brunswick Press, Boston, 2009. ↓2X

Annual report: AdNet Incorporated, *2010 Annual Report*, BCI, Inc., San Francisco, 2010.

Newspaper article: An, Sang Jin, "Banner Ad Frenzy," *The Wall Street Journal*, July 12, 2010, p. R6.

Book—two authors: Arlens, Rachel, and Seymour Schell, *E-Vertising*, New England Publishing, → hanging indent Cambridge, Mass., 2009.

Book—organization as author: *Directory of Internet Business Services*, International Corporate Libraries Assoc., New York, 2009.

WWW page: "eWebStats: Online Trends in the United States," *eWebStats*, August 11, 2010, <http://www.ewebstats.com/trends/ad>, accessed on September 7, 2010.

Journal article—paged continuously: Ingram, Fred, "Hiring Trends in Online Advertising," *Personnel Quarterly*, Vol. 30, September 2009, pp. 104-116.

Journal article—paged each issue: Johnson, Jennifer, "WebRatings Index Shows 8% Rise in Web Ads," *Advertising Today*, July 19, 2010, p. 18.

Online database: "Motivational Advertising Techniques," *Advertising Encyclopedia*, N.D., <http://www.adtech.com/motivational_advertising_techniques.html>, accessed on January 7, 2010.

Government document: National Institute of Psychology, *Who Clicks? An Analysis of Internet Advertising*, TNIP Publication No. ADM 82-1195, U.S. Government Printing Office, Washington, 2009.

E-mail: Williams, Dennis V., "Reaction to Analysis of Internet Ads," e-mail message, August 18, 2010.

C. MEMO REPORT

(page 1, with 2-line subject line, endnote references, and single-line list)

↓5X →tab

MEMO TO: Luis Torres, General Manager ↓2X

FROM: Jonathan R. Evans, Assistant Marketing Manager *jre*

DATE: January 19, 20--

2-line subject line **SUBJECT:** An Analysis of the Scope and Effectiveness of Current Online ↓1X
→tab Advertising in Today's Marketplace ↓2X

Online advertising uses the Internet and World Wide Web for the sole purpose of delivering marketing messages to customers. Some examples of online advertising are ads on search engine results pages, banner ads, interactive media ads, social network site advertising, online classified advertising, advertising networks, and e-mail marketing, including e-mail spam. ↓2X

One major benefit of online advertising is the immediate publishing of information and content that is not limited by geography or time. To that end, the emerging area of interactive advertising presents fresh challenges for advertisers.[i] (Endnote reference) Such challenges are opportunities for growth. ↓2X

GROWTH FACTORS ↓2X

Online business has grown in tandem with the expanding number of Internet users. That trend will only increase as time goes on. ↓2X

Uncertainty. The uncertainties surrounding advertising on the Internet remain one of the major impediments to the expansion. All of the Internet advertising industry is today in a state of flux.

Reasons for Not Advertising Online. A recent survey found two main reasons cited for not advertising online:[ii] ↓2X

Single-line list

1. The difficulty of determining return on investment.
2. The lack of reliable tracking and measurement data.

D. FORMATTING REPORTS

Margins, Spacing, and Indents. Begin the first page of each section (for example, the table of contents, first page of the body, and bibliography pages) 2 inches from the top of the page. Begin other pages 1 inch from the top. Use 1-inch default side and bottom margins for all pages. For a left-bound report, add 0.5 inch to the left margin. Single-space business reports. Double-space academic reports and indent paragraphs.

Titles and Headings. Center the title in 14-pt. font. Single-space multiline titles in a single-spaced report, and double-space multiline titles in a double-spaced report. Insert 1 blank line before and after all parts of a heading block (may include the title, subtitle, author, and/or date), and format all lines in bold. Format side headings in bold, at the left margin, with 1 blank line before and after them. Format paragraph headings at the left margin for single-spaced reports and indented for double-spaced reports in bold, followed by a period in bold and one space.

Citations. Format citations using Word's footnote (or endnote) feature.

Margins, Spacing, Headings, and Citations for APA- or MLA-Style Reports. See page R-10.

A. REPORT IN APA STYLE

(page 3; with header, 2-line title, byline, main heading, subheading, and citations)

top, bottom, and side margins: *default* (1")
double-space throughout

Online Advertising 3 **Header**

2-line title An Analysis of the Scope and Effectiveness

of Online Advertising

Byline Jonathan R. Evans

→ tab Online advertising uses the Internet for the sole purpose of delivering marketing messages to customers. Some examples of online advertising are ads on search engine results pages, banner ads, interactive media ads, online classifieds, advertising networks, and e-mail marketing (Gunderson, 2011, p. D1). **Citation**

One major benefit of online advertising is the immediate publishing of content that is not limited by geography or time. To end that, interactive advertising presents fresh challenges for advertisers (Newsome, 2010).

Main heading Growth Factors

Online business has grown in tandem with the expanding number of Internet users. That trend will only increase as time goes on (Arlens & Schell).

Subheading *Uncertainty* ← Italic

The uncertainties surrounding Internet advertising are impeding its expansion. A recent survey found two main reasons cited for not advertising online. The first is the difficulty of determining return on investment, especially in terms of repeat business and first-time shoppers. The second is the lack of reliable tracking and measurement data ("eWebStats," 2010).

B. REFERENCES IN APA STYLE

(page 14; with header)

top, bottom, and side margins: *default* (1")
double-space throughout

Online Advertising 14 **Header**

hanging indent ↓ References

Book—one author Adams, A. B. (2009). *Internet advertising and the upcoming electronic upheaval.*
→ hanging indent Boston: Brunswick Press.

Annual report AdNet Incoporated. (2010). *2010 annual report.* San Francisco: BCI, Inc.

Newspaper article An, S. J. (2010, July 12). Banner ad frenzy. *The Wall Street Journal,* p. R6.

Book—two authors Arlens, R., & Seymour, S. (2010). *E-vertising.* Cambridge, MA: New England Publishing.

Book—organization as author *Directory of business and financial services.* (2009). New York: International Corporate Libraries Association.

WWW page eWebStats: Advertising revenues and trends. (n.d.). New York: eMarketer. Retrieved August 11, 2010, from http://www.emarketer.com/ewebstats/2507manu.ad

Journal article—paged continuously Ingram, F. (2009). Trends in online advertising. *Personnel Quarterly, 20,* 804-816.

Journal article—paged each issue Johnson, J. (2010, July 19). WebRatings Index shows 4% rise in Web ads. *Advertising Today, 39,* 18.

Online database *Motivational advertising techniques.* (2010, January). *Advertising Encyclopedia.* Retrieved January 7, 2010, from http://www.adtech.com/ads.html

Government document National Institute of Psychology (2009). *Who clicks? An analysis of Internet advertising* (TNIP Publication No. ADM 82-1195). Washington, DC.

C. REPORT IN MLA STYLE

(page 1; with header, heading, 2-line title, and citations)

top, bottom, and side margins: *default* (1")
double-space throughout

Evans 1 **Header**

Heading Jonathan R. Evans

Professor Inman

Management 302

19 January 20--

2-line title An Analysis of the Scope and Effectiveness

of Online Advertising

→ tab Online advertising uses the Internet for the sole purpose of delivering marketing messages to customers. Some examples of online advertising are ads on search engine results pages, banner ads, interactive media ads, social network site advertising, online classifieds, and e-mail marketing (Gunderson D1). **Citation**

One major benefit of online advertising is the immediate publishing of information and content that is not limited by geography or time. To that end, interactive advertising presents fresh challenges for advertisers (Newsome 59).

Online business has grown in tandem with the expanding number of Internet users. That trend will only increase as time goes on (Arlens & Schell 376-379). The uncertainties surrounding Internet advertising remain one of the major impediments to the expansion. A recent survey found two main reasons cited for not advertising online. The first is the difficulty of determining return on investment. The second is the lack of reliable tracking and measurement data.

D. WORKS CITED IN MLA STYLE

(page 14; with header and hanging indent)

top, bottom, and side margins: *default* (1")
double-space throughout

Evans 14 **Header**

hanging indent ↓ Works Cited

Book—one author Adams, Ana. B. *Internet Advertising and the Upcoming Electronic Upheaval.*
→ hanging indent Boston: Brunswick Press, 2009.

Annual report AdNet Incoporated. *2010 Annual Report.* San Francisco: BCI, Inc., 2010.

Newspaper article An, Sang Jin. "Banner Ad Frenzy." *The Wall Street Journal,* 12 July 2010: R6.

Book—two authors Arlens, Rachel, and Seymour Schell. *E-vertising.* Cambridge, MA: New England Publishing, 2009.

Book—organization as author Corporate Libraries Association. *Directory of Business and Financial Services.* New York: Corporate Libraries Association, 2009.

WWW page "eWebStats: Advertising Revenues and Trends." 11 Aug. 2009. 7 Jan. 2010 <http://www.emarketer.com/ewebstats/ad>.

Journal article—paged continuously Ingram, Frank. "Trends in Online Advertising." *Personnel Quarterly* 20 (2010): 804-816.

Journal article—paged each issue Johnson, June. "WRI shows 4% rise in Web ads." *WebAds Today* 19 July 2010: 18.

Online database *Motivational Advertising Techniques.* 2010. Advertising Encyclopedia. 7 Jan. 2010 <http://www.adtech.com/ads.html>.

Government document National Institute of Psychology. *Who clicks?* TNIP Publication No. ADM 82-1195. Washington, DC. GPO: 2010.

E-mail Williams, Dan V. "Reaction to Internet Ads." E-mail to the author. 18 Aug. 2010.

Reference Manual

A. MEETING AGENDA

↓5X

14 pt **MILES HARDWARE EXECUTIVE COMMITTEE** ↓2X

12 pt ↓ **Meeting Agenda** ↓2X

June 7, 20-- ↓2X

Numbered list: default format

1. Call to order
2. Approval of minutes of May 5 meeting
3. Progress report on building addition and parking lot restrictions (Norman Hodges and Anthony Pascarelli)
4. May 15 draft of Five-Year Plan
5. Review of National Hardware Association annual convention
6. Employee grievance filed by Ellen Burrows (John Landstrom)
7. New expense-report forms (Anne Richards)
8. Announcements
9. Adjournment

B. MINUTES OF A MEETING

↓5X

14 pt **RESOURCE COMMITTEE** ↓2X

12 pt ↓ **Minutes of the Meeting** ↓2X

March 13, 20-- ↓1X

ATTENDANCE	The Resource Committee met on March 13, 20--, at the Airport Sheraton in Portland, Oregon, with all members present. Michael Davis, chairperson, called the meeting to order at 2:30 p.m. ↓1X
APPROVAL OF MINUTES	The minutes of the January 27 meeting were read and approved as presented.
OLD BUSINESS	The members of the committee reviewed the sales brochure on electronic copyboards and agreed to purchase one for the conference room. Cynthia Giovanni will secure quotations from at least two suppliers.
NEW BUSINESS	The committee reviewed a request from the Purchasing Department for three new computers. After extensive discussion regarding the appropriate use of the computers and software to be purchased, the committee approved the request.
ADJOURNMENT	The meeting was adjourned at 4:45 p.m. The next meeting is scheduled for April 13 in Suite B. ↓2X Respectfully submitted, ↓4X *D. S. Madsen* D. S. Madsen, Secretary

(Note: Table shown with "View Gridlines" active.)

C. ITINERARY

↓5X

14 pt **PORTLAND SALES MEETING** ↓2X

12 pt ↓ **Itinerary for Dorothy Turner** ↓2X

March 12-15, 20-- ↓1X

THURSDAY, MARCH 12 ↓1X	
5:10 p.m.-7:06 p.m.	Flight from Detroit to Portland; Northwest 83 (800-555-1212); e-ticket; Seat 8D; nonstop. ↓2X Jack Weatherford (Home: 503-555-8029; Office: 503-555-7631) will meet your flight on Thursday, provide transportation during your visit, and return you to the airport on Saturday morning. Airport Sheraton (503-555-4032) King-sized bed, nonsmoking room; late arrival guaranteed; Reservation No. 30ZM6-02. ↓1X
FRIDAY, MARCH 13	
9 a.m.-5:30 p.m.	Portland Sales Meeting 1931 Executive Way, Suite 10 Portland, OR 97211 (503-555-7631)
SATURDAY, MARCH 14	
7:30 a.m.-2:47 p.m.	Flight from Portland to Detroit; Northwest 360; e-ticket; Seat 9a; nonstop.

(Note: Table shown with "View Gridlines" active.)

D. LEGAL DOCUMENT

(with line numbers)

left tabs: 1″, 3.25″
right tab: 6.5″

← line numbers (court documents only)

STATE OF NEVADA → tab 6.5″ IN DISTRICT COURT ↓2X

COUNTY OF CLARK NORTHEAST JUDICIAL DISTRICT ↓2X

JOHN C. SMITH → tab 3.25″) → tab 6.5″ NO. ____ 1 space, 20 underscores
209 East Clark Avenue)
Las Vegas, NV 89155-1603)
)
→ tab 1″ Plaintiff, → tab 3.25″)
)
vs.) → tab 6.5″ SUMMONS
)
FAITH GEORGIA)
)
Defendant.) ↓2X

THE STATE OF NEVADA TO THE ABOVE-NAMED DEFENDANT: ↓2X

→ tab 1″ You are hereby summoned and required to appear and defend against the Complaint in this action, which is hereby served upon you by serving upon the undersigned an Answer or other proper response within twenty (20) days after the service of the Summons and Complaint upon you, exclusive of the day of service. ↓2X

If you fail to do so, judgment by default will be taken against you for the relief demanded in the Complaint.

SIGNED this ____ day of July, 20--. ↓2X

1 space; 5 underscores; 1 space → tab 3.25″ underscores to the right margin

Jim Roe → tab 6.5″ Attorney at Law
229 South Civic Way
Laughlin, NV 89029-2648
Telephone: 702-555-1205
Attorney for Plaintiff

A. RESUME

↓5X

Cambria 14 pt Bold ↓ **TERRY M. MARTINA** ↓2X

Cambria 12 pt Bold ↓ **250 Maxwell Avenue, Boulder, CO 80305**
Phone: 303-555-9311; e-mail: tmartina@ecc.edu ↓1X

Calibri 12 pt Bold ↓ ↓1X ↓1X Calibri 12 pt ↓

OBJECTIVE	Position in resort management anywhere in Colorado. ↓1X
EDUCATION	Edgewood Community College, Boulder, Colorado A.A. in hotel management to be awarded May 2011 → indent 0.5" Achieved grade point average of 3.1 (on 4.0 scale). Received Board of Regents tuition scholarship. ↓2X Central City High School, Denver, Colorado Graduated: May 2009 ↓1X
EXPERIENCE	*Assistant Manager, Burger King Restaurant* ← Calibri 12 pt Italic Boulder, Colorado May 2010 to Present → indent 0.5" In charge of balancing the cash register, closing the restaurant, and making night deposits. *Student Intern, Ski Valley Haven* Aspen, Colorado September to December 2009 Worked as an assistant to the manager. Gained experience in operating First-Guest software and produced daily occupancy reports. Received Outstanding Employee award.
ACTIVITIES	Activities pursued while attending college: • Volunteer tutor, Literacy Council of America • Secretary of ECC Hospitality Services Association
REFERENCES	Available upon request.

(Note: Table shown with "View Gridlines" active.)

B. APPLICATION LETTER IN BLOCK STYLE

(with return address)

↓5X
March 1, 20-- ↓4X

Mr. Lou Mansfield, Director
Human Resources Department
Rocky Resorts International
P.O. Box 1412
Denver, CO 80214 ↓2X

Dear Mr. Mansfield: ↓2X

Please consider me an applicant for the position of concierge for Suite Retreat, as advertised in last Sunday's *Denver Times*. ↓2X

I will receive my A.A. degree in hotel management from Edgewood Community College in May and will be available for full-time employment immediately. In addition to my extensive coursework in hospitality services and business, I've had experience in working for a ski lodge similar to Suite Retreats in Aspen. As a lifelong resident of Colorado and an avid skier, I would be able to provide your guests with any information they request.

After you've reviewed my enclosed resume, I would appreciate having an opportunity to discuss with you why I believe I have the right qualifications and personality to serve as your concierge. I can be reached at 303-555-9311. ↓2X

Sincerely, ↓4X

Terry M. Martina

Return address — Terry M. Martina
250 Maxwell Avenue, Apt. 8
Boulder, CO 80305 ↓2X

Enclosure

C. FORMATTING LISTS

Numbers or bullets are used in documents to call attention to items in a list and to increase readability. If the sequence of the list items is important, use numbers rather than bullets.

- Insert 1 blank line before and after the list.
- Use Word's default format for all lists in either single- or double-spaced documents, including lists in documents such as a meeting agenda. Any carryover lines will be indented automatically.
- Use the same line spacing (single or double) between lines in the list as is used in the rest of the document.

The three bulleted and numbered lists shown at the right are all formatted correctly.

D. EXAMPLES OF DIFFERENT TYPES OF LISTS

According to the Internet Advertising Bureau, the following are the most common types of advertising on the Internet:

- Banner ads that feature some type of appropriate animation to attract the viewer's attention and interest.
- Sponsorship, in which an advertiser sponsors a content-based Web site.
- Interstitials, ads that flash up while a page downloads.

There is now considerable controversy about the effectiveness of banner advertising. As previously noted, a central goal of banner advertisements is to

*****

According to the Internet Advertising Bureau, the following are the most common types of advertising on the Internet, shown in order of popularity:

1. Banner ads
2. Sponsorship
3. Interstitials

There is now considerable controversy about the effectiveness of banner advertising. As previously noted, a central goal of banner advertisements is to

*****

According to the Internet Advertising Bureau, the following are the most common types of advertising on the Internet:

- Banner ads that feature some type of appropriate animation to attract the viewer's attention and interest.
- Sponsorship, in which an advertiser sponsors a Web site.
- Interstitials, ads that flash up while a page downloads.

There is now considerable controversy about the effectiveness of banner advertising. As previously noted, a central goal of banner advertisements is to

A. BOXED TABLE

(with subtitle; bottom-aligned and braced column headings; left- and right-aligned columns; total line and table note)

center page ↓
center horizontally

Title: 14 pt — Subtitle: 12 pt ↓ — ↓1X — Braced column headings — align bottom ↓ — ↓1X — Total line — Table note

AUSTIN-REEVES PRINTER DEPOT Sales Trends for 20-- (000s omitted)				
	Annual Sales		Quarterly Sales	
Product	This Year	Last Year	This Quarter	Last Quarter
Ink-jet: color	$ 569	$ 841	$ 120	$ 99
Ink-jet: color portable	6	24	2	6
Ink-jet: black and white	273	588	71	147
Printer/copier combination	1,622	2,054	422	509
Black-and-white laser: standard	389	507	121	129
Black-and-white laser: premium	2,368	87	592	25
Color laser	409	230	100	70
Totals	$5,636	$4,331	$1,428	$985
Note: Sales for this quarter ended at midnight, December 31.				

B. OPEN TABLE

(with 2-line title; 2-line centered, bottom-aligned column headings; left- and right-aligned columns; column entries with dollar and percent signs)

center page ↓
center horizontally

2-line title: 14 pt / 12 pt ↓ — Row 1 — ↓1X — Row 2 — Row 3 ↓ — align bottom ↓ — ↓1X — 2-line column heading — 2 spaces for each digit — 5 spaces: 2 for each digit; 1 for each comma — Column A — Column B→

SUITE HOLIDAY RETREAT BOUTIQUE HOTELS New Lodging Rates			
Location	Rack Rate	Discount Rate	Saving
Bozeman, Montana	$ 95.75	$ 91.50	4.4%
Chicago, Illinois	159.00	139.50	12.3%
Dallas, Texas	249.50	219.00	12.2%
Las Vegas, Nevada	98.50	89.95	8.7%
Beverly Hills, California	1,179.00	950.00	19.4%
Minneapolis, Minnesota	115.00	95.00	17.4%
New York, New York	227.50	175.00	23.1%
Orlando, Florida	105.75	98.50	6.3%
Portland, Maine	93.50	93.50	0.0%
Seattle, Washington	143.75	125.75	12.5%

(Note: Table shown with "View Gridlines" active.)

C. RULED TABLE

(with table number, title, centered column headings, and total line)

center page ↓
center horizontally

Table number and title: 14 pt — ↓1X — 12 pt ↓ — align bottom ↓

Table 2. RESCUE ONE COMPUTER TECHNICAL SUPPORT	
Support Service	Fees to Date
Replacement parts	$ 9,200
Troubleshooting	12,850
Software support	5,095
Hardware support	8,032
Product literature	105
Technical documentation	150
Printer drivers	129
Total	$35,561

(Note: Table shown with "View Gridlines" active.)

D. FORMATTING TABLES

The three basic styles of tables are boxed, open, and ruled. Tables have vertical columns (Column A), horizontal rows (Row 1), and intersecting cells (Cell A1). Center a table vertically that appears alone on the page. Insert 1 blank line before and after a table that appears within a document. Automatically adjust column widths and horizontally center all tables.

Heading Block. Merge any cells in Row 1, and type the heading block. Center and bold throughout. Type the title in all-caps, 14-pt. font, and the subtitle in upper- and lowercase, 12-pt. font. If a table has a number, type *Table* in upper- and lowercase. Follow the table number with a period and 1 space. Insert 1 blank line below the heading block.

Column Headings. Center column headings. Type in upper- and lowercase and bold. Bottom-align all column headings if a row includes a 2-line column heading. Merge desired cells for braced headings.

Column Entries. Left-align text columns, and right-align number columns. Capitalize only the first word and proper nouns in column entries.

Column Entry Dollar and Percent Signs. Insert the dollar sign only before the amount in the first entry and before a total amount entry. Align the dollar sign with the longest amount in the column, inserting spaces after the dollar sign as needed (allowing for 2 spaces for each digit and 1 space for each comma). Repeat the percent sign for each number in each column entry (unless the column heading identifies the data as percentages).

Table Note and Total Line. For a note line, merge the cells of the last row and use "Note" followed by a colon. For a total line, add a top and bottom border, use "Total" or "Totals" as appropriate, and add a percent or dollar sign if needed.

A. FORMATTING BUSINESS FORMS

Many business forms can be created and filled in by using templates that are provided within commercial word processing software. Template forms can be used "as is" or they can be edited. Templates can also be used to create customized forms for any business.

When a template is opened, the form is displayed on screen. The user can then fill in the necessary information, including personalized company information. Data are entered into cells or fields, and you can move quickly from field to field with a single keystroke—usually by pressing TAB or ENTER.

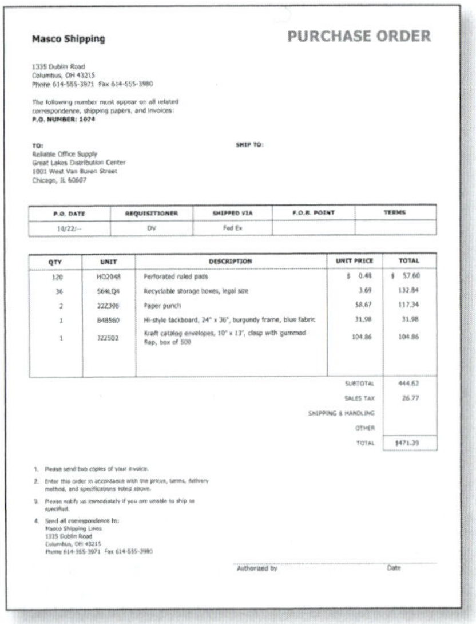

Masco Shipping PURCHASE ORDER

1335 Dublin Road
Columbus, OH 43215
Phone 614-555-3971 Fax 614-555-3980

The following number must appear on all related correspondence, shipping papers, and invoices:
P.O. NUMBER: 1074

TO:
Reliable Office Supply
Great Lakes Distribution Center
1001 West Van Buren Street
Chicago, IL 60607

SHIP TO:

P.O. DATE	REQUISITIONER	SHIPPED VIA	F.O.B. POINT	TERMS
10/22/--	DV	Fed Ex		

QTY	UNIT	DESCRIPTION	UNIT PRICE	TOTAL
120	HO2048	Perforated ruled pads	$ 0.48	$ 57.60
36	564LQ4	Recyclable storage boxes, legal size	3.69	132.84
2	222396	Paper punch	58.67	117.34
1	848560	Hi-style tackboard, 24" x 36", burgundy frame, blue fabric	31.98	31.98
1	322502	Kraft catalog envelopes, 10" x 13", clasp with gummed flap, box of 500	104.86	104.86
			SUBTOTAL	444.62
			SALES TAX	26.77
			SHIPPING & HANDLING	
			OTHER	
			TOTAL	$471.39

1. Please send two copies of your invoice.
2. Enter this order in accordance with the prices, terms, delivery method, and specifications listed above.
3. Please notify us immediately if you are unable to ship as specified.
4. Send all correspondence to:
   Masco Shipping Lines
   1335 Dublin Road
   Columbus, OH 43215
   Phone 614-555-3971 Fax 614-555-3980

Authorized by Date

B. U.S. POSTAL SERVICE ABBREVIATIONS

(for States, Territories, and Canadian Provinces)

States and Territories

Alabama	AL
Alaska	AK
Arizona	AZ
Arkansas	AR
California	CA
Colorado	CO
Connecticut	CT
Delaware	DE
District of Columbia	DC
Florida	FL
Georgia	GA
Guam	GU
Hawaii	HI
Idaho	ID
Illinois	IL
Indiana	IN
Iowa	IA
Kansas	KS
Kentucky	KY
Louisiana	LA
Maine	ME
Maryland	MD
Massachusetts	MA
Michigan	MI
Minnesota	MN
Mississippi	MS
Missouri	MO
Montana	MT
Nebraska	NE
Nevada	NV
New Hampshire	NH
New Jersey	NJ
New Mexico	NM
New York	NY
North Carolina	NC
North Dakota	ND
Ohio	OH
Oklahoma	OK
Oregon	OR
Pennsylvania	PA
Puerto Rico	PR
Rhode Island	RI
South Carolina	SC
South Dakota	SD
Tennessee	TN
Texas	TX
Utah	UT
Vermont	VT
Virgin Islands	VI
Virginia	VA
Washington	WA
West Virginia	WV
Wisconsin	WI
Wyoming	WY

Canadian Provinces

Alberta	AB
British Columbia	BC
Labrador	LB
Manitoba	MB
New Brunswick	NB
Newfoundland	NF
Northwest Territories	NT
Nova Scotia	NS
Ontario	ON
Prince Edward Island	PE
Quebec	PQ
Saskatchewan	SK
Yukon Territory	YT

C. PROOFREADERS' MARKS

Proofreaders' Marks	Draft	Final Copy
Omit space	data base	database
∨ or ∧ Insert	if he's going not	if he's not going,
Capitalize	Maple street	Maple Street
Delete	a final draft	a draft
# Insert space	allready to	all ready to
when Change word	and if you	and when you
/ Use lowercase letter	our President	our president
¶ Paragraph	... to use it.¶We can	... to use it. We can
... Don't delete	a true story	a true story
○ Spell out	the only 1	the only one
Transpose	they all see	they see all

Proofreaders' Marks	Draft	Final Copy
SS Single-space	SS first line second line	first line second line
ds Double-space	ds first line second line	first line second line
Move right	Please send	Please send
Move left	May I	May I
Bold	Column Heading	**Column Heading**
ital Italic	ital Time magazine	*Time* magazine
u/l Underline	u/l Time magazine	Time magazine
Move as shown	readers will see	readers will see

Language Arts for Business

(50 "must-know" rules)

PUNCTUATION

Commas

RULE 1
, direct address
(L. 21)

Use commas before and after a name used in direct address.

Thank you, John, for responding to my e-mail so quickly.
Ladies and gentlemen, the program has been canceled.

RULE 2
, independent clause
(L. 27)

The underline calls attention to a point in the sentence where a comma might mistakenly be inserted.

Use a comma between independent clauses joined by a coordinate conjunction (unless both clauses are short).

Ellen left her job with IBM, and she and her sister went to Paris.
But: Ellen left her job with IBM and went to Paris with her sister.
But: John drove and I navigated.

Note: An independent clause is one that can stand alone as a complete sentence. The most common coordinate conjunctions are *and*, *but*, *or*, and *nor*.

RULE 3
, introductory expression
(L. 27)

Use a comma after an introductory expression (unless it is a short prepositional phrase).

Before we can make a decision, we must have all the facts.
But: In 2004 our nation elected a new president.

Note: An introductory expression is a group of words that come before the subject and verb of the independent clause. Common prepositions are *to*, *in*, *on*, *of*, *at*, *by*, *for*, and *with*.

RULE 4
, direct quotation
(L. 41)

Use a comma before and after a direct quotation.

James said, "I shall return," and then left.

RULE 5
, date
(L. 51)

Use a comma before and after the year in a complete date.

We will arrive on June 2, 2006, for the conference.
But: We will arrive on June 2 for the conference.

RULE 6
, place
(L. 51)

Use a comma before and after a state or country that follows a city (but not before a ZIP Code).

Joan moved to Vancouver, British Columbia, in May.
Send the package to Douglasville, GA 30135, by Express Mail.
But: Send the package to Georgia by Express Mail.

RULE 7
, series
(L. 61)

Use a comma between each item in a series of three or more.

We need to order paper, toner, and font cartridges for the printer.

They saved their work, exited their program, and turned off their computers when they finished.

Note: Do not use a comma after the last item in a series.

RULE 8
, transitional expression
(L. 61)

Use a comma before and after a transitional expression or independent comment.

It is critical, therefore, that we finish the project on time.

Our present projections, you must admit, are inadequate.

But: You must admit our present projections are inadequate.

Note: Examples of transitional expressions and independent comments are *in addition to, therefore, however, on the other hand, as a matter of fact,* and *unfortunately.*

RULE 9
, nonessential expression
(L. 71)

Use a comma before and after a nonessential expression.

Andre, who was there, can verify the statement.

But: Anyone who was there can verify the statement.

Van's first book, *Crisis of Management,* was not discussed.

Van's book *Crisis of Management* was not discussed.

Note: A nonessential expression is a group of words that may be omitted without changing the basic meaning of the sentence. Always examine the noun or pronoun that comes before the expression to determine whether the noun needs the expression to complete its meaning. If it does, the expression is *essential* and does *not* take a comma.

RULE 10
, adjacent adjectives
(L. 71)

Use a comma between two adjacent adjectives that modify the same noun.

We need an intelligent, enthusiastic individual for this job.

But: Please order a new bulletin board for our main conference room.

Note: Do not use a comma after the second adjective. Also, do not use a comma if the first adjective modifies the combined idea of the second adjective and the noun (for example, *bulletin board* and *conference room* in the second example above).

Semicolons

RULE 11
; no conjunction
(L. 97)

Use a semicolon to separate two closely related independent clauses that are not joined by a conjunction (such as *and, but, or,* or *nor*).

Management favored the vote; stockholders did not.

But: Management favored the vote, but stockholders did not.

RULE 12
; series
(L. 97)

Use a semicolon to separate three or more items in a series if any of the items already contain commas.

Staff meetings were held on Thursday, May 7; Monday, June 7; and Friday, June 12.

Note: Be sure to insert the semicolon *between* (not within) the items in a series.

Hyphens

RULE 13
- number
(L. 57)

Hyphenate compound numbers between twenty-one and ninety-nine and fractions that are expressed as words.

Twenty-nine recommendations were approved by at least three-fourths of the members.

RULE 14
- compound adjective
(L. 67)

Hyphenate compound adjectives that come before a noun (unless the first word is an adverb ending in *-ly*).

We reviewed an up-to-date report on Wednesday.
But: The report was up to date.
But: We reviewed the highly rated report.

Note: A compound adjective is two or more words that function as a unit to describe a noun.

Apostrophes

RULE 15
' singular noun
(L. 37)

Use *'s* to form the possessive of singular nouns.

The hurricane's force caused major damage to North Carolina's coastline.

RULE 16
' plural noun
(L. 37)

Use only an apostrophe to form the possessive of plural nouns that end in *s*.

The investors' goals were outlined in the stockholders' report.
But: The investors outlined their goals in the report to the stockholders.
But: The women's and children's clothing was on sale.

RULE 17
' pronoun
(L. 37)

Use *'s* to form the possessive of indefinite pronouns (such as *someone's* or *anybody's*); do not use an apostrophe with personal pronouns (such as *hers, his, its, ours, theirs,* and *yours*).

She could select anybody's paper for a sample.
It's time to put the file back into its cabinet.

Colons

RULE 18
: explanatory material
(L. 91)

Use a colon to introduce explanatory material that follows an independent clause.

The computer satisfies three criteria: speed, cost, and power.

But: The computer satisfies the three criteria of_speed, cost, and power.

Remember this:_only one coupon is allowed per customer.

Note: An independent clause can stand alone as a complete sentence. Do not capitalize the word following the colon.

Periods

RULE 19
. polite request
(L. 91)

Use a period to end a sentence that is a polite request.

Will you please call me if I can be of further assistance.

Note: Consider a sentence a polite request if you expect the reader to respond by doing as you ask rather than by giving a yes-or-no answer.

Quotation Marks

RULE 20
" direct quotation
(L. 41)

Use quotation marks around a direct quotation.

Harrison responded by saying, "Their decision does not affect us."

But: Harrison responded by saying that their decision does not affect us.

RULE 21
" title
(L. 41)

Use quotation marks around the title of a newspaper or magazine article, chapter in a book, report, and similar terms.

The most helpful article I found was "Multimedia for All."

Italics (or Underline)

RULE 22
title or title
(L. 41)

Italicize (or underline) the titles of books, magazines, newspapers, and other complete published works.

Grisham's *The Brethren* was reviewed in a recent *USA Today* article.

GRAMMAR

Sentences

RULE 23
fragment
(L. 21)

Avoid sentence fragments.

Not: She had always wanted to be a financial manager. But had not had the needed education.

But: She had always wanted to be a financial manager but had not had the needed education.

Note: A fragment is a part of a sentence that is incorrectly punctuated as a complete sentence. In the first example above, "but had not had the needed education" is not a complete sentence because it does not contain a subject.

RULE 24
run-on
(L. 21)

Avoid run-on sentences.

Not: Mohamed is a competent worker he has even passed the MOS exam.
Not: Mohamed is a competent worker, he has even passed the MOS exam.
But: Mohamed is a competent worker; he has even passed the MOS exam.
Or: Mohamed is a competent worker. He has even passed the MOS exam.

Note: A run-on sentence is two independent clauses that run together without any punctuation between them or with only a comma between them.

Agreement

RULE 25
agreement singular
agreement plural
(L. 67)

Use singular verbs and pronouns with singular subjects; use plural verbs and pronouns with plural subjects.

I was happy with my performance.
Janet and Phoenix were happy with their performance.
Among the items discussed were our raises and benefits.

RULE 26
agreement pronoun
(L. 81)

Some pronouns (*anybody, each, either, everybody, everyone, much, neither, no one, nobody,* and *one*) are always singular and take a singular verb. Other pronouns (*all, any, more, most, none,* and *some*) may be singular or plural, depending on the noun to which they refer.

Each of the employees has finished his or her task.
Much remains to be done.
Most of the pie was eaten, but most of the cookies were left.

RULE 27
agreement intervening words
(L. 81)

Disregard any intervening words that come between the subject and verb when establishing agreement.

That box, containing the books and pencils, has not been found.
Alex, accompanied by Tricia and Roxy, is attending the conference and taking his computer.

RULE 28
agreement nearer noun
(L. 101)

If two subjects are joined by *or, either/or, neither/nor,* or *not only/but also,* make the verb agree with the subject nearer to the verb.

Neither the coach nor the players are at home.
Not only the coach but also the referee is at home.
But: Both the coach and the referee are at home.

Pronouns

RULE 29
nominative pronoun
(L. 107)

Use nominative pronouns (such as *I, he, she, we, they,* and *who*) as subjects of a sentence or clause.

The programmer and he are reviewing the code.
Barb is a person who can do the job.

RULE 30
objective pronoun
(L. 107)

Use objective pronouns (such as *me, him, her, us, them,* and *whom*) as objects of a verb, preposition, or infinitive.

The code was reviewed by the programmer and him.
Barb is the type of person whom we can trust.

Adjectives and Adverbs

RULE 31
adjective/adverb
(L. 101)

Use comparative adjectives and adverbs (*-er, more,* and *less*) when referring to two nouns or pronouns; use superlative adjectives and adverbs (*-est, most,* and *least*) when referring to more than two.

The shorter of the two training sessions is the more helpful one.
The longest of the three training sessions is the least helpful one.

Word Usage

RULE 32
accept/except
(L. 117)

***Accept* means "to agree to"; *except* means "to leave out."**

All employees except the maintenance staff should accept the agreement.

RULE 33
affect/effect
(L. 117)

***Affect* is most often used as a verb meaning "to influence"; *effect* is most often used as a noun meaning "result."**

The ruling will affect our domestic operations but will have no effect on our Asian operations.

RULE 34
farther/further
(L. 117)

***Farther* refers to distance; *further* refers to extent or degree.**

The farther we drove, the further agitated he became.

RULE 35
personal/personnel
(L. 117)

***Personal* means "private"; *personnel* means "employees."**

All personnel agreed not to use e-mail for personal business.

RULE 36
principal/principle
(L. 117)

***Principal* means "primary"; *principle* means "rule."**

The principle of fairness is our principal means of dealing with customers.

MECHANICS

Capitalization

RULE 37
≡ sentence
(L. 31)

Capitalize the first word of a sentence.

Please prepare a summary of your activities.

RULE 38
≡ proper noun
(L. 31)

Capitalize proper nouns and adjectives derived from proper nouns.

Judy Hendrix drove to Albuquerque in her new Pontiac convertible.

Note: A proper noun is the official name of a particular person, place, or thing.

RULE 39
≡ time
(L. 31)

Capitalize the names of the days of the week, months, holidays, and religious days (but do not capitalize the names of the seasons).

On Thursday, November 25, we will celebrate Thanksgiving, the most popular holiday in the fall.

RULE 40
≡ noun #
(L. 77)

Capitalize nouns followed by a number or letter (except for the nouns *line, note, page, paragraph,* and *size*).

Please read Chapter 5, which begins on page 94.

RULE 41
≡ compass point
(L. 77)

Capitalize compass points (such as *north, south,* or *northeast*) only when they designate definite regions.

From Montana we drove south to reach the Southwest.

RULE 42
≡ organization
(L. 111)

Capitalize common organizational terms (such as *advertising department* and *finance committee*) only when they are the actual names of the units in the writer's own organization and when they are preceded by the word *the*.

The report from the Advertising Department is due today.

But: Our advertising department will submit its report today.

RULE 43
≡ course
(L. 111)

Capitalize the names of specific course titles but not the names of subjects or areas of study.

I have enrolled in Accounting 201 and will also take a marketing course.

Number Expression

RULE 44
general
(L. 47)

In general, spell out numbers zero through ten, and use figures for numbers above ten.

We rented two movies for tonight.

The decision was reached after 27 precincts sent in their results.

RULE 45
 # figure
(L. 47)

Use figures for

- **Dates. (Use *st, d,* or *th* only if the day comes before the month.)**

  The tax report is due on April 15 (not *April 15th*).

  We will drive to the camp on the 23d (or *23rd* or *23*[rd]) of May.

- **All numbers if two or more *related* numbers both above and below ten are used in the same sentence.**

  Mr. Carter sent in 7 receipts, and Ms. Cantrell sent in 22.

  But: The 13 accountants owned three computers each.

- **Measurements (time, money, distance, weight, and percent).**

  The $500 statue we delivered at 7 a.m. weighed 6 pounds.

- **Mixed numbers.**

  Our sales are up 9½ (or *9.5*) percent over last year.

RULE 46
 # word
(L. 57)

Spell out

- **A number used as the first word of a sentence.**

  Seventy-five people attended the conference in San Diego.

- **The shorter of two adjacent numbers.**

  We have ordered 3 two-pound cakes and one 5-pound cake for the reception.

- **The words *million* and *billion* in round numbers (do not use decimals with round numbers).**

  Not: A $5.00 ticket can win $28,000,000 in this month's lottery.

  But: A $5 ticket can win $28 million in this month's lottery.

- **Fractions.**

  Almost one-half of the audience responded to the question.

Abbreviations

RULE 47
abbreviate none
(L. 67)

In general business writing, do not abbreviate common words (such as *dept.* or *pkg.*), compass points, units of measure, or the names of months, days of the week, cities, or states (except in addresses).

Almost one-half of the audience indicated they were at least 5 feet 8 inches tall.

Note: Do not insert a comma between the parts of a single measurement.

RULE 48
abbreviate measure
(L. 87)

In technical writing, on forms, and in tables, abbreviate units of measure when they occur frequently. Do not use periods.

14 oz   5 ft 10 in   50 mph   2 yrs 10 mo

RULE 49
abbreviate lowercase
(L. 87)

In most lowercase abbreviations made up of single initials, use a period after each initial but no internal spaces.

a.m.   p.m.   i.e.   e.g.   e.o.m.

Exceptions: mph   mpg   wpm

RULE 50
abbreviate ≡
(L. 87)

In most all-capital abbreviations made up of single initials, do not use periods or internal spaces.

OSHA   PBS   NBEA   WWW   VCR   MBA

Exceptions: U.S.A.   A.A.   B.S.   Ph.D.   P.O.   B.C.   A.D.

Getting Started

Refer to Getting Started and Lessons 21 through 24 (Orientation to Word Processing A, B, C, and D) as needed throughout this course. This information will not be repeated.

GDP—Word Settings

REFER TO

WM Appendix A, Using Microsoft Word in the Workplace

Microsoft Windows and Microsoft Word are distributed in a variety of versions with various default settings already in place. GDP (*Gregg Document Processing*) course software opens Word files with controlled settings in place so you will experience a predictable, trouble-free word processing environment during this course. However, you must also change a few Word option settings listed in Appendix A before beginning any work.

Certain parts of illustrations (title bar information, style choices, and tabs) might vary slightly from your Word screens due to automatic updates from Microsoft and user customizations. These differences are not cause for concern.

Word Manual Conventions

This *Microsoft Office Word 2016 Manual* (your Word Manual) accompanies *Gregg College Keyboarding & Document Processing* (your textbook) and includes step-by-step directions and helpful illustrations for all Word features. Use these handy resources during this course and in the workplace.

Typically, you will study the Formatting section in the textbook, launch Word via GDP, study the related Word features in the Word Manual and complete the hands-on Practice exercises, and then type the desired jobs in the Document Processing section of the textbook. Word features are introduced on a "need-to-know" basis. After completing this course successfully, you will be proficient in keyboarding and able to use Word to produce a wide variety of mailable business documents.

The following conventions are used in this manual:

- Commands, tabs, groups, buttons, and other names or keyboard combinations used in step-by-step directions are shown in bold. For example, "From the **Home** tab, **Font** group, click the **Bold** button."

- Keyboard key names are shown in all-caps and bold; for example, "Press **ENTER** 1 time."
- Words you actually type are shown in a different font to distinguish them. For example, "Type `Agenda` as the report title."
- To execute keyboard combinations, press and hold down the first key while you tap the second key; then release both keys. For example, "On the keyboard, press **CTRL+S** to save a file."
- Certain key combinations that use the function keys (**F1, F2**, etc., on the top row of the keyboard) might require the **FN** (function) key to be held along with the keyboard combination; for example, **SHIFT+F3** as opposed to **FN+SHIFT+F3**. Check your keyboard documentation.
- Formatting marks are shown in illustrations—verify that formatting marks in your jobs match the illustrations.

REFER TO
WM L. 24, Show/Hide Formatting

When you see these icons, do this:

Attention:	Study this important, broad-based information.
Help:	Read supporting information.
Tip:	Review handy tips for using Word.
Hands-On:	Launch Word via GDP, and complete the Practice exercise.
Download File:	Return to GDP to download a file.
GO TO Textbook:	Return to the textbook to complete document processing jobs.
REFER TO:	Research related information in the textbook, Reference Manual, Word Manual, or GDP.

- *L* stands for *Lesson.*
- *R* stands for *Reference Manual.*
- *WM* stands for *Word Manual.*
- *GDP* stands for *Gregg Document Processing* (the course software).

The following terms (for a right-handed mouse) are used in this manual:

- **Point:** Move the mouse until the mouse pointer on the screen is pointing to and resting over the desired item.
- **Click:** Point to an item; then press and quickly release the left mouse button without moving the mouse.
- **Double-click:** Point to an item; then press and quickly release the left mouse button twice without moving the mouse.
- **Drag:** Point to an item, hold down the left mouse button while moving the mouse, and release at the end of the selection.

- **Right-click:** Point to an item; then press and quickly release the right mouse button.
- **Select:** Drag across characters, double-click, and so forth to highlight text.

Appendix A, B, and C

- Refer to Appendix A, Using Microsoft Word in the Workplace, for Word settings you must change or verify.
- Refer to Appendix B, Using GDP for Document Processing, for an index of GDP features relevant to document processing jobs and their order of introduction in the Word Manual.
- Refer to Appendix C, Saving a Word File in PDF Format, for steps to save a Word document in PDF format.

GDP—Help

REFER TO
GDP—Help

Explore GDP Help as directed or anytime you need to familiarize yourself with relevant GDP features.

Orientation to Word Processing—A

LESSON 21

GDP—Start Word

REFER TO
GDP—Help (document processing)

See GDP Help for steps to launch Word via GDP to complete Practice exercises starting in Lesson 21 and document processing jobs starting in Lesson 25.

OPENING WORD FILES

REFER TO
WM Appendix A, Using Microsoft Word in the Workplace, GDP—Word Settings
WM L. 103, Compatibility Mode

Before beginning any work, set the Word options outlined in Appendix A, GDP—Word Settings.

- Depending upon your Windows settings, file extensions may or may not appear in Word's title bar and in the Windows Open dialog box. Refer to Windows Help for steps to display file extensions.
- Refer to your browser's Help for steps to download, open, and save files.
- If any Word file opens and a Protected View warning displays, click Enable Editing. If necessary, click View, Edit Document.
- If any Word file opens with *[Read Only]* in the title bar, save the file using a different file name or location.
- If any Word file opens with *[Compatibility Mode]* in the title bar, the Word version you are using is newer than the Word version used to create the document. You do not need to convert any files until Lesson 103.
- Look for important notes on GDP screens for information related to a lesson or job.

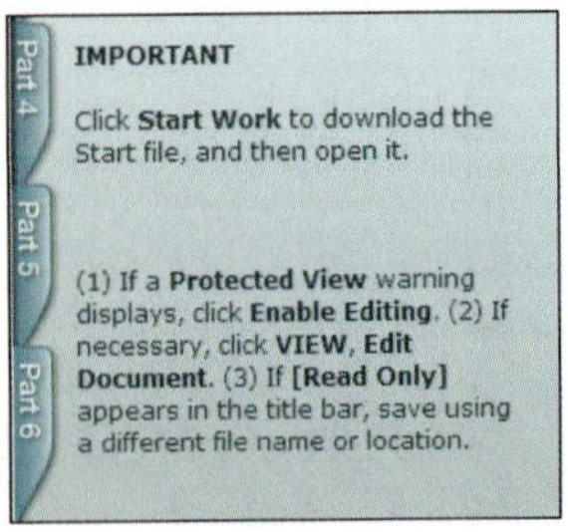

GDP screen notes

PRACTICE 21 (1 of 7)

1. From GDP's Lesson 21E screen, click **Start Work**; download and open *Document1* (a blank, unnamed file) following your browser's steps.

   In future Practice exercises, GDP will typically launch Word and open a document with an assigned name and content in place.

2. Study this illustration and the description of each feature and identify each feature on your own screen:

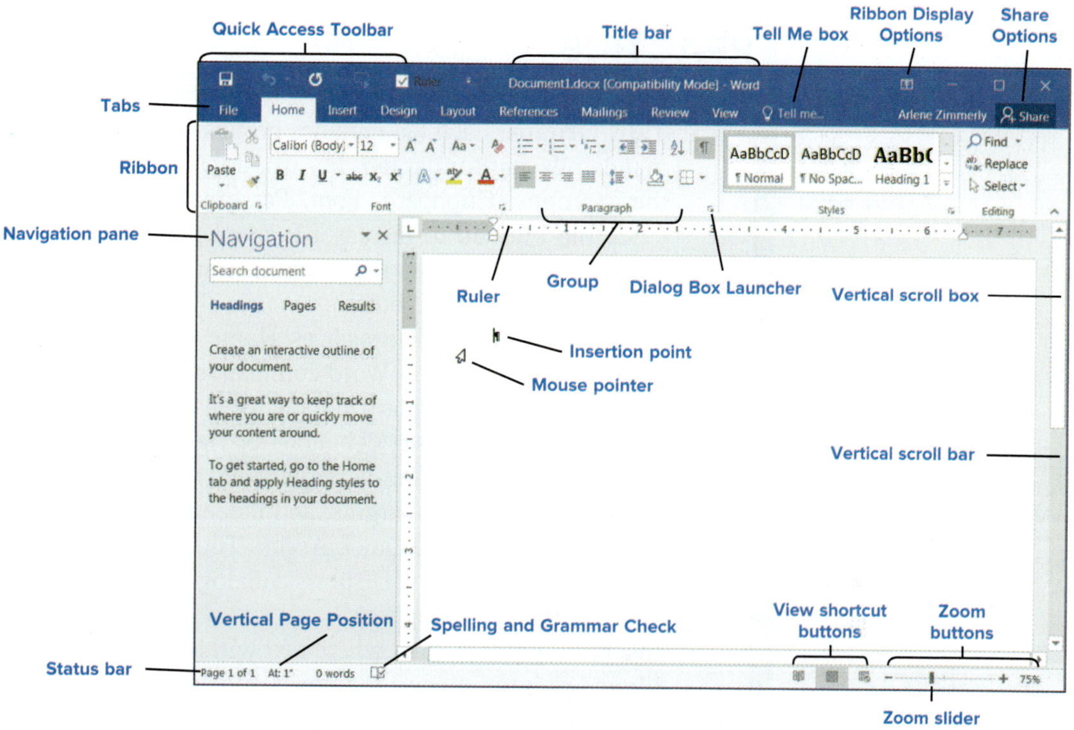

REFER TO

WM L. 21, GDP—Start Word
WM L. 103, Compatibility Mode
WM Appendix A, Using Microsoft Word in the Workplace, GDP—Word Settings, Normal Style

PRACTICE (continued)

Screens for Word documents opened via GDP appear slightly different from screens for new Word 2016 documents opened outside of GDP. These cosmetic differences are not cause for concern. See Lesson 21 and Appendix A for details.

- **Quick Access Toolbar.** Displays frequently used commands, such as Save and Undo. You can add or remove Word commands to customize it to your preferences.
- **Title bar.** Displays the name of the current document and the application program. Any new, unsaved file is assigned a generic name, such as *Document1*.
- **Tell Me box.** Searches for help for typed keywords.
- **Ribbon Display Options.** Displays options to auto-hide the Ribbon, show the Ribbon tabs only, or show the Ribbon tabs and commands.
- **Share Options.** Displays options for sharing.

PRACTICE (continued)

Back button

- **Tabs/Groups**. Each tab includes groups of frequently used commands relevant to that tab. For example, the Home tab includes these groups: Clipboard, Font, Paragraph, Styles, and Editing. Click the File tab to display file management features, such as Info, New, Open, Save, Print, and Close. To exit File view, press ESC or click the Back button.
- **Ribbon**. Displays tabs, such as Home, Insert, and Layout, for quick access to popular Word commands organized into groups.
- **Navigation pane**. Displays initially when a new, blank document is opened. Click the Close (X) button (top right of the pane) to close it.

REFER TO

WM L. 21, Choosing Commands, From the Quick Access Toolbar
WM L. 45, Tab Set—Ruler Tabs

- **Ruler**. Displays or hides horizontal and vertical rulers for convenient access to tabs, margins, and indent settings; you can add a Ruler checkbox to the Quick Access Toolbar for convenience.
- **Dialog Box Launcher**. Displays a dialog box or task pane for that group with relevant options.
- **Insertion point**. Shows where text will be inserted next.
- **Mouse pointer**. Shows the position of the mouse. The context-sensitive pointer changes dynamically with the task at hand.
- **Vertical scroll box**. Displays different parts of a document as you drag it up or down.
- **Vertical scroll bar**. Displays one screen of the document at a time as you click on it.

REFER TO

WM Appendix A, Using Microsoft Word in the Workplace, GDP—Word Settings, Status Bar

- **Status bar**. Displays information about a document, such as the current page and number of words. See Appendix A for steps to display the status bar.
- **Vertical Page Position**. Displays the vertical page position of the insertion point as measured from the top of the page.

REFER TO

WM L. 24, Spelling and Grammar Check

- **Spelling and Grammar Check**. Displays the Spelling pane to begin a review of possible errors.
- **View shortcut buttons**. Display different document views, such as Read Mode, Print Layout, and Web Layout.

  Use Word's default Print Layout view (the second View shortcut button on the status bar) unless otherwise directed.

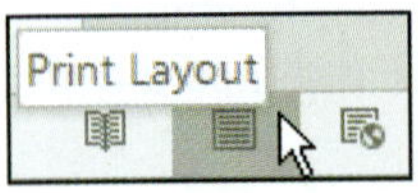

Print Layout view button

- **Zoom buttons**. Apply different zoom settings.
- **Zoom slider**. Displays a faraway or close-up view when you drag the slider arrow or click the minus or plus signs to the left or right of the slider.

Note: Keep this document open and continue reading.

Choosing Commands

A command directs Word to perform some action; for example, you can click a button to print a document or insert a table. You can execute commands via the Ribbon, Mini toolbars, shortcut menus, or shortcut keys.

FROM THE RIBBON

Click the Home tab, and roll your mouse scroll button to move from one tab to the next. Click any button in a group to execute a given command or display a submenu. Click any list arrow to display more options. Click any Dialog Box Launcher diagonal arrow to open a related dialog box.

To display a ScreenTip: Point to a button (or any item) in each group, and pause briefly. Read the related information.

Point to a button and pause to see a **ScreenTip** and any relevant keyboard shortcut.

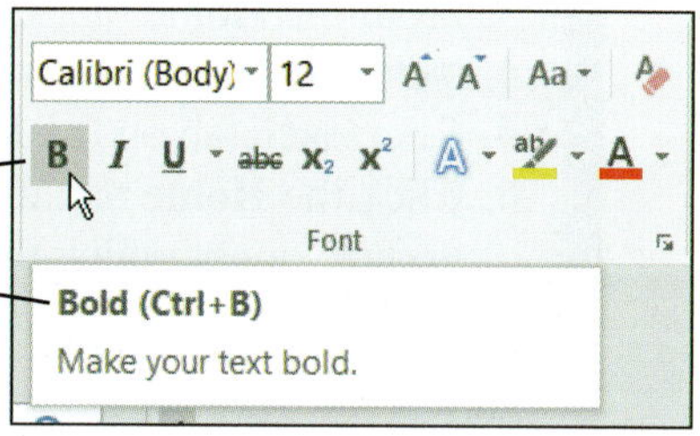

Word's Live Preview shows you how formatting options such as font colors and styles will look if applied. For example, if you select text and pause over a button (click the drop-down list for a font color and point to a color in a gallery), a Live Preview of the new formatting appears in the related text. When you point to the next choice, the Live Preview updates. Click the desired choice to apply it.

By selecting text (the text displayed in red was selected first) and then pointing to a formatting choice, you can see a Live Preview of that option.

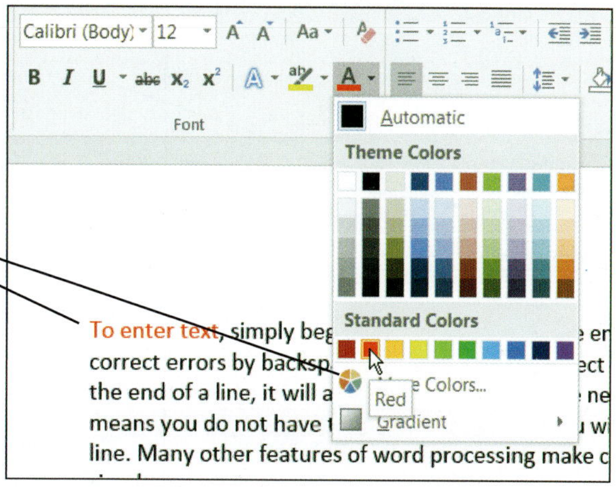

Ribbon Display Options button

To increase the screen space for the document to more easily view the Live Preview: Double-click any tab to collapse the **Ribbon** groups. To expand the groups, double-click that tab again.

Or: Click the **Ribbon Display Options** button in the upper right-hand corner of the Word window and click any desired option.

PRACTICE 21 (2 of 7)

1. From the **Ribbon**, click the **Home** tab.
2. From the **Quick Access Toolbar**, point to any button, and note the **ScreenTip**.
3. From the **Home** tab, **Font** group, click the **Dialog Box Launcher**.
4. Note the commands in the **Font** dialog box, and click **Cancel**.
5. Click each tab on the **Ribbon**; note the group names for each tab.
6. Click the **Home** tab; double-click the **Home** tab to collapse the groups; double-click the **Home** tab again to expand the groups.

Note: Keep this document open and continue reading.

FROM THE MINI TOOLBARS OR SHORTCUT MENUS

Frequently-used commands appear in Mini toolbars for quick access. For example, if you select some text and point to the top part of the selected text, a Mini toolbar appears. Point to the Mini toolbar to brighten it. Right-click selected text to display the Mini toolbar and a context-sensitive shortcut menu.

Point to or right-click the selected text to display the Mini Font toolbar and a context-sensitive shortcut menu.

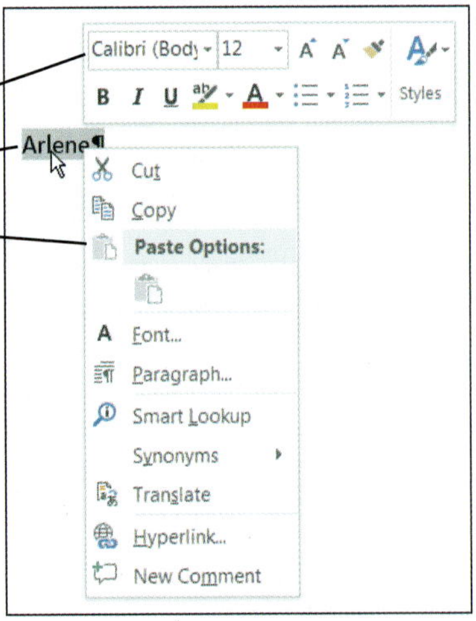

PRACTICE 21 (3 of 7)

1. Type your first name, and double-click it to select it; note the **Mini Font** toolbar that displays immediately after you double-click.
2. Deselect the text.
3. Right-click over the text, and note the related choices in the shortcut menu.

Note: Keep this document open and continue reading.

FROM THE KEYBOARD

Use keyboard combination shortcuts (for example, hold down CTRL+C to copy) to execute a command.

PRACTICE 21 (4 of 7)

1. From the **Ribbon**, click the **Home** tab.
2. From the **Font** group, point to the **Bold** button, and note the **ScreenTip** and the key combination shortcut, **CTRL+B**.
3. From the Font group, point to the **Italic** button, and note the **ScreenTip** and the key combination shortcut, **CTRL+I**.

Note: Keep this document open and continue reading.

FROM THE QUICK ACCESS TOOLBAR

The Quick Access Toolbar (QAT) is located above the Ribbon. This customizable toolbar displays frequently used commands, such as Save and Undo. You can add your favorite commands to the toolbar.

To add a favorite command to the QAT: Right-click a favorite command; then click **Add to Quick Access Toolbar**.

Or: Click the list arrow to the right of the **QAT**; then click the desired choice. Click **More Commands** to add or remove other commands. **Quick Print, Print Preview and Print**, and **Ruler** are recommended choices.

To remove a command from the QAT: Click the list arrow to the right of the **QAT**; then uncheck the desired choice.

Or: Right-click the command on the **QAT**, and click **Remove from Quick Access Toolbar**.

PRACTICE 21 (5 of 7)

1. Click the **Home** tab on the **Ribbon**.
2. From the **QAT**, click the **Undo** button repeatedly until you return to a blank screen.
3. Click the list arrow to the right of the **QAT** and check **Quick Print** (or verify that **Quick Print** is checked); note the new **Quick Print** icon on the toolbar, which sends your entire document to the default printer immediately when clicked.
4. Click the list arrow to the right of the **QAT**, and uncheck **Quick Print**; note the **Quick Print** icon is removed.
5. From the **Home** tab, **Font** group, right-click the **Bold** button, and click **Add to Quick Access Toolbar**.
6. From the **QAT**, right-click the **Bold** button, and click **Remove from Quick Access Toolbar**.
7. Keep this document open, but go to GDP's Lesson 21E screen to download *practice-21* to complete the second part of this lesson; then return here to continue reading.

Note: Keep this document open.

File—Open

To open a file:

1. From the **File** tab, click **Open**, or press **CTRL+O**.

   When you click the File tab, Open, Recent, a list of recently opened file names appears. To open a recent document, click the desired file name. To keep a file in the Recent Documents list for quick access, point to the file name, and click the Pin button to the right of the document name. Note that the document name is repositioned under the Pinned list. To release (unpin) a document, click that document's Pin button again.

2. Under the **Open** pane, click **This PC**; below that, click **Browse**; note that the **Open** dialog box appears.
3. Browse to the desired location and file; double-click the desired file to open it.

   Consult Windows Help for steps to browse to a file. If the desired file does not display, you likely have a file filter in effect. Consult Windows Help for steps to display All Files (*.*) when you are browsing.

PRACTICE 21 (6 of 7)

In future Practice exercises, GDP will typically launch Word and automatically open a document with an assigned name and content in place ready for your input. In this exercise, you will open a file manually for practice.

1. From GDP's Lesson 21E screen; click **Download File**; download and open *practice-21* following your browser's steps—click **Enable Editing** if necessary.
2. Note that the title bar displays the file name *practice-21*, and the document opens with one paragraph already typed.

   The title bar will also display *[Compatibility Mode]* after the file name. You do not have to be concerned with this mode until Lesson 103.

3. Note that two Word documents are now opened simultaneously—an unnamed, blank document and *practice-21*.

Note: Keep both documents open and continue reading below.

REFER TO
WM L. 103, Compatibility Mode

GDP—Quit Word

REFER TO
GDP—Help (document processing)

See GDP Help for steps to quit Word, to end or repeat a Practice exercise, or to end or repeat a document processing job and return to GDP. From this point forward when you see *Go to Textbook* and *Return to GDP* at the end of a Practice exercise, follow the standard steps to quit Word and close all documents. These directions will not be repeated.

PRACTICE 21 (7 of 7)

Practice exercises are not uploaded to GDP. Consult with your instructor regarding saving or submitting completed Practice files outside of GDP.

1. Close all documents and close Word. (*Hint:* Click the **Close** button in the upper right-hand corner of the Word window.)
2. If you are prompted to save changes, click **Don't Save**.
3. Return to GDP.

GO TO
Textbook

Orientation to Word Processing—B

LESSON 22

Document Navigation

The insertion point (a blinking vertical bar) indicates where text will appear upon your next keystroke. After scrolling, click at the desired point in the document to move the insertion point. Do not confuse the mouse pointer with the blinking vertical insertion point (also known as the "cursor"). The mouse pointer is typically an arrow or I-beam symbol showing the location of the mouse pointer over the screen.

To navigate through a document:

To Navigate	Via the Mouse	Via the Keyboard
Anywhere	Click where desired to position the cursor.	Use the arrow keys to move the cursor.
Through the document	Click the scroll bar (the area above or below the scroll box) to display the previous or next screen.	Press **PAGE UP** or **PAGE DOWN** to move up or down one screen.
To a specific page	Drag the **vertical scroll box** until the desired page appears in the **Page number ScreenTip**.	Press **CTRL+F**; from the **Navigation** pane, **Search** document box, click the list arrow, **Go To**; from the **Go To** tab, **Enter page number** box, type the desired page number; click **Go To, Close**.
To the begin-ning or end of a document	Drag the **vertical scroll box** to the top or bottom of the **vertical scroll bar**.	Press **CTRL+HOME** or **CTRL+END** to move to the start or end of a document.
To the beginning or end of a line	Click at the beginning or end of the line.	Press **HOME** to move to the beginning of a line or **END** to move to the end.
Through the pages		Press **CTRL+PAGE DOWN** or **CTRL+PAGE UP** to browse up or down a page at a time.

Page number ScreenTip

PRACTICE 22 (1 of 5)

1. From GDP's Lesson 22E screen, click **Start Work** to download and open *Document1* (a blank, unnamed file) following your browser's steps; then click **Download File** to download and open *practice-22*, a one-paragraph file.
2. In the *practice-22* file, locate the mouse pointer (an I-beam symbol) and the insertion point (in front of the first word).
3. Move the mouse pointer over the **Ribbon**; note that it changes from an I-beam to an arrow.
4. Press **CTRL+END** to move the insertion point to the end of the document.
5. Move the insertion point just to the left of the "T" in "This" in line 3.
6. Press **BACKSPACE**; then press the **SPACE BAR** to replace the deleted space.
7. Press **DELETE**; then type T to replace the deleted letter.
8. Move to the beginning of the same line (line 3).
9. Move to the beginning of the document.

Note: Keep this document open and continue reading.

File—Save

To save a file for the first time:

1. From the **File** tab, click **Save**.

   Or: From the **Quick Access Toolbar**, click **Save**.

   Or: On the keyboard, press **CTRL+S**.

2. From the **Save As** pane, click **This PC**; click **Browse** below that to save to a different location.
3. After the **Save As** dialog box appears, browse to the desired folder.

   The folder choice listing varies depending on user customizations and Microsoft updates.

4. If necessary, click the list arrow in the **Save as type** box, and click **Word Document (*.docx)** to save the file as a Word 2016 document. Word automatically adds the extension *.docx* to your file name.
5. Type the desired file name in the **File name** box, and click **Save**.

Word automatically inserts a file name in the File name box, which usually includes the first few words in the document. The highlighted temporary name is replaced with your first keystroke.

To save an existing document: Click the **File** tab, **Save**.

Or: From the **Quick Access Toolbar**, click the **Save** button.

Or: On the keyboard, press **CTRL+S**.

To save an existing document under a different name or in a different location: Click the **File** tab, and click **Save As**. From the **Save As** pane, click **This PC**; below that, click **Browse**. From the **Save As** window, in the **File** name box, the existing document name will be highlighted. Browse to a new location if desired, type the new file name, and click **Save**.

REFER TO

WM Appendix C, Saving a Word File in PDF Format

See Appendix C for steps to save a Word document in PDF format.

PRACTICE 22 (2 of 5)

When you launch Word via GDP to begin a document processing job, typically a document with an assigned name opens automatically. When you use Save, you will not need to type a file name because the file was already assigned a specific name. However, in this exercise, you will use the Save and Save As commands to practice assigning a file name.

1. Move to the end of the *practice-22*, and press **ENTER** 2 times.
2. Type your first name and last name.
3. From the **File** tab, click **Save As**.
4. Under the **Save As** pane, click **This PC**; below that, click **Browse** and browse to the desired location—feel free to save the file in the **Downloads** folder; or under **Recent Folders**, click the desired folder.
5. Save this file with the new file name *student-22*, and click **Save**. Your screen should now look similar to the illustration in the next step.

   If you are prompted to upgrade your document, click **Cancel**. From the **Save As** dialog box, check **Maintain compatibility with previous versions of Word** on the bottom left of the dialog box; verify that the file name in the **File name** box is correct; click **Save**.

PRACTICE (continued)

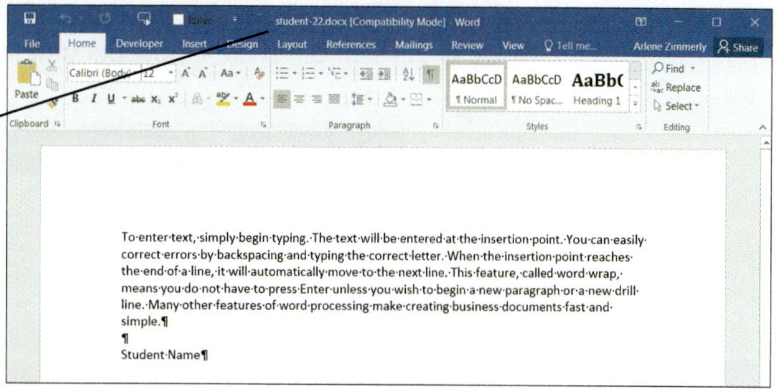

Note that the file name changes to *student-22* after saving. The file extension *.docx* may not display depending upon your Windows settings.

Note: Keep this document open and continue reading.

File—Close

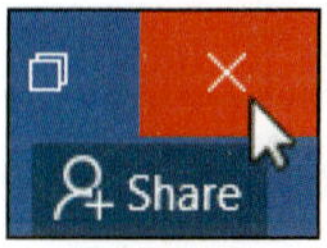

Close button

To close a file: From the **File** tab, click **Close**, or press **CTRL+W**.

Or: Click the **Close** button in the upper-right-hand corner of the Word window.

If the file is a new, unsaved document or an existing document to which you made changes, you will be prompted to save the document. Follow the prompts to save or discard the file as desired.

PRACTICE 22 (3 of 5)

1. Move the insertion point to the top of *student-22*, and type this:

   Hello!

2. Press **ENTER 2** times to insert 1 blank line after the new text.
3. Close *student-22* (do *not* close Word) by carefully following one of the steps just explained—click **Don't Save** so that changes are discarded and the original file remains intact. (*Hint:* Press **CTRL+W** to ensure that you close *student-22* but leave Word open.)
4. Note that *student-22* closes, and Word is still open.

Note: Keep Word open and continue reading.

File—New

To close the Word file but keep Word open: On the keyboard, press **CTRL+W**. Or click the **File** tab, and click **Close**. Then, either open an existing document or create a new document to continue working.

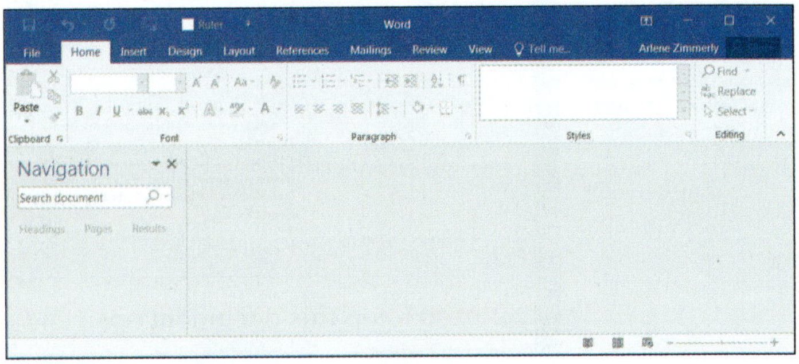

To create a new document: Press **CTRL+N**, or click the **File** tab, **New**; click **Blank document** from the list of templates.

PRACTICE 22 (4 of 5)

1. Press **CTRL+N** to create a new blank document, and type your name.
2. Note the generic file name in the title bar.
3. Open the file named *practice-22*, which you downloaded previously from the Lesson 22D GDP screen. (*Hint:* The file is probably in the *Downloads* folder on your computer.)

Note: Keep both documents open and continue reading.

Switch Windows

To switch windows:

1. Click the **View** tab.
2. From the **Window** group, click the **Switch Windows** button, and click the desired document window from the displayed list of open documents.

   Or: Press **CTRL+F6** (or **FN+CTRL+F6**) repeatedly to toggle through available windows.

Maximize button

Or: From the **View** tab, **Window** group, click the **Arrange All** button to tile all open windows. To return each window to normal size, click the **Maximize** button in the upper-right-hand corner of each window as you switch among them, or double-click the title bar.

Or: Click the desired document button on the **Windows taskbar**.

PRACTICE 22 (5 of 5)

1. Click the **View** tab; from the **Window** group, click **Switch Windows**; from the drop-down list, click the desired document.
2. Press **CTRL+F6** (or **FN+CTRL+F6**) repeatedly to toggle through the open document windows.
3. From the **View** tab, **Window** group, click **Arrange All** to tile all open document windows vertically.
4. Double-click the title bar in the top window to return it to normal size.
5. Close all files without saving, and return to GDP.

GO TO Textbook

Orientation to Word Processing—C

LESSON **23**

Select Text

To modify existing text: Select the desired text—the selected text appears highlighted; then make any desired changes, such as italicizing, moving, or deleting the text.

Selected text is highlighted

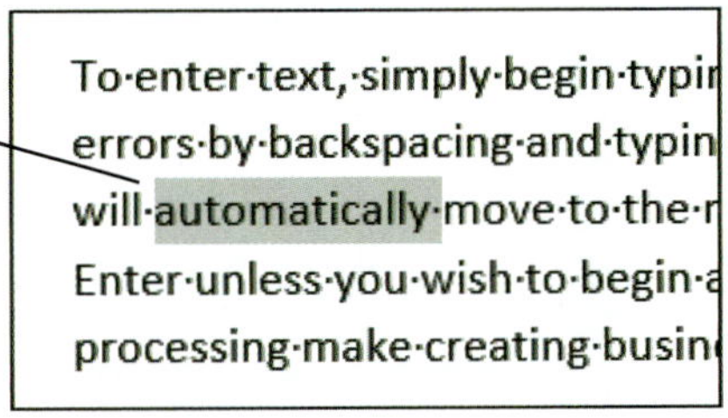

To select (highlight) text using the mouse:

To Select	Do This
Any amount of text	Point and drag over the text you want to select.
Any amount of continuous text	Position the insertion point at the beginning of the desired text. Hold down **SHIFT**; press the right and down arrow keys to extend the selection precisely, or click at the end of the selection.
A word (and the space after it)	Double-click the word.
A line	Click in the **Selection bar** (the blank area in the margin just to the left of the typed line).
A sentence (and the space after if another sentence follows)	Hold down **CTRL** and click anywhere in the sentence.
A paragraph	Double-click in the **Selection bar** to the left of the paragraph (or triple-click anywhere in the paragraph).
The entire document	Triple-click anywhere in the **Selection bar** or press **CTRL+A**.

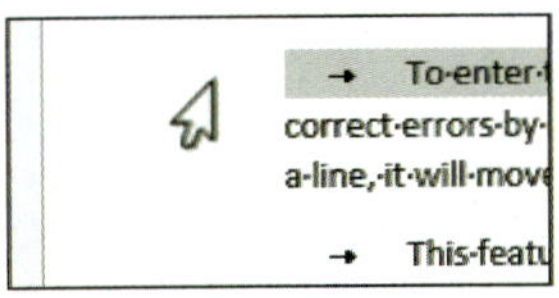

Selection bar area

To deselect text (remove highlight): Click anywhere on the screen or press any arrow key.

PRACTICE 23 (1 of 4)

1. From GDP's Lesson 23I screen, click **Start Work**; download and open *practice-23* (a one-paragraph file) following your browser's steps.
2. Move the insertion point to the beginning of the document.
3. Press **TAB** to indent the first line of the paragraph.

   If an AutoCorrect Options lightning bolt button appears after pressing TAB, click it; then click Stop Setting Indent on Tabs and Backspace. Refer to Appendix A for details.

REFER TO

WM Appendix A, Using Microsoft Word in the Workplace, GDP—Word Settings, AutoFormat As You Type Options, Tabs and Indents

4. Note that the first line is indented by 0.5". Select "automatically" in the third line by double-clicking anywhere in the word; then delete the word by pressing **BACKSPACE**.
5. Move the insertion point immediately to the left of "T" in "This" in line 3. Delete the space to the left by pressing **BACKSPACE**; then start a new paragraph at this point by pressing **ENTER** 2 times.

   If the second paragraph is indented automatically when you press ENTER, see the explanation in step 3 and change Word settings.

6. Select the second paragraph by double-clicking the **Selection bar** area left of the paragraph or by triple-clicking anywhere in the paragraph.

Selection bar area.

→ To·enter·text,·simply·begin·typing.·The·text·will·be·entered·at·the·insertion·point.·You·can·easily·correct·errors·by·backspacing·and·typing·the·correct·letter.·When·the·insertion·point·reaches·the·end·of·a·line,·it·will·move·to·the·next·line.¶
¶
This·feature,·called·word·wrap,·means·you·do·not·have·to·press·Enter·unless·you·wish·to·begin·a·new·paragraph·or·a·new·drill·line.·Many·other·features·of·word·processing·make·creating·business·documents·fast·and·simple.¶

7. Select the entire document by pressing **CTRL+A**. Deselect the document by clicking anywhere on the screen or by pressing any directional arrow key.
8. Select the words "word processing" in the last sentence. In their place, type `Microsoft Word for Windows`. Your text should now look similar to this:

→ To·enter·text,·simply·begin·typing.·The·text·will·be·entered·at·the·insertion·point.·You·can·easily·correct·errors·by·backspacing·and·typing·the·correct·letter.·When·the·insertion·point·reaches·the·end·of·a·line,·it·will·move·to·the·next·line.¶
¶
This·feature,·called·word·wrap,·means·you·do·not·have·to·press·Enter·unless·you·wish·to·begin·a·new·paragraph·or·a·new·drill·line.·Many·other·features·of·Microsoft·Word·for·Windows·make·creating·business·documents·fast·and·simple.¶

Note: Keep this document open and continue reading.

Bold

Bold text is darker so it stands out. The Bold button "toggles." Clicking the button once applies bold and clicking again removes it.

To bold text as you type:

Bold button

1. From the **Home** tab, **Font** group, click the **Bold** button, or press **CTRL+B**.
2. Type the text you want to appear in bold.
3. Click the **Bold** button, or press **CTRL+B** again to turn off bold; note that the text appears in bold on the screen.

To bold existing text:

1. Select the text you want to appear in bold (or click inside a single word).
2. Click the **Bold** button or press **CTRL+B**.

To remove bold formatting:

1. Select the desired bolded text (or click inside a single word).
2. Click the **Bold** button or press **CTRL+B**.

PRACTICE 23 (2 of 4)

1. Move to the end of the second paragraph. Press the **SPACE BAR** 1 time after the period, turn on bold, and type this: **Amazing!**
2. Select "word wrap" in line 4, and bold both words.
3. In line 6, remove the bold formatting from "Amazing!" including the exclamation point.
4. In the second sentence of the last paragraph, select and bold "Word for Windows."
5. In the second sentence of the last paragraph, click inside the word "Microsoft"; bold the word without selecting it.
6. Press **TAB** at the start of the second paragraph to indent it. Your screen should now look similar to this:

→ To·enter·text,·simply·begin·typing.·The·text·will·be·entered·at·the·insertion·point.·You·can·easily·correct·errors·by·backspacing·and·typing·the·correct·letter.·When·the·insertion·point·reaches·the·end·of·a·line,·it·will·move·to·the·next·line.¶
¶
→ This·feature,·called·**word·wrap**,·means·you·do·not·have·to·press·Enter·unless·you·wish·to·begin·a·new·paragraph·or·a·new·drill·line.·Many·other·features·of·**Microsoft·Word·for·Windows**·make·creating·business·documents·fast·and·simple.·Amazing!¶

Note: Keep this document open and continue reading.

Undo/Redo Commands

To cancel a command before it has been executed: Press **ESC**, click elsewhere on the screen, or tap any directional arrow key.

Undo button

To undo the most recent action: From the **Quick Access Toolbar**, click the **Undo** button; or press **CTRL+Z**.

To undo an action other than the most recent one: Click the **Undo** button or **CTRL+Z** repeatedly, or click the list arrow to the right of the **Undo** button to display a list of recent actions. The most recent action appears at the top of the list. Select and click the action you want to undo. Clicking an action anywhere below the first one undoes all actions up to and including the selected action.

Repeat button

To repeat the most recent action: From the **Quick Access Toolbar**, click the **Repeat** button, or press **CTRL+Y**.

The Repeat button is inactive until some action can be repeated or undone. Then it toggles between Redo and Repeat as you work. Point to the Repeat button to display a ScreenTip that identifies the action to be repeated.

Redo button

To redo the most recent action: From the **Quick Access Toolbar**, click the **Redo** button.

The Redo button does not appear until some action has first been undone so it can be redone. Point to the Redo button to display a ScreenTip that identifies the action to be redone.

PRACTICE 23 (3 of 4)

1. Move the insertion point to the end of the document; press **ENTER** 2 times to begin a new paragraph; press **TAB** to indent the first line of the new paragraph. Type this sentence:

   ```
   Word processing makes sense (and cents) in the
   workplace.
   ```

2. Use **Undo** to undo (remove) the sentence you just typed.
3. Use **Redo** to reinsert the sentence.

PRACTICE (continued)

4. Double-click "Enter" in the second paragraph to select it; press **CAPS LOCK**, retype it in all-caps, and release **CAPS LOCK**. Your screen should look similar to this:

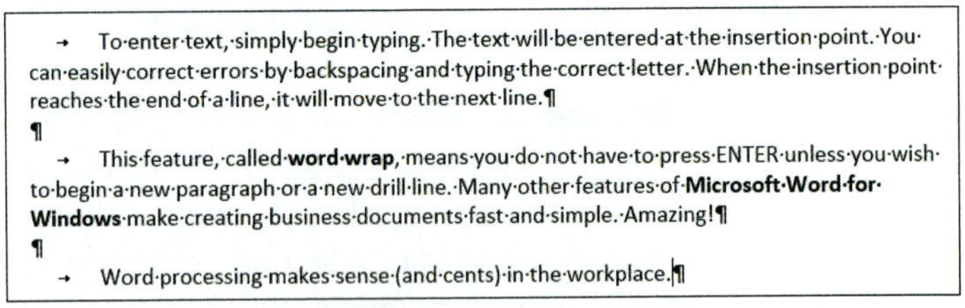

→ To·enter·text,·simply·begin·typing.·The·text·will·be·entered·at·the·insertion·point.·You·can·easily·correct·errors·by·backspacing·and·typing·the·correct·letter.·When·the·insertion·point·reaches·the·end·of·a·line,·it·will·move·to·the·next·line.¶

¶

→ This·feature,·called·**word·wrap**,·means·you·do·not·have·to·press·ENTER·unless·you·wish·to·begin·a·new·paragraph·or·a·new·drill·line.·Many·other·features·of·**Microsoft·Word·for·Windows**·make·creating·business·documents·fast·and·simple.·Amazing!¶

¶

→ Word·processing·makes·sense·(and·cents)·in·the·workplace.¶

Note: Keep this document open and continue reading.

Help

To get help via F1: On the keyboard, press **F1** (or **FN+F1**).

To get help via the Tell me search feature:

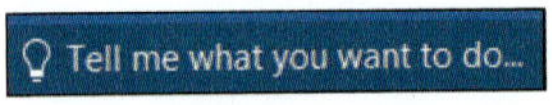

Tell me box

1. Type any desired keywords in the **Tell me** box in the title bar; then click each option on the list below the box one by one; for example, type bold in the **Tell me** box; click **Bold** to apply bold at that point in the document—note that the **Bold** button is now active.
2. Click **Smart Lookup on "bold"** or explore other buttons to access related feature help.
3. Type other keywords, and explore the **Tell me** box options on your own.

Help button via dialog box

To get help via a dialog box: For example, from the **Home** tab, **Font** group, click the **Dialog Box Launcher** arrow to open the **Font** dialog box; click the **Help** button (the question mark in the upper-right-hand corner of the title bar in the dialog box to the left of the **Close** button).

Or: With the dialog box open, on the keyboard, press **F1** (or **FN+F1**).

PRACTICE 23 (4 of 4)

Explore any Help features of interest on your own. Your exact steps to use Help may differ slightly from these ones.

1. Type `bold` in the **Tell me** box; note the drop-down list of possible actions.
2. Click any related actions of interest from the list.
3. From the **Home** tab, **Font** group, click the **Dialog Box Launcher**; click the **Help** button, and read any related information.
4. Save the changes to *practice-23*, and return to GDP.

GO TO Textbook

Orientation to Word Processing—D

Print Preview

To preview a document before printing:

1. From the **File** tab, click **Print**; or press **CTRL+F2** (or **FN+CTRL+F2**).
2. Note that your formatted document appears as a full page on the right side of the screen, and note the options under **Print**, **Printer**, and **Settings**.
3. Note the **Zoom** slider in the lower-right-hand corner of the screen, which you can use to adjust the zoom level of the print preview for that document.
4. Press **ESC** or click the **Back** button to return to the document to make any desired document edits.

REFER TO
WM L. 24, Zoom

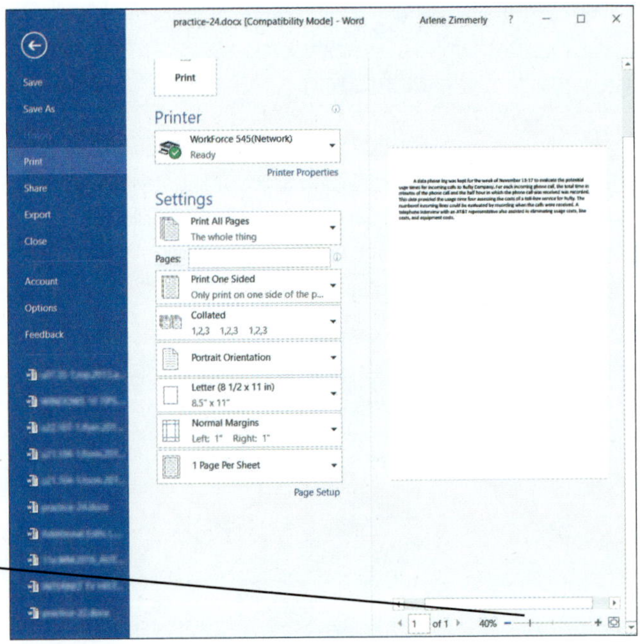

Zoom slider

PRACTICE 24 (1 of 7)

1. From GDP's Lesson 24E screen, click **Start Work**, and follow your browser's prompts to download and open *practice-24* (a one-paragraph file with deliberate errors).
2. From the **File** tab, click **Print**. Your screen should look similar to the illustration on page 24.
3. Drag the **Zoom** slider left and right to adjust the zoom level.
4. Press **ESC** or click the **Back** arrow on the top of the left pane to return to the document.

Note: Keep this document open and continue reading.

Spelling and Grammar Check

Word's automatic spelling check compares typed words with Word's built-in dictionary. A red wavy underline appears below words not in the dictionary. Such words are not necessarily misspelled. Omitted words, misused words, or typographical errors that form a new word (such as "sing" for "sign") are often missed by Word's spelling check! Always proofread documents carefully before submitting them.

Word's automatic grammar check uses a blue wavy underline below words that might be used in the wrong context—for example, using "loose" instead of "lose." Only one feature in Word's grammar check (Frequently confused words) should be active during this course due to inconsistencies and inaccuracies in other automatic grammar check features. Make sure Word options for checking spelling and grammar have been set as described next.

REFER TO

WM Appendix A, Using Microsoft Word in the Workplace, GDP—Word Settings, Spelling and Grammar Check

To enable spelling and grammar options: From the **File** tab, click **Options**; from the **Word Options** window, left pane, click the **Proofing** tab; under **When correcting spelling and grammar in Word**:

- Uncheck **Mark grammar errors as you type** and uncheck **Check grammar with spelling**.
- Verify that **Check spelling as you type** and **Frequently confused words** are checked; click **OK**.

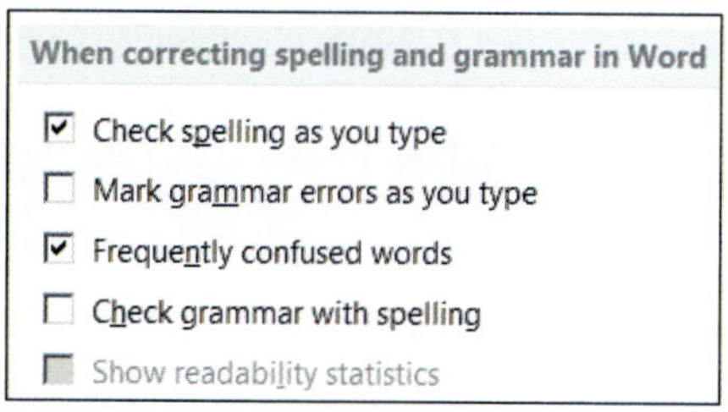

To correct a spelling error immediately: Right-click the word marked with the red or blue wavy line to display suggested corrections; click the correctly spelled word or a relevant choice, such as **Ignore**, **Ignore All**, or **Add to Dictionary**.

Spelling & Grammar button

Proofing Errors icon

To manually check spelling and grammar:

1. From the **Review** tab, **Proofing** group, click the **Spelling & Grammar** button. Or press **F7** (or **FN+F7**).

   Or: On the status bar, click the **Proofing Errors** icon when errors are present as indicated by an "X" on the icon. Note the **ScreenTip**: "Word found proofing errors. Click or tap to correct them." Click the button to move to each error. If no errors are found, the button displays a check mark, and the **ScreenTip** displays: "No proofing errors."

2. Note that Word scrolls through the document. If Word finds a possible error, the **Spelling** pane is automatically displayed.
3. Each time Word stops for a spelling error, do one of the following:
   - If the highlighted word is spelled correctly, click **Ignore** (or **Ignore All** if you want the speller to ignore all occurrences of this word in your document).
   - To add the word in question to the custom dictionary so that it will not be marked again, click **Add**.

     Use caution to avoid adding incorrectly spelled words to the dictionary. Once you click Ignore, Word will no longer mark that text as an error even if you spell-check the document again. Consult Word help for steps to remove words from the built-in dictionary. Word may not behave as expected in the Practice exercise if words have been added to Word's dictionary.

   - If a word in the **Suggestions** list has the correct spelling, select that word, and then click **Change** or **Change All** as desired.

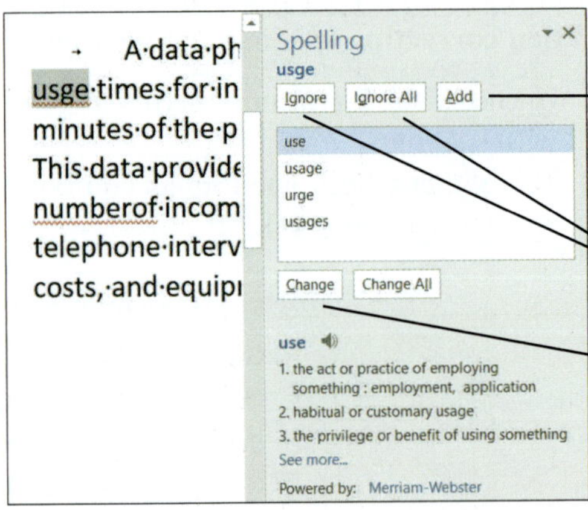

Click **Add** to add the word to the custom dictionary so the word won't be marked again. If you click **Ignore** for a misspelled word such as "usge" or if you click **Add** for a name such as "Rufty," Word will not mark those words as possible spelling errors.

Click **Ignore** or **Ignore All** if the word is spelled correctly.

Click **Change** to change the highlighted word in the document to the highlighted word in the spelling list.

4. Each time Word stops for a grammar check for a frequently confused word, do one of the following:
   - Compare the description of the error with the suggested correction in the list of suggestions.
   - If the change is applicable, click **Change**.
   - If the change is not applicable, click **Ignore**.
5. If you interrupt your spell check, click **Resume** to continue the spell check. When the dialog box appears confirming the spelling and grammar check is complete, click **OK**.

AUTOCORRECT

REFER TO

WM Appendix A, Using Microsoft Word in the Workplace, GDP—Word Settings, AutoCorrect Options, Capitalization

Word will automatically correct some common typographical errors immediately after you type them, often without your noticing. For example, if you type "teh" and press the SPACE BAR, Word will automatically change "teh" to "the" on the fly (as you type). Give it a try.

Word will automatically capitalize the first letter of sentences unless you have changed the automatic capitalization setting. See Appendix A for details on changing your settings.

PRACTICE 24 (2 of 7)

Word's automatic spelling check compares typed words with Word's built-in dictionary. If this feature does not behave as expected, simply read the steps that follow for basic concepts.

1. Verify that your spelling and grammar check options are properly set as explained in the Spelling and Grammar Check section in this lesson.
2. Move the insertion point to the end of the document, press the **SPACE BAR** 1 time, type this sentence, and press **CTRL+HOME**.

   ```
   The bottom line is to avoid loosing money
   unnecessarily.
   ```

3. Note any words marked with a red wavy underline and a blue wavy underline. Adjust your zoom level for a closer look.

→ A·data·phone·log·was·kept·for·the·week·of·November·13-17·to·evaluate·the·potential·usge·times·for·incoming·calls·to·Rufty·Company.·For·each·incoming·phone·call,·the·total·time·in·minutes·of·the·phone·call·and·the·half·hour·in·which·the·phone·call·was·received·was·recorded.·This·data·provided·the·usage·time·four·assessing·the·costs·of·a·toll-free·service·for·Rufty.·The·numberof·incoming·lines·could·be·evaluated·by·recording·when·the·calls·were·received.·A·telephone·interview·with·an·AT&T·representative·also·assisted·in·eliminating·usage·costs,·line·costs,·and·equipment·costs.·The·bottom·line·is·to·avoid·loosing·money·unnecessarily.¶

PRACTICE (continued)

4. From the **Review** tab, **Proofing** group, click the **Spelling & Grammar** button, or on the keyboard, press **F7** (or **FN+F7**).
   a. Word highlights and displays "usge" in the document and displays "usage" in the **Spelling Pane** as one of the suggested choices; click "usage" and click **Change** to accept this suggestion.
   b. In the **Spelling Pane**, Word displays "Rufty" and suggests replacements; however, "Rufty" is the correct spelling for the company; note that "Rufty" occurs twice in the document; click **Ignore All** so that Word will not mark this word again; note that all instances of "Rufty" are no longer displayed with a red, wavy underline.
   c. In the **Spelling Pane**, Word displays "numberof"; click "number of"; click **Change**.
   d. In the **Grammar Pane**, Word displays "loosing" and displays definitions for the correct word "losing"; click **Change**.
   e. When the dialog box appears confirming the spelling and grammar check is complete, click **OK**.
   f. Carefully proofread the document again and correct each of these contextual errors: At the end of line 3 and the start of line 4, "was recorded" should be "were recorded"; in line 4, "four" should be "for." Correct the spelling in these instances.

5. Your lines should now look similar to the following illustration. Save *practice-24*.

→ A·data·phone·log·was·kept·for·the·week·of·November·13-17·to·evaluate·the·potential·usage·times·for·incoming·calls·to·Rufty·Company.·For·each·incoming·phone·call,·the·total·time·in·minutes·of·the·phone·call·and·the·half·hour·in·which·the·phone·call·was·received·were·recorded.·This·data·provided·the·usage·time·for·assessing·the·costs·of·a·toll-free·service·for·Rufty.·The·number·of·incoming·lines·could·be·evaluated·by·recording·when·the·calls·were·received.·A·telephone·interview·with·an·AT&T·representative·also·assisted·in·eliminating·usage·costs,·line·costs,·and·equipment·costs.·The·bottom·line·is·to·avoid·losing·money·unnecessarily.¶

Note: Keep this document open and continue reading.

Show/Hide Formatting

When you press a nonprinting key, Word inserts a nonprinting formatting mark into the document. Formatting marks are shown in illustrations to help you verify that the keystrokes you used in your job are correct.

Mark	Press	To Insert
¶	ENTER	Paragraph break
↵	SHIFT+ENTER	Line break
→	TAB	Paragraph indent
•	SPACE BAR	Space

The directions "insert 1 hard return" or "press ENTER 1 time" are synonymous. Word defines a paragraph as any text or graphic that is followed by a ¶ mark.

Show/Hide ¶ button

To display formatting marks on the screen: From the **Home** tab, **Paragraph** group, click the **Show/Hide** ¶ button, or press **CTRL+SHIFT+8**.

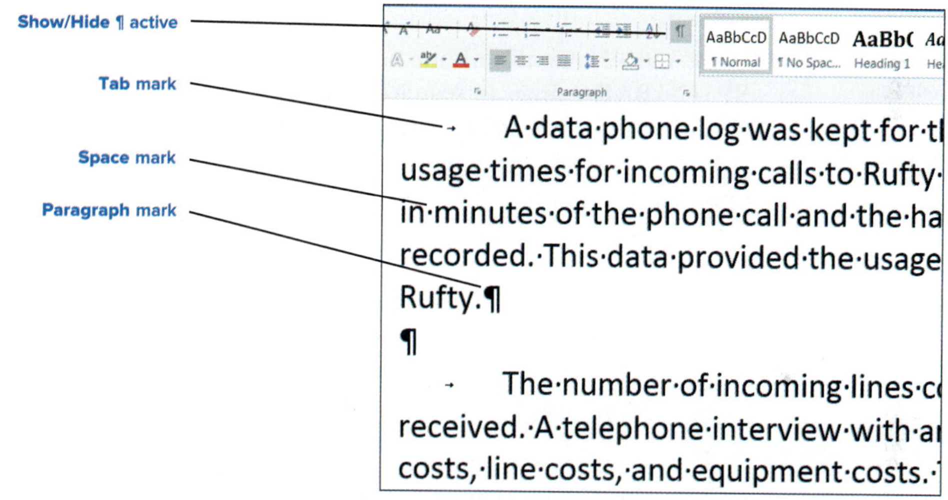

PRACTICE 24 (3 of 7)

1. From the **Home** tab, **Paragraph** group, click the **Show/Hide** ¶ button, or press **CTRL+SHIFT+8** to display the formatting marks.
2. Move to the end of the first sentence of the document, and press **SHIFT+ENTER**.
3. Point to the different formatting marks shown on the screen—the tab mark, the line break you just inserted, the space mark, and the paragraph mark.
4. Delete the line break you inserted in step 2.

Note: Keep this document open and continue reading.

Navigation Pane—Search

Navigation Pane Search document box

Use the Navigation Pane Search document box to search for characters (letters or words), spaces, and punctuation marks. Electronic searching is a powerful proofreading tool to help you find trailing spaces (one or more spaces following a word just before the end of a paragraph) and extra spaces after a punctuation mark, between words, or between sentences.

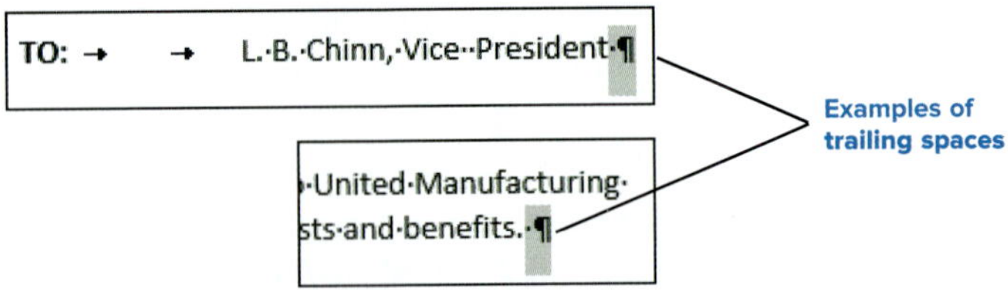

To use the Navigation Pane to search for extra spaces:

REFER TO
WM L. 69, Find and Replace

1. Click in the **Navigation Pane Search document** box, and press the **SPACE BAR** 2 times to search for any extra, undesired spaces.
2. Note that all instances of 2 spaces are highlighted in the document.

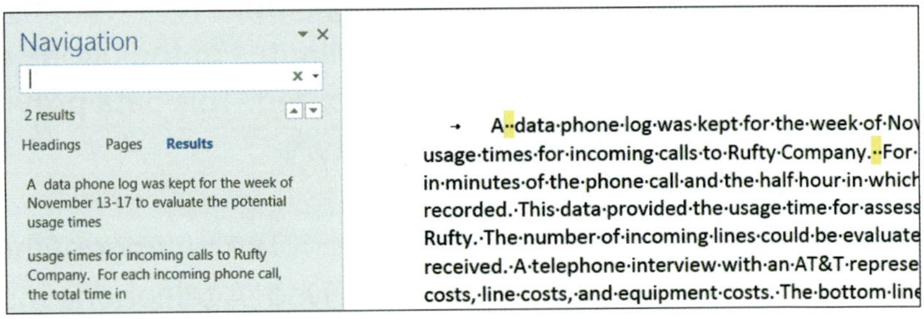

3. Click in the document at the point of the first match; edit as desired; click the **Next Search Result** down arrow under the search box; continue editing in like manner until you're done.

To use the Navigation Pane to search for trailing spaces:

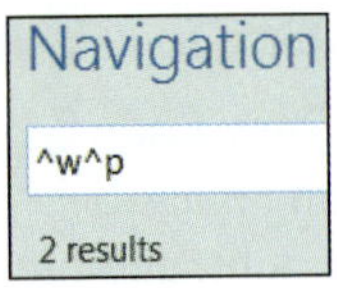

Search codes

1. In the **Navigation Pane Search document** box, press **SHIFT+6**; type `w`; press **SHIFT+6**; type `p`.

   Pressing SHIFT+6 inserts a caret (^) code; "w" represents a white space and "p" represents a paragraph mark.

2. Click the **Next Search Result** down arrow under the search box.

3. Note that the first trailing space is highlighted and indicated under **Results**.

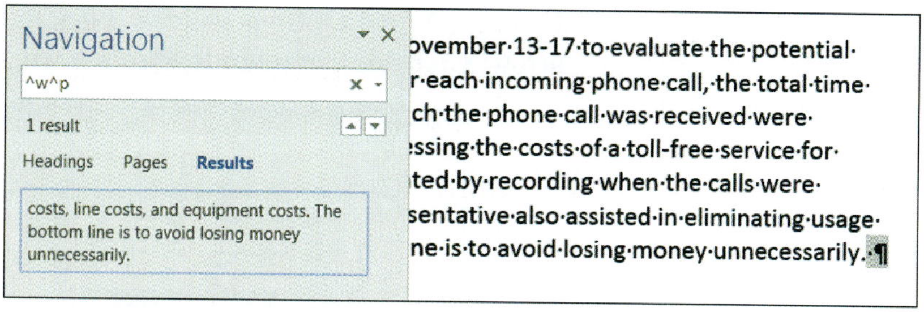

4. Correct errors using the same routine you used for extra spaces.

PRACTICE 24 (4 of 7)

1. In the first sentence, type an extra space after "A" (the first word in the sentence) and after the period in "Company" at the end of the sentence.
2. Click in the **Navigation Pane Search document** box, and press the **SPACE BAR** 2 times to search for any extra, undesired spaces.
3. Click in the document at the point of the first match; edit as needed; click the down arrow under the search box; continue editing in like manner until you're done.
4. Press **CTRL+END**, and type an extra space after the period at the end of the paragraph.
5. In the **Navigation Pane Search document** box, delete the spaces, press **SHIFT+6**; type `w`; press **SHIFT+6**; type `p`.
6. Click the **Next Search Result** down arrow under the search box; click in the document, and edit as needed.

Note: Keep this document open and continue reading.

Speak

Use Speak to listen to a selection of text as it is read aloud. Listening to what you have typed as you read your original copy is a highly effective proofreading practice. Listen for wording that doesn't make contextual sense, and focus in particular on numbers and names. Speak is available only when you add the Speak button to the Quick Access Toolbar.

To add the Speak button to the Quick Access toolbar:

1. From the **Quick Access Toolbar** list arrow, click **More Commands**.
2. From the **Word Options** window, click the **Choose commands from** list arrow; click **All Commands**; scroll down to **Speak**; click **Add >>**, **OK**.

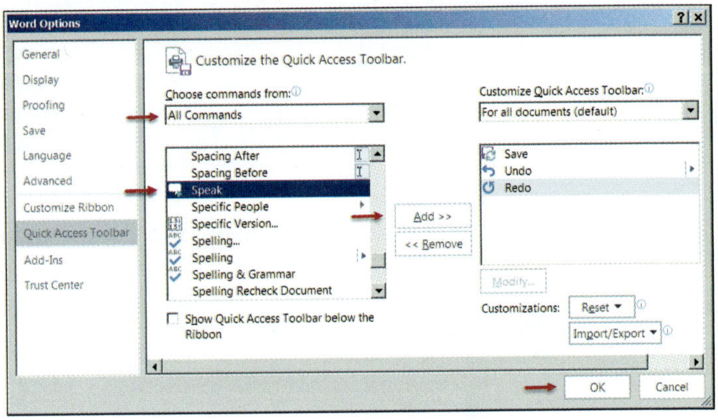

To use the Speak button to listen to selected text:

1. Select the desired text; from the **Quick Access Toolbar**, click the **Speak** button.

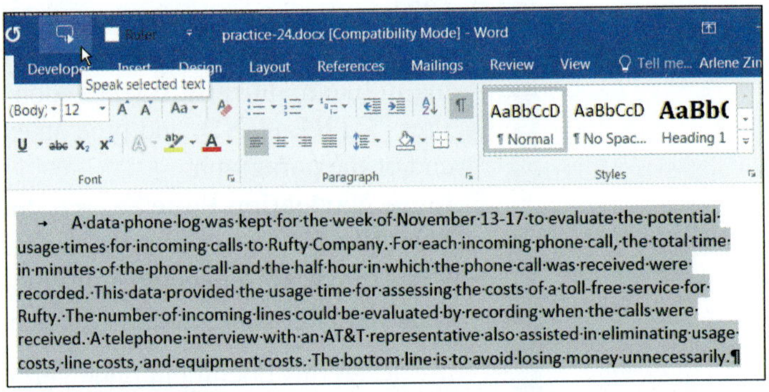

2. Note that **Speak** reads the selected text, and the **Speak** button displays an "X" badge until all selected text has been read; listen carefully for any contextual errors and watch for typos; edit the Practice exercise accordingly.

Speak button with X badge

Whenever the X badge is displayed on the Speak button, click Speak to pause speaking the selected text. Click Speak again to resume speaking of selected text from the beginning. Note the X badge disappears when reading is paused or when reading is finished.

PRACTICE 24 (5 of 7)

1. Add the **Speak** button to the **Quick Access Toolbar**.
2. In the second line, delete “Rufty”; after “Company,” change “For each” to “Four every.”
3. Press **CTRL+A** to select the entire document.
4. Click the **Speak** button as you keep your eyes on the correct copy below:

> → A·data·phone·log·was·kept·for·the·week·of·November·13-17·to·evaluate·the·potential·usage·times·for·incoming·calls·to·Rufty·Company.·For·each·incoming·phone·call,·the·total·time·in·minutes·of·the·phone·call·and·the·half·hour·in·which·the·phone·call·was·received·were·recorded.·This·data·provided·the·usage·time·for·assessing·the·costs·of·a·toll-free·service·for·Rufty.·The·number·of·incoming·lines·could·be·evaluated·by·recording·when·the·calls·were·received.·A·telephone·interview·with·an·AT&T·representative·also·assisted·in·eliminating·usage·costs,·line·costs,·and·equipment·costs.·The·bottom·line·is·to·avoid·losing·money·unnecessarily.¶

5. Listen carefully for the contextual errors you added in step 2; pause **Speak** at each error, correct the error, reselect text to be read, and continue in like manner until you’re done.
6. Save changes to *practice-24*, and close the file.
7. Go to GDP’s Lesson 24E screen to download *practice-24-zoom* to complete the remainder of this lesson; then return here to continue reading.

Zoom

Zoom in for a magnified look at details or zoom out to display one page or multiple pages on one screen. Adjust zoom settings via the View tab, Zoom group options or use the Zoom bar on the status bar.

To adjust the zoom level using the View tab:

Zoom group buttons

1. From the **View** tab, **Zoom** group, click the **Zoom** button to open the **Zoom** dialog box.

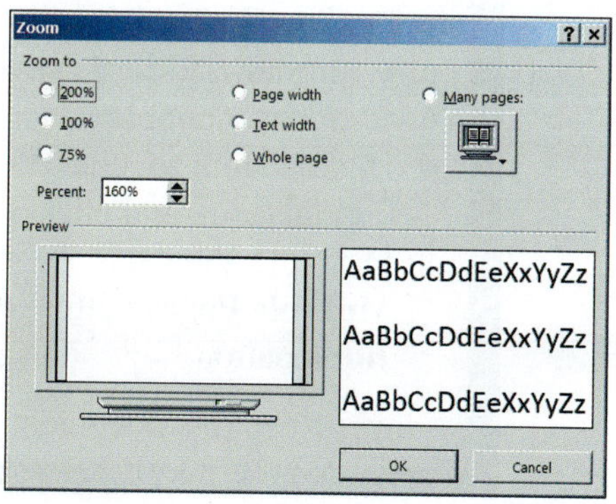

2. Experiment with the choices under **Zoom to**.
3. As you click a **Zoom to** option, note the **Preview**.
4. Click the desired zoom; click **OK**.
5. On the **Ribbon**, note and experiment with the buttons in the **Zoom** group for **One Page**, **Multiple Pages**, and **Page Width**.

In the Zoom level button on the Zoom slider, the term *Whole page* is used rather than *One Page*. The functionality is identical.

To adjust the zoom level using the Zoom bar on the status bar:

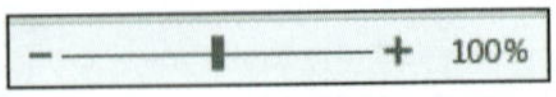

Zoom Out (–)
Zoom Slider (|)
Zoom In (+)
Zoom level (%)

1. Click the **Zoom level** button (the % on the slider on the **Zoom** bar) to display the **Zoom** dialog box. This is the same dialog box you can access via the **View** tab, **Zoom** group, **Zoom** button.
2. Click the **Zoom Out** (–) and **Zoom In** (+) buttons as desired.
3. Drag the **Zoom slider** (|) left or right as desired.

To hide the marginal white space at the top and bottom of a page, point to the top or bottom edge of any page until the mouse pointer displays double boxed arrows pointing down and up and double-click. Repeat these steps to undo that action.

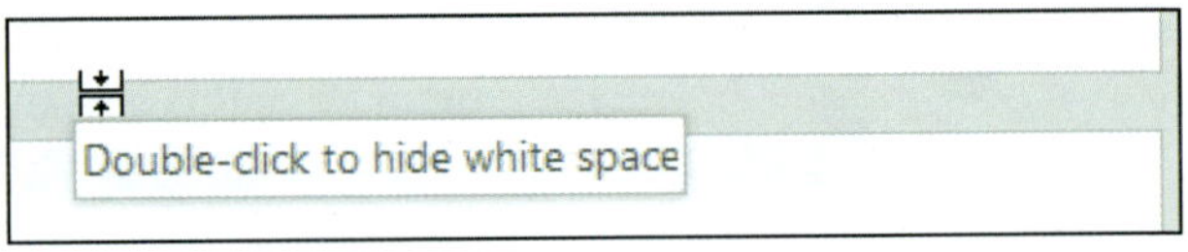

PRACTICE 24 (6 of 7)

1. From GDP's Lesson 24E screen, click the **Download File** button, and follow your browser's prompts to download and open *practice-24-zoom* (a multipage business report file).
2. Click the **Zoom Out** (–) button repeatedly until two whole pages display.
3. Click the **Zoom In** (+) button repeatedly until the **Zoom** level button shows **100%**.
4. Drag the **Zoom slider** (|) until the **Zoom level** button shows about **300%**.
5. With **Show/Hide ¶** active, note the formatting marks.
6. Click the **Zoom level** (%) button to display the **Zoom** dialog box.
7. Under **Zoom to**, click **Whole Page**, **OK**; click the **Zoom level** (%) button again, and click **Text Width**, **OK**.
8. From the **View** tab, **Zoom** group, click the **One Page** button, the **Multiple Pages** button, the **Page Width** button, and finally, the **100%** button.

Note: Keep this document open and continue reading.

Print

To print the document displayed on the screen:

1. From the **File** tab, click **Print**, or press **CTRL+P**.

   See Lesson 21 for steps to add the Quick Print button and the Print Preview and Print button to the Quick Access Toolbar. Use the Quick Print button to immediately print a copy of the entire document, or use the Print Preview and Print button to open the Print window.

2. Click the desired print options under **Print**, **Printer**, and **Settings**.

REFER TO

WM L. 21, Choosing Commands, From the Quick Access Toolbar

Click the **Print All Pages** list arrow; then click desired choice.

Click in the **Pages** box and type the desired page range; for example, type "1-2" to print pages 1 though 2; type "2" to print only page 2.

To print the page currently displayed in **Print Preview**, browse to the desired page; click the **Print All Pages** list arrow, and click **Print Current Page**.

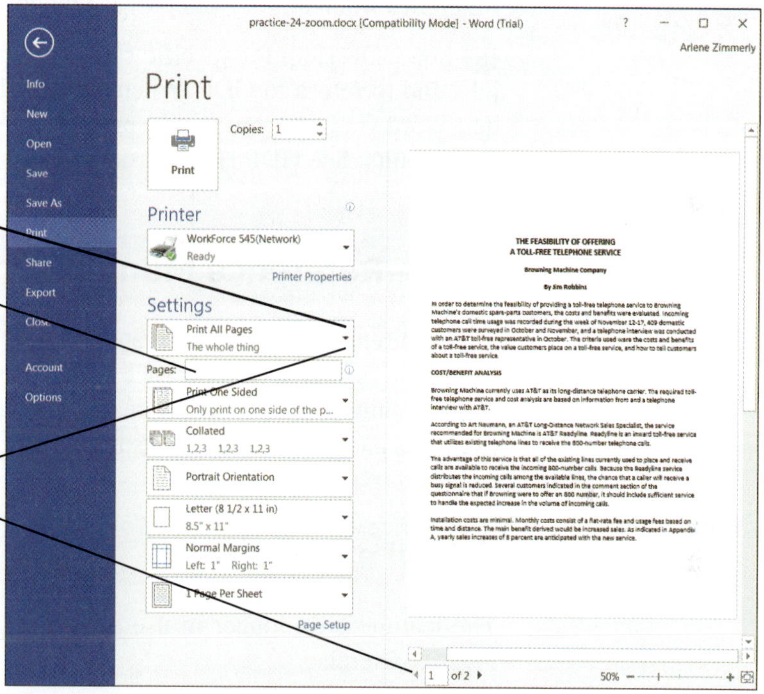

PRACTICE 24 (7 of 7)

Always check with your instructor before printing anything!

1. Print one copy of *practice-24-zoom*.
2. Close *practice-24-zoom*, and return to GDP.

GO TO Textbook

E-Mail Messages

25

LESSON

GDP—Scoring

REFER TO

WM L. 21, GDP—Start Word | GDP—Quit Word
GDP—Help (keystroking scoring)

Document processing jobs begin in Lesson 25 with Correspondence 25-1. From now on, you will use several GDP features routinely (Scoring and the Reference Manual, for example) as you complete your work.

See GDP Help for specific steps to begin and end document processing jobs and to return to GDP. When you finish a document processing job and quit Word via GDP, you will be prompted to score your document and review your results. See GDP Help for details.

GDP—Reference Manual

The Reference Manual is available in your textbook and in this manual. An electronic, searchable Reference Manual is available via GDP's Reference Manual button. Refer to this resource routinely as you complete Practice exercises and document processing jobs.

E-Mail a Document

The feature is no longer in use in the 11th Edition. Please continue to the Practice exercise.

PRACTICE 25 (1 of 1)

REFER TO

WM Appendix A, Using Microsoft Word in the Workplace, GDP—Word Settings
WM L. 32, Widow/Orphan Control

Follow these procedures routinely from now on. These directions will no longer be repeated.

- Verify or set all Word options as outlined in Appendix A, Using Microsoft Word in the Workplace, GDP—Word Settings.
- Before you complete any Practice exercise, first read the related Formatting section in your textbook.

PRACTICE (continued)

- Click Start Work; download and open the start file so you are ready to begin with step 1.
- Activate Show/Hide ¶ to display nonprinting formatting marks—refer to illustrations to verify nonprinting keystrokes.
- Spell-check, proofread, and preview your document for errors, including undesirable page breaks. Close any open documents, and save as desired or as directed.

1. From GDP's Lesson 25G screen, click **Start Work**, and follow your browser's prompts to download and open *practice-25* (an unformatted e-mail message).
2. Arrange the e-mail message in correct format as shown in Lesson 25F, E-Mail Messages, in the textbook by pressing **ENTER** to insert blank lines where applicable.
3. Click directly before "Uploading" in the first paragraph; type this paragraph, and then press **ENTER** 2 times:

   As soon as you complete Lesson 10, please schedule a technique check with me. I'll send you an appointment schedule tomorrow. Choose a convenient appointment time and reply to my e-mail message when you have made a selection.

   In Word, lines wrap automatically to a second line as you approach the right margin. Do not press ENTER when you see a line break in the copy to be typed, which inserts a hard return and forces an incorrect line break. Press ENTER only between paragraphs, not within a paragraph. Refer to the illustration in step 8.

4. Click directly after "me" just before the period at the end of the first sentence, and type this:

   --the sooner, the better

5. Note that after you type both hyphens (--) followed by "the" and then press the **SPACE BAR**, a solid em dash (—) appears.

   In Word, two consecutive hyphens typed between words within a line should be converted automatically to a solid em dash when you space after the word following the dash.

6. Click directly after the last character in the e-mail address, and press **ENTER**; note that the e-mail address is converted to a hyperlink.

REFER TO

WM Appendix A, Using Microsoft Word in the Workplace, GDP—Word Settings, AutoFormat As You Type Options, Dashes

REFER TO

WM Appendix A, Using Microsoft Word in the Workplace, GDP—Word Settings, AutoFormat As You Type Options, Hyperlinks

PRACTICE (continued)

Hyperlinks are generated automatically when you press the SPACE BAR, type a punctuation mark and press the SPACE BAR, or press ENTER after an e-mail address or Web address in a line.

7. Type this on the line below the e-mail address:

   `Phone: 323-555-4000`

8. Click the **Show/Hide ¶** button to view ¶ formatting marks. Verify you have pressed **ENTER** and inserted spaces as shown. Your e-mail message should look similar to this:

```
Hi,·Students:¶
¶
As·soon·as·you·complete·Lesson·10,·please·schedule·a·technique·check·with·me—the·sooner,·the·better.·I'll·send·you·an·appointment·schedule·tomorrow.·Choose·a·convenient·appointment·time·and·reply·to·my·e-mail·message·when·you·have·made·a·selection.¶
¶
Uploading·your·lessons·on·time·and·on·a·regular·basis·is·absolutely·critical·to·your·success·in·an·online·course.·The·grace·period·for·turning·in·your·work·ends·next·week,·so·work·hard·this·week·to·get·on·schedule.·Send·me·an·e-mail·message·if·you·have·any·questions.¶
¶
Professor·Charlene·Morimoto¶
E-mail:·cmorimoto@fastmail.net¶
Phone:·323-555-4000¶
```

9. Save changes to *practice-25*, and return to GDP.

GO TO Textbook

Envelopes and Labels

LESSON 28

Envelopes

REFER TO
WM L. 115, Mail Merge—Envelopes

Envelopes may be typed individually or inserted automatically into a letter via Word's envelope feature. In this lesson, you will create standard No. 10 business envelopes.

- In Lesson 81, you will learn about DL envelopes (metric size) for international correspondence.
- In Lesson 115, you will generate multiple envelopes with different delivery addresses automatically by creating a single envelope as a main document, linking it to a data source with multiple recipients, and merging these two elements.

To insert a No. 10 envelope:

1. From the **Mailings** tab, **Create** group, click the **Envelopes** button—wait a few seconds for the dialog box to appear.

Select the lines of the inside address first; then use the Envelope feature to add the envelope to the document.

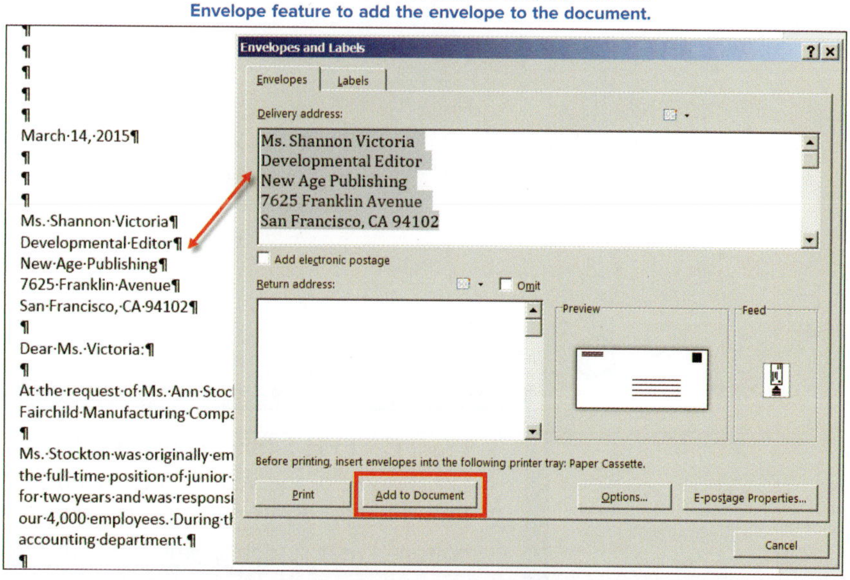

2. Note that the **Envelopes and Labels** dialog box opens with the **Envelopes** tab active; the **Delivery address** box should display the inside address automatically—edit the address if necessary.

3. Type a return address; or if your envelope has a printed return address, delete information in the **Return address** box; or check **Omit** above the **Return address** box.
4. Click **Add to Document** to save the envelope with the document.

   Or: Insert an envelope in the correct position into your printer, and click **Print**—the **Envelopes and Labels** dialog box closes automatically and the envelope should print; the envelope will not be saved with the document.

5. Note that the **Envelopes and Labels** dialog box closes automatically, and the envelope is inserted above the letter.

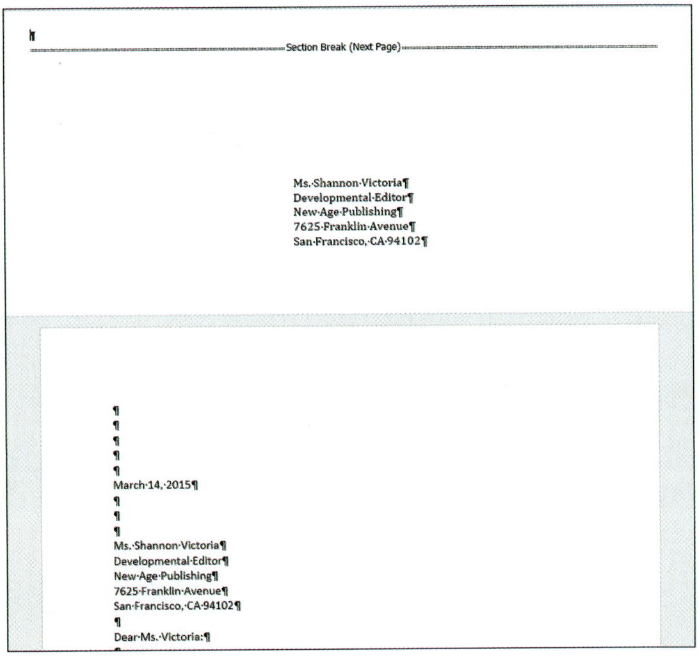

PRACTICE 28 (1 of 2)

1. Press **ENTER** 5 times above the date to position it at 2"; change the last 2 digits of the year to the current year in black font color.
2. From the **Mailings** tab, **Create** group, click the **Envelopes** button—your screen should look similar to the illustration on page 39.

PRACTICE (continued)

3. Check the **Omit** box to omit any return address, and click **Add to Document**; view the envelope at the top of the page—your screen should look similar to the illustration on page 40.
4. Press **CTRL+W** to close the file, but leave Word open. (Click **Save** to save changes if desired; Word will remain open but no document will be displayed.) Do not go to GDP.

Note: With Word open, continue reading.

View Gridlines

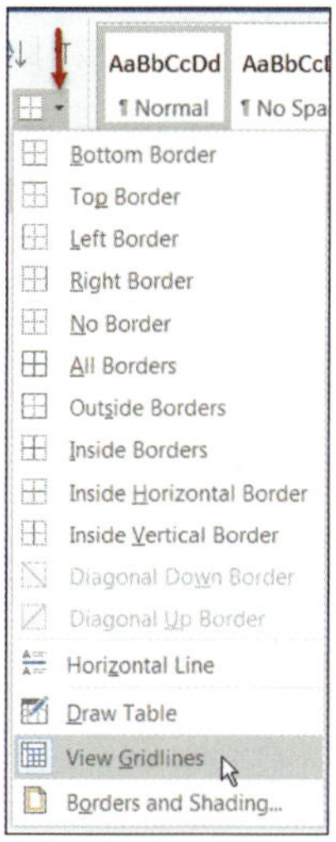

Borders button

Word's label feature automatically opens a selected label product with a table structure customized to that label. Because labels don't generally include borders, use View Gridlines to display gridlines around the cell boundaries.

To view table gridlines:

1. From the **Home** tab, **Paragraph** group, click the list arrow next to the **Borders** button.

   Click the list arrow next to the Borders button, not the Borders button itself—if you click the Borders button, you will apply the currently displayed border to the table or selected cell.

2. From the drop-down menu, click **View Gridlines**.

   Or: Click inside an existing table structure. The on-demand **Table Tools** tab appears on the ribbon with on-demand **Design** and **Layout** tabs below it. Click the **Layout** tab. From the **Table** group, click **View Gridlines**.

   Or: From the **Design** tab, **Borders** group, click the list arrow below the **Borders** button; click **View Gridlines**.

Labels

REFER TO
WM L. 115, Mail Merge—Labels
GDP—Help (mailing labels)

Labels can be affixed to blank envelopes in place of a typed return address or delivery address. It is more convenient to print a page of labels and affix them to an envelope than it is to adjust your printer and insert envelopes.

You can create a single label, a full page of labels with the same address, or a full page of labels with different addresses. In Lesson 115, Mail Merge, you will create labels with different delivery addresses automatically by creating a single label as a main document, linking it to a data source with variable label information, and merging the two.

Many brands and sizes of labels are available via office supply retailers. Note the brand, the label number, and/or the label dimensions of the desired label because you will be asked to specify the label brand and number when you create labels.

To print a single label:

1. Open a new Word file; from the **Mailings** tab, **Create** group, click the **Labels** button.
2. Type the mailing address in the **Address** box; clear the check box for **Use return address**, if necessary; click **Single label**.
3. Click the **Options** button to open the **Label Options** dialog box.

Click the desired vendor from the **Label vendors** box.

Note the product details under **Label information.**

Click the desired product from the **Product number** box.

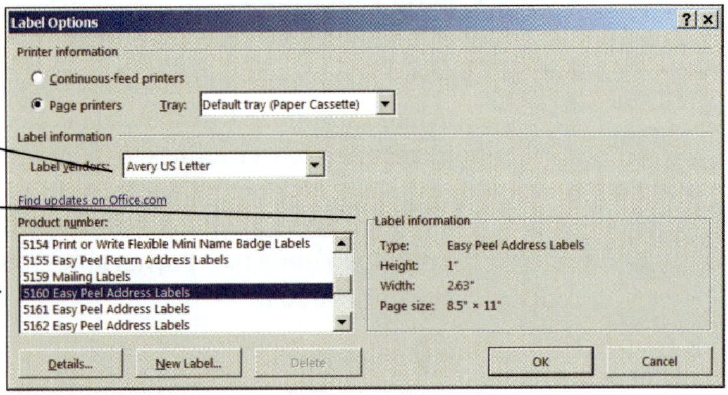

4. Under **Label vendors**, click **Avery US Letter** (or the desired vendor).
5. Under **Product number**, click **5160** (or the desired product number); click **OK**, **Print**.

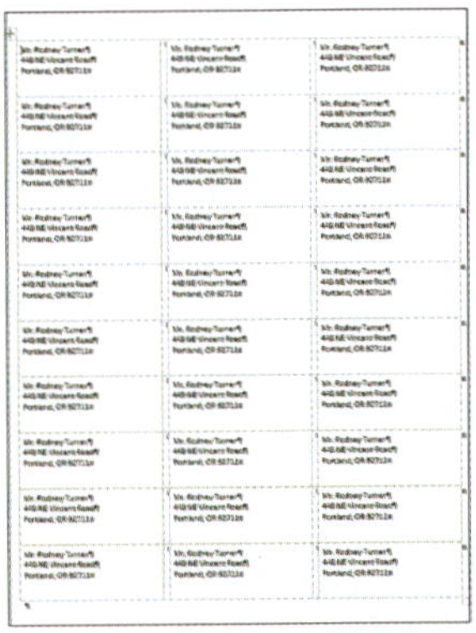

Avery US Letter 5160 label

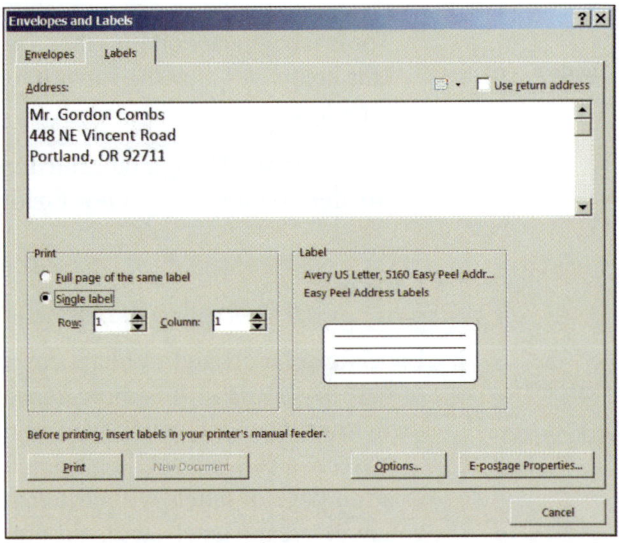

To print a full page of the same label:

1. Follow all the steps in the previous section except in step 2, click **Full page of the same label**.
2. For the final step, click **New Document**, and print the document.

REFER TO
WM L. 22, File—Save

The new document is assigned a generic file name (*Labels1*, for example); save the file with a new name as desired.

To create a page of labels with different information on each label:

1. Follow all the steps in the previous section except delete any text in the **Address** box.
2. For the final step, click **New Document**, and print the document.
3. Type different label information in each cell of the table as desired.

PRACTICE 28 (2 of 2)

1. Press **CTRL+N** to open a new Word file; from the **Mailings** tab, **Create** group, click the **Labels** button.
2. From the **Envelopes and Labels** dialog box, **Labels** tab, select and delete any text that might appear in the **Address** box; if needed, clear the check box for **Use return address**; directly under the **Address** box, under **Print**, click **Full page of the same label**.
3. Click the **Options** button; under **Label vendors**, scroll to and click **Avery US Letter**; under **Product number**, click **5160 Easy Peel Address Labels**; click **OK**.
4. From the **Envelopes and Labels** dialog box, click **New Document** to display a full page of empty labels; note the generic file name of *Labels1*. (The number at the end of the generic file name might be higher than 1.)
5. From the **Home** tab, **Paragraph** group, click the **Show/Hide ¶** button to hide formatting marks.
6. From the **Home** tab, **Paragraph** group, click the list arrow next to the **Borders** button; from the drop-down menu, click **View Gridlines** to toggle off the feature and hide gridlines. You should see a blank page—now you can see the importance of understanding these features.
7. From the **Home** tab, **Paragraph** group, click the list arrow next to the **Borders** button; from the drop-down menu, click **View Gridlines** again to display the nonprinting gridlines; click the **Show/Hide ¶** button to display formatting marks.

PRACTICE (continued)

8. Click in the first label, and type the first address block—press **ENTER** 1 time between lines.

   Ms. Renee Milfuggia
   Stevenson Corporation
   1479 Monroe Street
   Gastonia, NC 28054

9. Press **TAB** twice, or click in the next label (middle label in first row); type the second address block.

   Mr. Cal Rigoletto
   1014 South Marietta Street
   Grove City, PA 16127

10. Your finished labels should look similar to this. Close this document—save changes if desired.

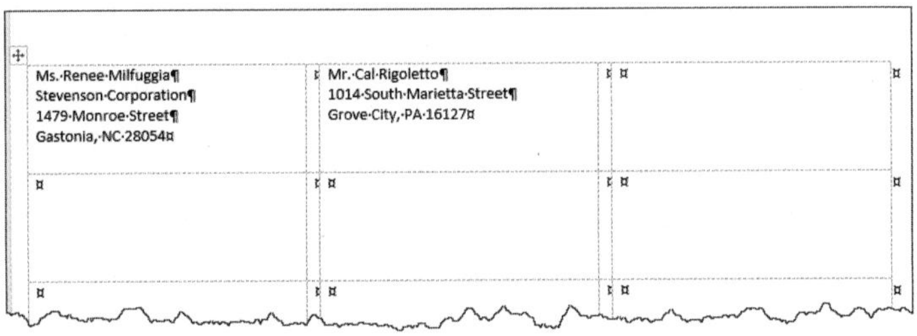

11. Close any other open document, and return to GDP.

GO TO Textbook

Memos and E-Mail With Attachments

LESSON 29

E-Mail—Attachment Notations

GO TO Textbook

This feature is no longer in use in the 11th Edition. Please skip this feature and return to GDP and the textbook.

Correspondence Review

LESSON 30

Italic and Underline

To italicize or underline text as you type:

I
Italic button

U
Underline button

1. From the **Home** tab, **Font** group, click the **Italic** or **Underline** button, or press **CTRL+I** (italic) or **CTRL+U** (underline).
2. Type the text you want italicized or underlined; then click the **Italic** or **Underline** button again to turn off italic or underline.

! Be careful not to underline any surrounding spaces.

plain text

italic text

underlined text

To italicize or underline existing text:

1. Select the text to be italicized or underlined; or for a single word, simply click inside the word.
2. Click the **Italic** or **Underline** button, or press **CTRL+I** or **CTRL+U**.

? The Italic and Underline buttons toggle. Click the button once to activate the feature and again to deactivate it. To undo this formatting, select the text and then click the desired button.

PRACTICE 30 (1 of 1)

1. Type the first sentence—underline "not" and italicize the book title, *To Kill a Mockingbird*; press **ENTER** 2 times, and type the second sentence exactly as shown without underline or italics applied:

   I will not have time to read *To Kill a Mockingbird* before Friday.
   I will have time to read This Old House.

2. In the second sentence, underline "will" and italicize the book title "This Old House." Your copy should look like this:

   I will not have time to read *To Kill a Mockingbird* before Friday.

   I will have time to read *This Old House*.

3. In the first sentence, remove the underline from *not*; then undo the action to replace the underline.
4. Save changes to *practice-30*, and return to GDP.

GO TO Textbook

One-Page Business Reports 31

LESSON

Alignment

Four paragraph alignment options are available:

- **Left:** Aligns text flush with the left margin.
- **Right:** Aligns text flush with the right margin.
- **Center:** Centers the text between the left and right margins.
- **Justify:** Aligns text evenly between the left and the right margins by adjusting spacing between words.

To change paragraph alignment:

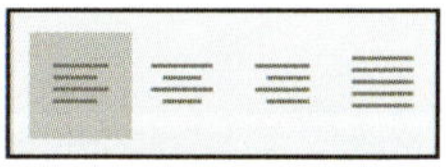

Alignment buttons
Align Left button active

1. Click in the desired line or paragraph, or select the desired text.
2. From the **Home** tab, **Paragraph** group, click the desired alignment button.

   Or: On the keyboard, press **CTRL+L** (left alignment); **CTRL+E** (center alignment); **CTRL+R** (right alignment); or **CTRL+J** (justified alignment).

PRACTICE 31 (1 of 2)

1. Turn on **Show/Hide ¶**; with the insertion point at the top of the document, press **ENTER** 5 times.
2. Type `MICHIGAN AVENUE VETERINARY CLINIC (DRAFT)` (the report title) in all-caps.

   Press the CAPS LOCK key on your keyboard, type the desired text in all-caps, and press CAPS LOCK again to release it.

3. Note that the **Vertical Page Position** on the status bar indicates the title is correctly positioned 2" from the top of the page.

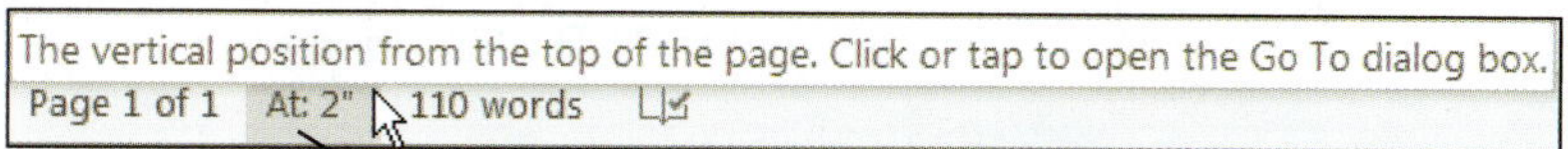

Vertical Page Position on the status bar

If the Vertical Page Position does not appear on the status bar, change your status bar setting. See Appendix A for steps.

REFER TO

WM Appendix A, Using Microsoft Word in the Workplace, GDP—Word Settings, Status Bar

PRACTICE (continued)

4. Press **ENTER** 2 times; type `Recent Trends` (the report subtitle).
5. Press **ENTER** 2 times, type `Marcus Smith` (the writer's name); press **ENTER** 2 times.
6. Note that all the newly typed lines are left aligned.
7. Select the title, subtitle, and byline; bold and center the lines.
8. Click in paragraph 1, and press **CTRL+J** to activate justified alignment; note that all lines in that paragraph are aligned flush with both the left and right margins.
9. Click in paragraph 2, **CTRL+R** to change to right alignment; note that all lines in that paragraph are flush with the right margin and the left side is jagged. Your document should look similar to this:

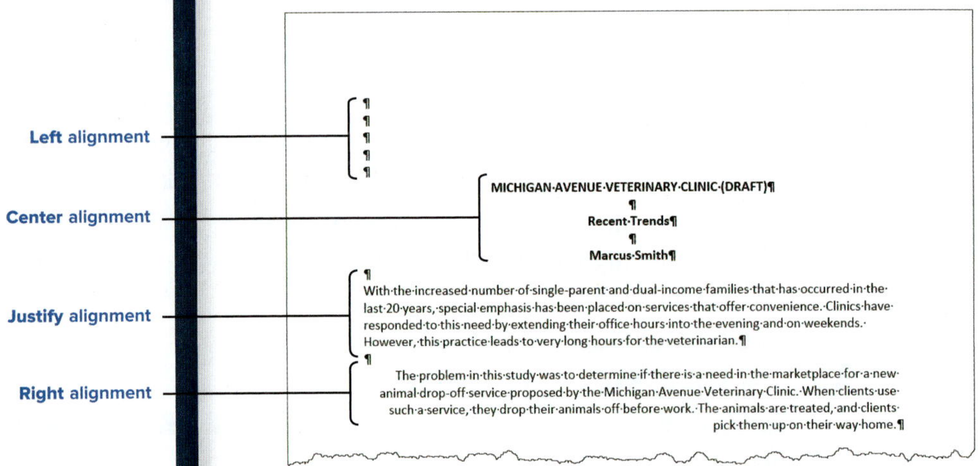

10. Save changes to *practice-31.*

Note: Keep this document open, and continue reading.

Font—Size

Font size is measured in point size (the height of a character). Thus, 1 point (pt.) is equal to 1/72 of an inch—a 12-pt. font is 1/6 of an inch tall.

10-pt. Font Size

12-pt. Font Size

18-pt. Font Size

24-pt. Font Size

To change the font size:

Font Size box

Increase Font Size button

Decrease Font Size button

1. Click where you want to begin the desired font size (or select the text you want to change).
2. From the **Home** tab, **Font** group, click the down arrow to the right of the **Font Size** box; click the desired font size.

   Or: Click the **Increase Font Size** or **Decrease Font Size** buttons as desired.

   Or: On the keyboard, press **CTRL+D** to open the **Font** dialog box. From the **Font** tab, under **Size**, click the desired font size; click **OK**.

PRACTICE 31 (2 of 2)

1. Set alignment to left in both paragraphs.
2. Select the title, and change the font size to 14 point.
3. Click before "The" in the first line of the second paragraph.
4. Type the side heading PROBLEM in all-caps and press **ENTER** 2 times; bold the side heading. Your document should look similar to this:

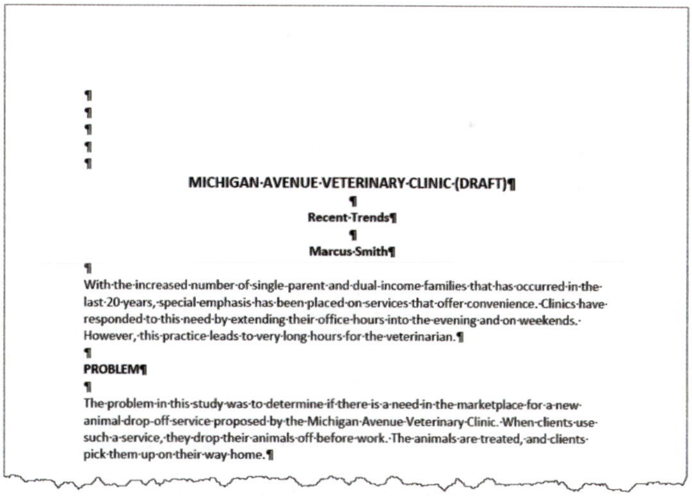
¶
¶
¶
¶
¶
MICHIGAN AVENUE VETERINARY CLINIC (DRAFT)¶
¶
Recent Trends¶
¶
Marcus Smith¶
¶
With the increased number of single-parent and dual-income families that has occurred in the last 20 years, special emphasis has been placed on services that offer convenience. Clinics have responded to this need by extending their office hours into the evening and on weekends. However, this practice leads to very long hours for the veterinarian.¶
¶
PROBLEM¶
¶
The problem in this study was to determine if there is a need in the marketplace for a new animal drop-off service proposed by the Michigan Avenue Veterinary Clinic. When clients use such a service, they drop their animals off before work. The animals are treated, and clients pick them up on their way home.¶

5. Save changes to *practice-31*, and return to GDP.

GO TO Textbook

Multipage Business Reports

Page Number

REFER TO

R-8A—8B
WM L. 47, Headers

A *header* is any information (a page number, for example) that appears at the top of designated pages in a document. The Page Number feature inserts a page number field inside the header, which increases the page number automatically from page to page, whereas a manually typed page number never changes.

The page number on the first page of multipage documents is usually suppressed (removed from view), meaning the page number appears only on the second and subsequent pages. In this lesson you will use the Page Number gallery to choose a plain page number with the desired alignment already in place in the header.

To insert a header with a right-aligned page number:

1. From the **Insert** tab, **Header & Footer** group, click **Page Number**, **Top of Page**, **Plain Number 3**, from the design gallery to insert a right-aligned page number.

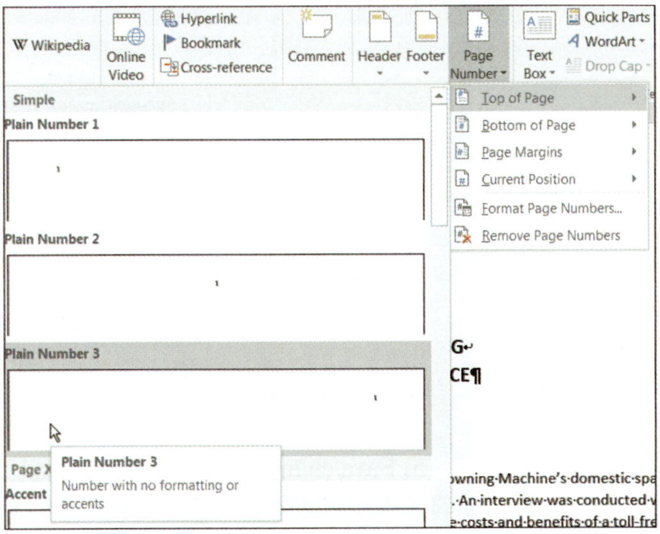

2. Note that you are now inside the **Header** section with the automatic page number highlighted and right alignment set; note the display of the on-demand **Header & Footer Tools** tab and **Design** tab.

To suppress the page number on the first page of a multipage document while you are still inside the header:

1. From the **Header & Footer Tools** tab, **Design** tab, **Options** group, check **Different First Page**.
2. Note that you are still in the **First Page Header** section, and the page number does not display because it has been suppressed—the page number is still visible on subsequent pages.

To suppress the page number on the first page of a multipage document after you have closed the header:

1. Right-click over the header area on any page, click **Edit Header**.
2. From the **Header & Footer Tools** tab, **Design** tab, **Options** group, check **Different First Page**.

To close a header and return to the document body: Double-click anywhere outside the **Header** area.

Or: From the **Header & Footer Tools** tab, **Design** tab, **Close** group, click the **Close Header and Footer** button.

To edit a header: Double-click anywhere over the header area, or right-click over the header area and click **Edit Header**; edit as desired and close the header.

To remove a header: If you have suppressed the header on the first page, click anywhere inside the body of the second page. From the **Insert** tab, **Header & Footer** group, click **Header**; from the menu at the bottom of the gallery, click **Remove Header**.

If you have not suppressed the header on the first page, it wouldn't matter what page you are on when you remove the header. If a header is not behaving as expected and you want to delete header content, press CTRL+A inside the header; press CTRL+X.

PRACTICE 32 (1 of 2)

1. Insert a right-aligned plain page number in the page header. (*Hint:* From the **Insert** tab, **Header & Footer** group, click **Page Number**, **Top of Page**, **Plain Number 3** from the design gallery.)
2. Suppress the page number on page 1. (*Hint:* From the **Header & Footer Tools** tab, **Design** tab, **Options** group, check **Different First Page**.)

PRACTICE (continued)

3. Close the header.
4. From the **File** tab, click **Print**.
5. Adjust the zoom level until 2 pages display.
6. Preview both pages of the document—the page number should be suppressed on the first page and appear right aligned on the second page.

REFER TO
WM L.24, Zoom

Note the page number is suppressed on page 1 and displayed on page 2.

Adjust the **Zoom** until you can see 2 pages at once.

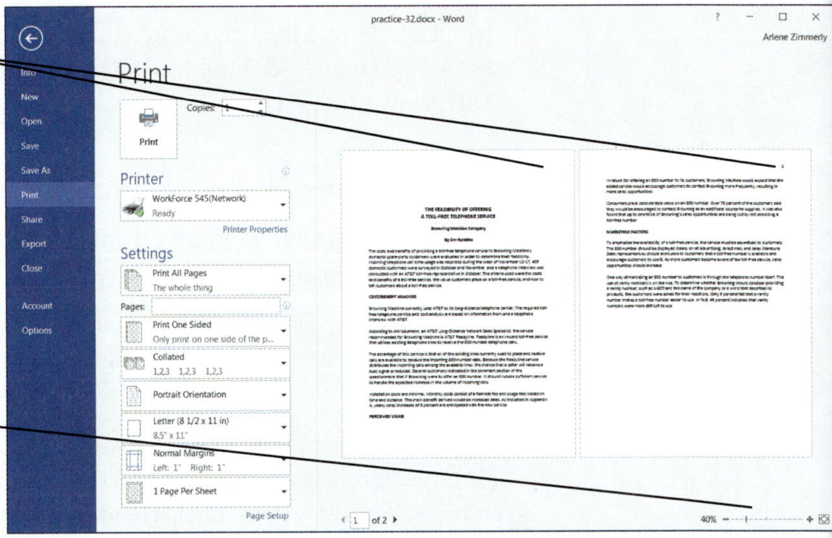

7. Click the **Back** button to return to the document.
8. Save changes to *practice-32*.

Note: Keep this document open, and continue reading.

Page Break

This feature is no longer in use in the 11th Edition. Please skip this feature and continue to Widow/Orphan Control.

Widow/Orphan Control

As you type, Word automatically starts a new page when the text on the current page approaches the bottom margin. This page break changes as text is added and deleted. Some automatic page breaks are not desirable. A one-liner *orphan* is a single line at the bottom of a page. A one-liner *widow* is a single line of a paragraph at the top of a page.

- Generally speaking, at least 2 continuous lines should remain at the bottom of a page and at least 2 continuous lines should be carried over to the top of the next page.
- Never end a page with a single line of a new paragraph or a heading followed by no text.
- You may begin a page with a heading on a line by itself, but never begin a page with 1 line of a paragraph.

An *orphan* is a single line at the bottom of a page.

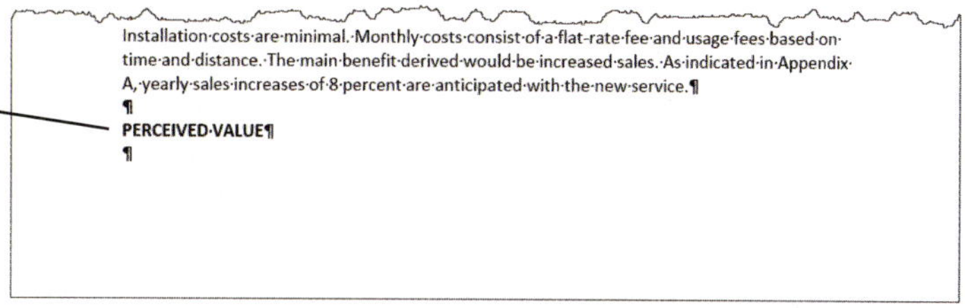

Installation·costs·are·minimal.·Monthly·costs·consist·of·a·flat-rate·fee·and·usage·fees·based·on·time·and·distance.·The·main·benefit·derived·would·be·increased·sales.·As·indicated·in·Appendix·A,·yearly·sales·increases·of·8·percent·are·anticipated·with·the·new·service.¶

¶

PERCEIVED·VALUE¶

¶

A *widow* is a single line of a paragraph from the preceding page at the top of a page.

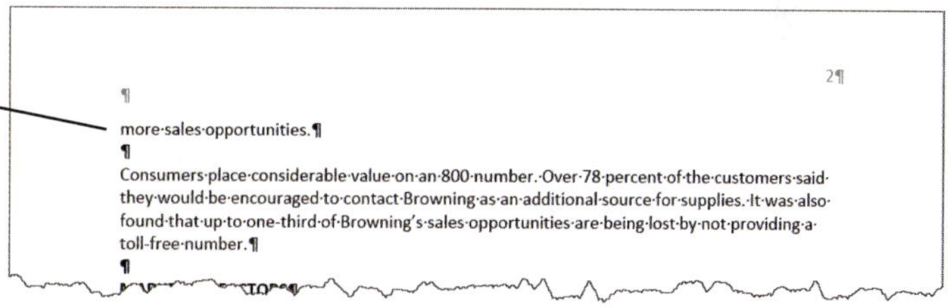

2¶

¶

more·sales·opportunities.¶

¶

Consumers·place·considerable·value·on·an·800·number.·Over·78·percent·of·the·customers·said·they·would·be·encouraged·to·contact·Browning·as·an·additional·source·for·supplies.·It·was·also·found·that·up·to·one-third·of·Browning's·sales·opportunities·are·being·lost·by·not·providing·a·toll-free·number.¶

¶

The Widow/Orphan Control feature is in effect by default. However, this feature does not always keep a side heading together with the paragraph that follows it. A "Keep with next" option keeps these lines together so that a single heading will not appear as a one-liner at the bottom of a page.

If any document processing jobs include one-liners, use the Widow/Orphan control feature and other Pagination features to fix them to avoid GDP scoring errors.

To verify Widow/Orphan control and to fix one-liners:

1. From the **Home** tab, **Paragraph** group, click the **Dialog Box Launcher**.
2. From the **Paragraph** dialog box, **Line and Page Breaks** tab, under **Pagination**, verify that **Widow/Orphan control** is checked; click **OK**.
3. Turn on **Show/Hide ¶** so that you can see formatting symbols.
4. Select the lines you wish to keep together. In this example, select the heading at the bottom of the first page through the first line of the paragraph that follows it.
5. From the **Home** tab, **Paragraph** group, click the **Dialog Box Launcher**.
6. From the **Paragraph** dialog box, click the **Line and Page Breaks** tab.
7. Under **Pagination**, check **Keep with next**; click **OK**.

Do not check Keep lines together, or you could get unexpected results.

Check **Widow/Orphan control** and **Keep with next**.

Select lines to be kept with next.

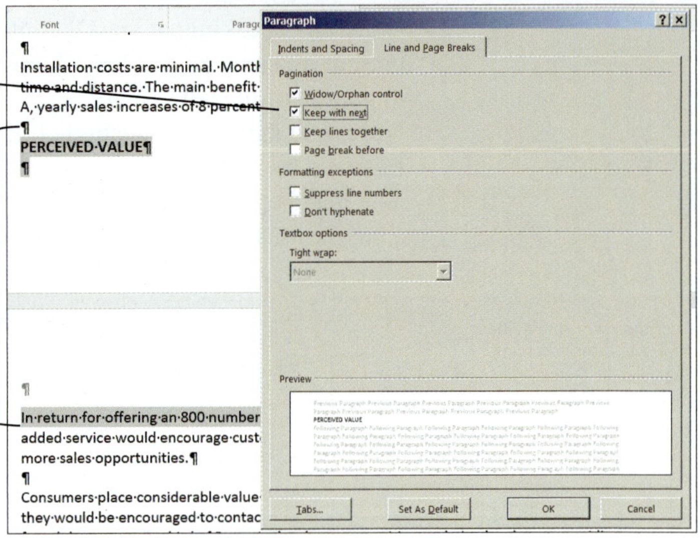

8. Note that the selected lines remain together and appear at the top of page 2.
9. Note that square bullets (nonprinting formatting marks) appear next to the selected lines as a visual cue that these lines have been formatted to remain together on the same page.

Square bullets (nonprinting formatting marks) appear next to the lines with **Keep with next** formatting as visual verification that these lines will always remain together.

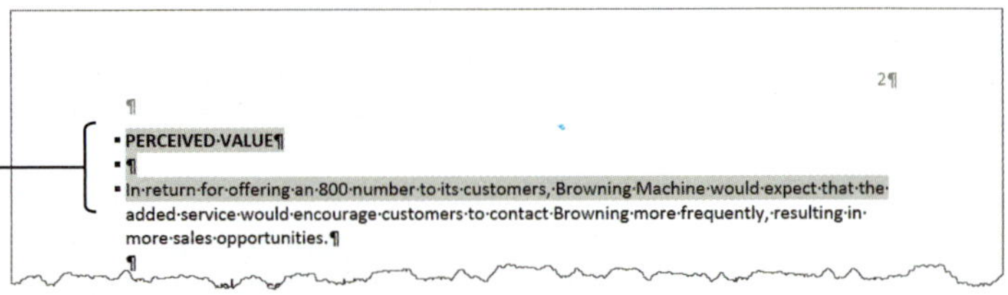

To release Widow/Orphan control on selected lines:

1. Turn on **Show/Hide ¶** to see the formatting symbols.
2. Look for lines with the square bullet formatting marks, and select the lines you wish to release.
3. From the **Home** tab, **Paragraph** group, click the **Dialog Box Launcher**.
4. From the **Paragraph** dialog box, click the **Line and Page Breaks** tab.
5. Under **Pagination**, uncheck **Keep with next**; click **OK**.

PRACTICE 32 (2 of 2)

1. Select the lines you wish to keep together; in this case, select the heading at the bottom of the first page through the first line of the paragraph below it.
2. From the **Home** tab, **Paragraph** group, click the **Dialog Box Launcher**; from the **Paragraph** dialog box, click the **Line and Page Breaks** tab; under **Pagination**, check **Keep with next**; click **OK**.
3. Note that square bullets (nonprinting formatting marks) appear next to the selected lines at the top of the second page as a visual cue that these lines have been formatted to remain together on the same page.
4. Release the lines that have been formatted to stay together.
5. Undo that action so that the lines are once again formatted to stay together. (*Hint:* Press **CTRL+Z**.) Your final document should look similar to this:

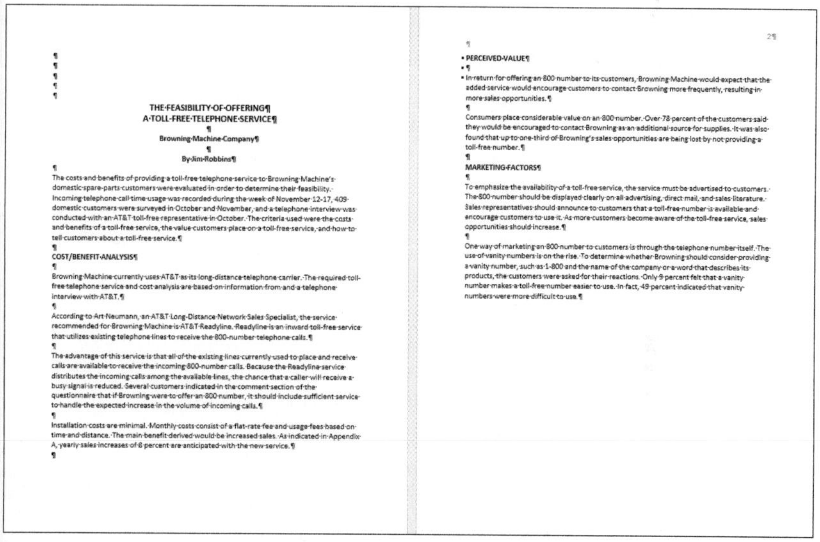

THE FEASIBILITY OF OFFERING
A TOLL-FREE TELEPHONE SERVICE

Browning Machine Company

By Jim Robbins

The costs and benefits of providing a toll-free telephone service to Browning Machine's domestic spare-parts customers were evaluated in order to determine their feasibility. Incoming telephone call time usage was recorded during the week of November 12-17, 409 domestic customers were surveyed in October and November, and a telephone interview was conducted with an AT&T toll-free representative in October. The criteria used were the costs and benefits of a toll-free service, the value customers place on a toll-free service, and how to tell customers about a toll-free service.

COST/BENEFIT ANALYSIS

Browning Machine currently uses AT&T as its long-distance telephone carrier. The required toll-free telephone service and cost analysis are based on information from and a telephone interview with AT&T.

According to Art Neumann, an AT&T Long-Distance Network Sales Specialist, the service recommended for Browning Machine is AT&T Readyline. Readyline is an inward toll-free service that utilizes existing telephone lines to receive the 800-number telephone calls.

The advantage of this service is that all of the existing lines currently used to place and receive calls are available to receive the incoming 800-number calls. Because the Readyline service distributes the incoming calls among the available lines, the chance that a caller will receive a busy signal is reduced. Several customers indicated in the comment section of the questionnaire that if Browning were to offer an 800 number, it should include sufficient service to handle the expected increase in the volume of incoming calls.

Installation costs are minimal. Monthly costs consist of a flat-rate fee and usage fees based on time and distance. The main benefit derived would be increased sales. As indicated in Appendix A, yearly sales increases of 8 percent are anticipated with the new service.

2

PERCEIVED VALUE

In return for offering an 800 number to its customers, Browning Machine would expect that the added service would encourage customers to contact Browning more frequently, resulting in more sales opportunities.

Consumers place considerable value on an 800 number. Over 78 percent of the customers said they would be encouraged to contact Browning as an additional source for supplies. It was also found that up to one-third of Browning's sales opportunities are being lost by not providing a toll-free number.

MARKETING FACTORS

To emphasize the availability of a toll-free service, the service must be advertised to customers. The 800 number should be displayed clearly on all advertising, direct mail, and sales literature. Sales representatives should announce to customers that a toll-free number is available and encourage customers to use it. As more customers become aware of the toll-free service, sales opportunities should increase.

One way of marketing an 800 number to customers is through the telephone number itself. The use of vanity numbers is on the rise. To determine whether Browning should consider providing a vanity number, such as 1-800 and the name of the company or a word that describes its products, the customers were asked for their reactions. Only 9 percent felt that a vanity number makes a toll-free number easier to use. In fact, 49 percent indicated that vanity numbers were more difficult to use.

6. Save changes to *practice-32*, and return to GDP.

GO TO Textbook

Rough-Draft Business Reports With Lists

33

LESSON

Bullets and Numbering

REFER TO
R-12C–12D

Use bullets or numbers to call attention to listed items and to increase readability. If the list sequence is important, use numbers; if not, use bullets. List items are automatically indented from the left margin.

Word's default list indent will be used for lists in Practice exercises and document processing jobs in this course.

To add bullets or numbers and to end a list:

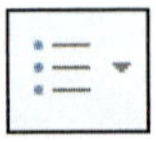

Bullets button

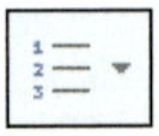

Numbering button

1. Press **ENTER** as needed to insert 1 blank line above the list.
2. From the **Home** tab, **Paragraph** group, click the **Bullets** or **Numbering** button, and type your list of items pressing **ENTER** 1 time after each item.

   Click the list arrow on either button to view a Bullet Library or Numbering Library if you want to use a different style of bullet or number.

3. Note that a new bullet or number appears each time you press **ENTER**.
4. To end the list, press **ENTER** 2 times. (The second time you press **ENTER**, the numbers or bullets end, and your insertion point moves back to the left margin.)

   Or: Press **ENTER** 1 time and click the highlighted **Bullets** or **Numbering** button 1 time to release it. Your insertion point should move back to the left margin.

5. Press **ENTER** as many times as needed to insert 1 blank line below the list.

If the list feature is behaving erratically, undo all previous actions until the list disappears. Type your list unformatted with each list item on a separate line and 1 blank line above and below the list. Select only the lines to be formatted as a list. From the Home tab, Paragraph group, click either the Bullets or Numbering button. If the list has unexpected indention, from the Home tab, Paragraph group, try clicking the Increase Indent or Decrease Indent button.

To remove bullets or numbers from an existing list:

Decrease Indent button

1. Select the desired list or click anywhere inside the desired line.
2. Click either the **Bullets** or **Numbering** button as desired.
3. If necessary, from the **Home** tab, **Paragraph** group, click the **Decrease Indent** button to position the text at the left margin.

To change the number of a list item to any desired number:

1. Point to the desired number in the list, and click to select it.
2. Note that all the numbers in the list are highlighted, and the number you clicked is highlighted in a different color.
3. Right-click over the highlighted list number to display the shortcut menu.
4. Click **Restart at 1** to restart numbering; or click **Continue Numbering** to continue numbering from a previous list in the document; or click **Set Numbering Value**, and type the desired value in the **Set value to** box.

   If necessary, click the Numbering button twice right after this to reset the line number value on the selected lines.

To move a list item:

REFER TO

WM Appendix A, Using Microsoft Word in the Workplace, GDP—Word Settings, AutoFormat As You Type Options, Tabs and Indents

1. Click in the line to be moved (or select multiple list items if desired).
2. Press **ALT+SHIFT+↑** (the directional up arrow on the keyboard) or **ALT+SHIFT+↓** (the directional down arrow) as desired.

If you press the TAB or BACKSPACE key after typing a list and an unwanted indentation appears, follow the steps in Appendix A to change the related AutoFormat option.

PRACTICE 33 (1 of 1)

1. Select the 4 sentences in the middle of the document that end with question marks; format them as a numbered list by clicking the **Numbering** button; note that numbers are added and the entire list is indented.
2. Deselect the list, and move the insertion point to the end of the document. (*Hint:* Press **CTRL+END**.)
3. Click the **Bullets** button, and type the following three list items pressing **ENTER** 1 time between each sentence except the last one:

```
Provide a better understanding of the need for this
service.
Define some of the mechanics of the service.
Provide direction on how to introduce this service.
```

PRACTICE (continued)

4. Press **ENTER** 3 times after the last bulleted item—note that the bullets end after you press **ENTER** 2 times and the insertion point is positioned at the left margin. Then type this paragraph:

   `Although cat owners also represent a large client base for the veterinarian, they were excluded from this study because cats do not have to be licensed.`

5. Click anywhere inside the last bulleted item, and click the **Bullets** button; note that the bullet is removed as well as the indent; click the **Bullets** button again to reverse this action.
6. Move to the end of the last sentence in the document, press the **SPACE BAR** 1 time; type the following sentence, and press **ENTER** 2 times:

   `Two more questions must be asked:`

7. Click the **Numbering** button and type each question on a separate line:

   `Should cat owners be surveyed?`
   `Should the same questions be asked?`

8. Click directly over the first number in this list, right-click to display the shortcut menu, and click **Continue Numbering**. Note that these sentences are renumbered to 5 and 6.
9. Click directly over the "5" to select it, right-click to display the shortcut menu, and click **Restart at 1**. Note that the items 5 and 6 are renumbered to 1 and 2. Your document should look similar to this:

The·following·problem·was·addressed·in·this·study·to·determine·the·value·of·this·proposed· service·to·dog·owners:·What·is·the·feasibility·of·offering·an·animal·drop-off·service·to·dog· owners·who·are·customers·of·the·Michigan·Avenue·Veterinary·Clinic?·First,·these·four· questions·must·be·addressed:¶
¶
1.→ How·much·value·will·the·new·service·provide·to·dog·owners?¶
2.→ How·many·potential·clients·will·transfer·from·their·existing·veterinarian·to·take· advantage·of·this·new·service?¶
3.→ What·drop-off·hours·and·pick-up·hours·are·preferred?¶
4.→ What·level·of·additional·personnel·and·boarding·facilities·will·be·required·to·offer·this· service?¶
¶
The·purpose·of·this·study·is·to·determine·if·the·Michigan·Avenue·Veterinary·Clinic·should·invest· the·resources·needed·to·introduce·and·maintain·a·new·animal·drop-off·service.·The·proposed· study·would·provide·these·results:¶
¶
•→ Provide·a·better·understanding·of·the·need·for·this·service.¶
•→ Define·some·of·the·mechanics·of·the·service.¶
•→ Provide·direction·on·how·to·introduce·this·service.¶
¶
Although·cat·owners·also·represent·a·large·client·base·for·the·veterinarian,·they·were·excluded· from·this·study·because·cats·do·not·have·to·be·licensed.·Two·more·questions·must·be·asked:¶
¶
1.→ Should·cat·owners·be·surveyed?¶
2.→ Should·the·same·questions·be·asked?¶

PRACTICE (continued)

10. Click in the last numbered item in the document; then press **ALT+SHIFT+↑**; note that "Should the same questions be asked?" is now the first item in the list; press **ALT+SHIFT+↓** to reverse this move.
11. Save changes to *practice-33*, and return to GDP.

GO TO Textbook

Multipage Academic Reports With Lists

LESSON 34

Line Spacing

REFER TO
R-8C–8D

In academic reports, set line spacing to double to add an extra blank line between typed lines within a paragraph. If a document is double spaced, any inserted tables will also be double spaced. Line spacing for the inserted table must be manually changed to single.

If you change line spacing at the beginning of a document, all paragraphs typed from that point forward adopt the new spacing. If you change the line spacing later in the document, only paragraphs from that point forward adopt the new line spacing; if you select an existing paragraph or table and change line spacing, only the line spacing for that selection is changed.

To change line spacing for selected text/table or an entire document: On the keyboard, select the desired text; then use the desired shortcut:

Line Spacing	Shortcut
Single	**CTRL+1**
1.5 lines	**CTRL+5**
Double	**CTRL+2**

Line and Paragraph Spacing button

Or: From the **Home** tab, **Paragraph** group, click the list arrow on the **Line and Paragraph Spacing** button, and click the desired line spacing option.

Click the list arrow on the **Line and Paragraph Spacing** button to see the spacing in use.

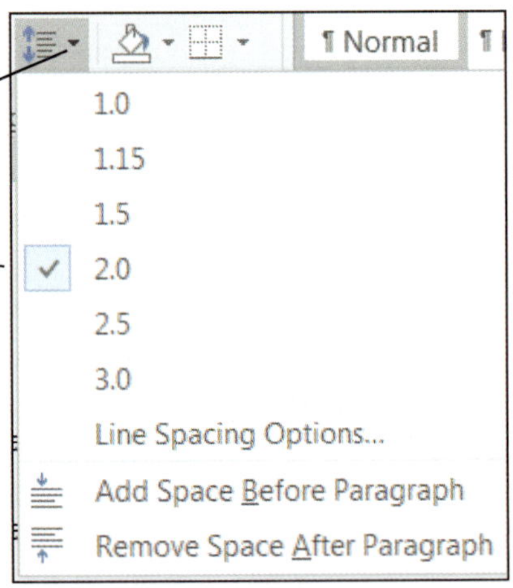

PRACTICE 34 (1 of 1)

1. Select the entire document with **CTRL+A**; press **CTRL+2** to change to double-spacing.
2. With **Show/Hide ¶** on, delete the extra blank lines above and below both lists.
3. Click in front of each paragraph, and press **TAB**.

   If you press TAB to indent a paragraph and do not see a TAB formatting mark appear (→) in your document, change Word's AutoFormat As You Type option. See Appendix A for steps.

4. Click inside the first paragraph; press **CTRL+1**; note the paragraph line spacing changes to single; undo that action. (*Hint:* Press **CTRL+Z**.)
5. The body of your document should look similar to this:

> → The following problem was addressed in this study to determine the value of this proposed service to dog owners: What is the feasibility of offering an animal drop-off service to dog owners who are customers of the Michigan Avenue Veterinary Clinic? First, these four questions must be addressed:¶
>
> 1.→ How much value will the new service provide to dog owners?¶
> 2.→ How many potential clients will transfer from their existing veterinarian to take advantage of this new service?¶
> 3.→ What drop-off hours and pick-up hours are preferred?¶
> 4.→ What level of additional personnel and boarding facilities will be required to offer this service?¶
>
> → The purpose of this study is to determine if the Michigan Avenue Veterinary Clinic should invest the resources needed to introduce and maintain a new animal drop-off service. The proposed study would provide these results:¶
>
> •→ Provide a better understanding of the need for this service.¶
> •→ Define some of the mechanics of the service.¶
> •→ Provide direction on how to introduce this service.¶
>
> → Although cat owners also represent a large client base for the veterinarian, they were excluded from this study because cats do not have to be licensed.¶

6. Save changes to *practice-34*, and return to GDP.

REFER TO

WM Appendix A, Using Microsoft Word in the Workplace, GDP—Word Settings, AutoFormat As You Type Options, Tabs and Indents

GO TO Textbook

More Rough-Draft Reports

35 LESSON

Cut and Copy

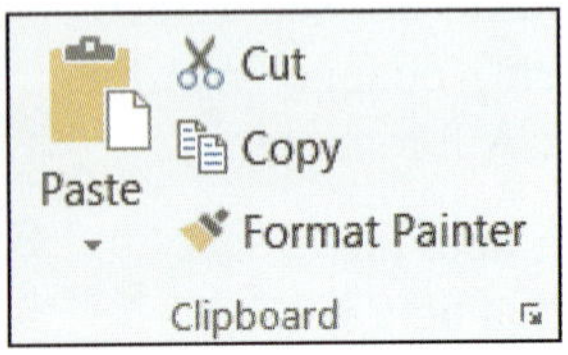

Cut, **Copy**, and **Paste** buttons

Clipboard Status notice

Cut, Copy, and Paste buttons are found on the Home tab, Clipboard group. Cutting removes selected items from the document and places them on the Clipboard. (If you use DELETE on the keyboard to delete a selection, the deletion is not added to the Clipboard collection.) Copying adds a copy of selected text or objects to the Clipboard. Pasting from the Clipboard (or via the Paste button) inserts cut or copied text and objects at the insertion point.

The Microsoft Office Clipboard allows you to collect up to 24 cut or copied items and paste them into any Office file—Word, Excel, etc. When an item has been successfully added to the Clipboard collection, you will see a Clipboard Status notice at the bottom of the Clipboard pane. If the Office Clipboard is not active, only the most recently copied or cut item remains in the Clipboard for pasting.

Another way to move text is to select it, point to the selected text, and drag and drop it into place in the desired location.

CLIPBOARD

To display the Clipboard in the left pane:

1. From the **Home** tab, in the **Clipboard** group, click the **Dialog Box Launcher**.
2. Click any item under **Click an item to paste** to paste it into your document at the insertion point.
3. Click the **Options** button at the bottom of the pane to select any desired options for displaying the **Clipboard**.

   Check the Collect Without Showing Office Clipboard option when you need to conserve screen real estate but still want to collect items.

To clear the Clipboard: Click the **Clear All** button.

If you see a Clipboard status notice stating that an item could not be added to the Clipboard, you have exhausted your system's memory. Clear the Clipboard, and try cutting or copying again.

To close the Clipboard: Click the **Close** button at the top of the pane.

CUT

To cut text:

1. From the **Home** tab, **Clipboard** group, click the **Dialog Box Launcher** to display the **Clipboard**.
2. In your document, select the text you want to cut and move.

Select the text to be cut and pasted.

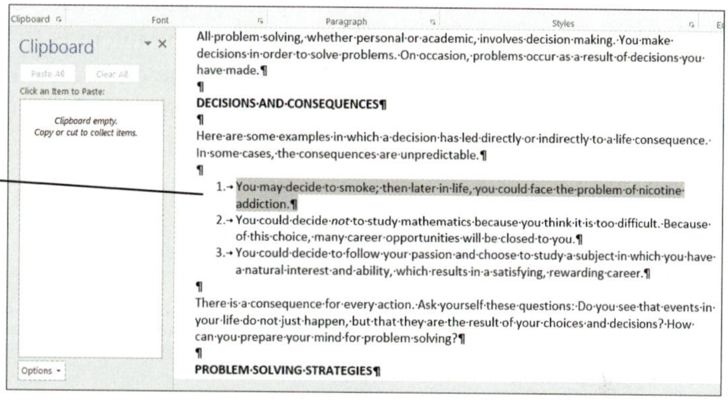

3. From the **Home** tab, **Clipboard** group, click the **Cut** button, or press **CTRL+X**. Note that the cut item is added to the **Clipboard**.

The selected sentence cut previously is automatically added to the **Clipboard** for reuse.

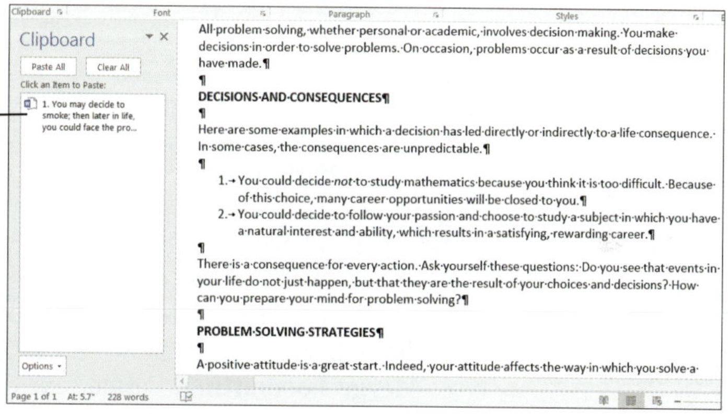

COPY

To copy text to the Clipboard:

1. From the **Home** tab, **Clipboard** group, click the **Dialog Box Launcher** to display the **Clipboard**.
2. In your document, select the text you want to copy.
3. From the **Home** tab, **Clipboard** group, click the **Copy** button, or press **CTRL+C**; note that the copied item is added to the **Clipboard**.

Paste

To paste text:

1. From the **Home** tab, **Clipboard** group, click the **Dialog Box Launcher** to display the **Office Clipboard**.
2. Position the insertion point where you want to insert the text. (In the example that follows, the intent is to move the first numbered item that was cut previously to the end of the list.)
3. From the **Clipboard** pane, click the desired item to paste it in its new location, or press **CTRL+V** to paste the last copied item.

   Or: From the **Home** tab, **Clipboard** group, click the **Paste** button to paste the most recently copied or cut item.

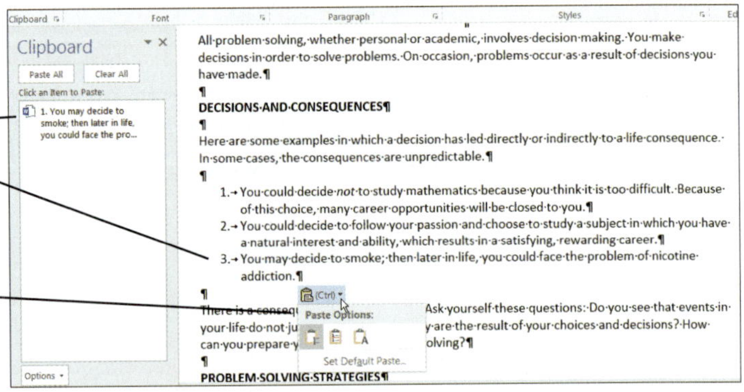

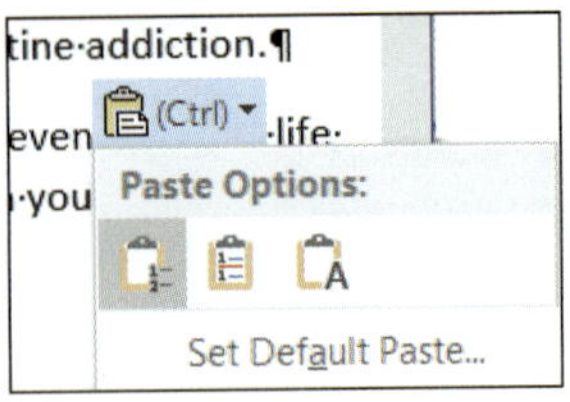

Paste Options button

4. Click the **Paste Options** button, and choose a desired paste option:

   The Paste Options list is context-sensitive—choices change depending on the circumstances. Point to or click each paste option to preview the results.

   - **Keep Source Formatting.** Pasted text will appear exactly as it did in the source.
   - **Merge Formatting.** Pasted text will match the text that surrounds it. (This option is usually the one that will consistently give you desired results.)
   - **Use Destination Styles.** Pasted text will change itself to match the formatting style of the surrounding text in the destination. Bolding and italics will be retained.
   - **Use Destination Theme.** Pasted item will adopt the destination theme attributes (fonts, colors, etc.) for that theme.
   - **Keep Text Only.** All formatting (bullets, numbers, italics, bolding, indents, pictures, and so forth) will be removed from the pasted text; the pasted text will change itself to match the formatting of the surrounding text in the destination.

- **Continue List.** The pasted list item is merged with the existing list and automatically renumbered.
- **New List.** The pasted list item becomes the last item on the list, but numbering is restarted.

Press ESC to make the Paste Options button disappear.

PRACTICE 35 (1 of 1)

1. Display the **Clipboard** and clear it.
2. Turn on **Show/Hide ¶**, and select the first numbered item ("You may decide to smoke . . .") including the paragraph symbol at the end. (*Hint:* Click inside the sentence; press **CTRL** and click.)

   The list number is not highlighted in the selection because it was created using the Numbering feature as opposed to typing it manually. However, the number will be cut along with the text because you included the paragraph symbol in the selection.

3. Cut the selected list item; note that the remaining list items are renumbered, and the cut item appears in the **Clipboard** list.
4. Click in blank line just below the second item in the list; paste the cut list item; note that the pasted list item is renumbered "3."
5. Click the **Paste Options** button, and click **New List**; note that the pasted item is numbered "1."

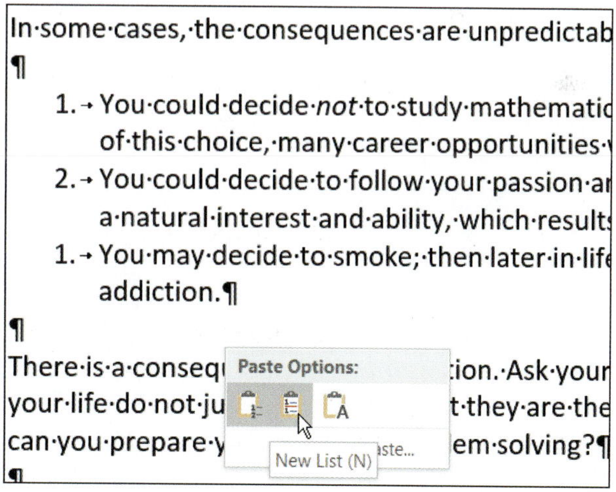

6. Click the **Paste Options** button, and click **Continue List**; note that the pasted item is numbered "3."
7. Press **ESC** to make the **Paste Options** button disappear.

PRACTICE (continued)

8. Click inside the third numbered item; press **ALT+SHIFT+↑** to move it up to the second numbered item; press **ALT+SHIFT+↓** to move it back to the third numbered item.
9. The order of the numbered list items in your document should be identical to the order here:

> Here are some examples in which a decision has led directly or indirectly to a life consequence. In some cases, the consequences are unpredictable.¶
> ¶
> 1.→ You could decide *not* to study mathematics because you think it is too difficult. Because of this choice, many career opportunities will be closed to you.¶
> 2.→ You could decide to follow your passion and choose to study a subject in which you have a natural interest and ability, which results in a satisfying, rewarding career.¶
> 3.→ You may decide to smoke; then later in life, you could face the problem of nicotine addiction.¶
> ¶
> There is a consequence for every action. Ask yourself these questions: Do you see that events in

10. Save changes to *practice-35*, and return to GDP.

GO TO Textbook

Boxed Tables

Table—Insert

Vertical columns in tables are identified by a letter (*Column A*, for example). Horizontal rows are identified by a number (*Row 1*, for example). A table cell is identified by the intersection of column letter and row number (*Cell A1*, for example). Thus, "President" in the following example appears in Cell A1—the intersection of Column A and Row 1.

	Column A	Column B	
Row 1	President¤	Juanita·Cortez¤	¤
Row 2	Secretary¤	Rhonda·Butler¤	¤
Row 3	Treasurer¤	Rachel·Corker¤	¤
Row 4	Sponsor¤	Leon·South¤	¤

¶

A table cell creates fixed boundaries with cell padding (the white space between the cell border and the text) similar to margins in a document. Text wraps within a cell when the cell is not wide enough to accommodate it.

Word applies borders by default to all the cells when a table is created. *Boxed* tables have borders all around. *Open* tables don't have borders. *Ruled* tables have a border on the top and bottom of Row 2 and the bottom of the last row only. You will learn to remove borders in open tables in Lesson 37 and to use table styles to create ruled tables automatically in Lesson 80.

REFER TO
R-5A, R-8B, R-13A–3B
WM L. 37, Table—Borders
WM L. 80, Table—Styles

To insert a table:

1. Position the insertion point where you want the table to start.
2. From the **Insert** tab, **Tables** group, click the **Insert Table** button; then drag to create a table with the desired number of columns and rows

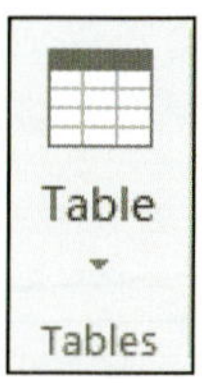

Insert Table button

A 3×4 table (3 columns by 4 rows) is shown in the next illustration. Note that as you drag to create the table, a Live Preview appears in the background. When you release the mouse, the table is inserted.

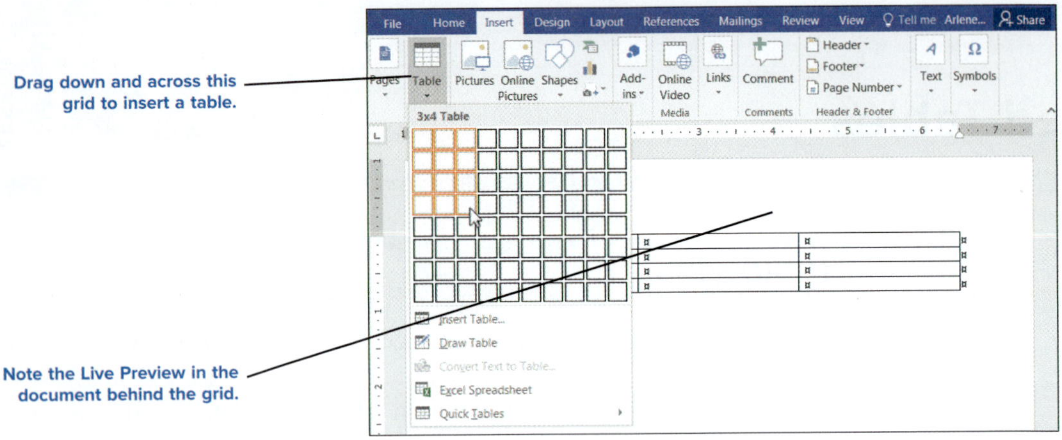

Or: From the **Insert** tab, **Tables** group, click the **Table** button, **Insert Table**. The **Insert Table** dialog box appears; make the desired choices for the number of rows and columns, and click **OK**.

3. Turn on **Show/Hide ¶**; note that the insertion point is in Cell A1, the **Table Move** handle appears above Cell A1, and **table end-of-cell markers** appear at the beginning of each cell and outside the last cell in any row. (These table formatting codes will be important in later lessons.)

An *on-demand* Table Tools tab appears above the Ribbon with a Design tab and Layout tab below it whenever you click inside a table. Tabs disappear when you click outside a table.

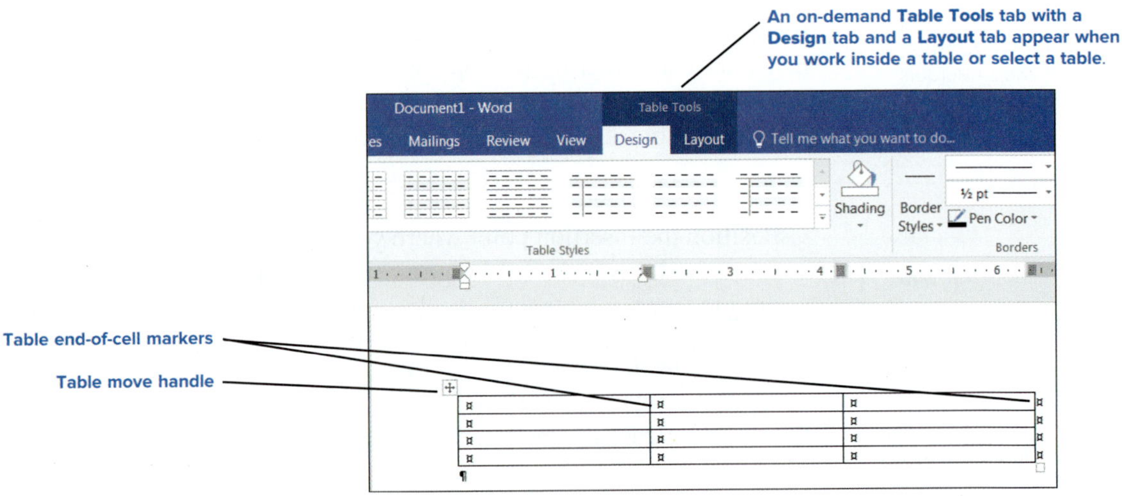

4. Type text inside the cells as desired. Note that cells expand automatically to accommodate longer text.

If you press ENTER by accident, an additional blank line will be added to the cell. Press BACKSPACE or CTRL+Z to delete the unwanted line.

To move the insertion point from cell to cell: Click the desired cell with the mouse, or press **TAB**.

To move the insertion point to the previous cell: Press **SHIFT+TAB**.

To move the insertion point up or down the rows: Use the directional arrow keys.

To insert an additional row: Click in the last cell, and press **TAB**.

Or: Turn on **Show/Hide ¶**, click immediately to the right of any row just before the **table end-of-cell marker**, and press **ENTER**.

Or: Click inside the table anywhere; point to the selection area just to the left of an outside border of a cell until the **Insert Control** button appears—it looks like a plus sign with extended space between rows. Click the **Insert Control** button as many times as desired.

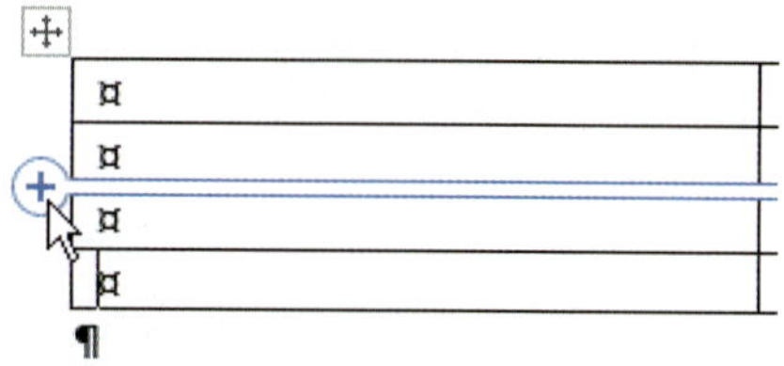

To delete a row or column: Select the desired row or column; right-click and click **Delete Rows** or **Delete Columns**, or press **CTRL+X**.

To move a row up or down: Click inside the row to be moved (or select multiple rows if desired); then press **ALT+SHIFT+↑** or **ALT+SHIFT+↓**.

Or: Select the row (or multiple rows if desired), and drag and drop it into place.

To insert an additional column: Click inside the desired column; from the **Table Tools**, **Layout** tab, **Rows & Columns** group, click **Insert Left** or **Insert Right**.

Or: Click inside the table anywhere; point to the selection area just above a column until the **Insert Control** button appears—it looks like a plus sign with extended space between columns; click the **Insert Control** button as many times as desired.

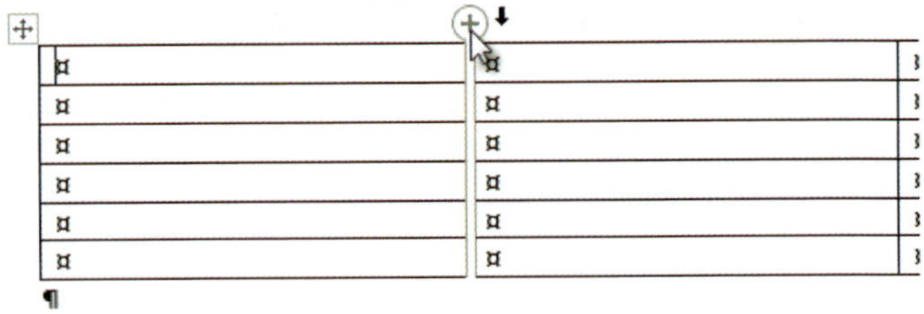

To move a column left or right: Select the column by holding the mouse over the top of the column until you see the black down arrow; click the column to select it, hold the mouse pointer over the column, and then drag and drop the column into place.

TABLE—DELETE

To select and delete a table:

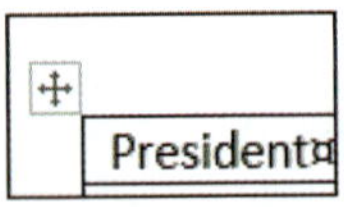

Table Move handle

Point to the table until the **Table Move** handle (4-headed arrow) appears on the top left of the table; click it to select the table—you can also select from the **Table Tools**, **Layout** tab, **Table** group, **Select** button, **Select Table**; press **CTRL+X**.

Or: Click inside the table; from the **Table Tools**, **Layout** tab, **Rows & Columns** group, **Delete** button, click **Delete Table**.

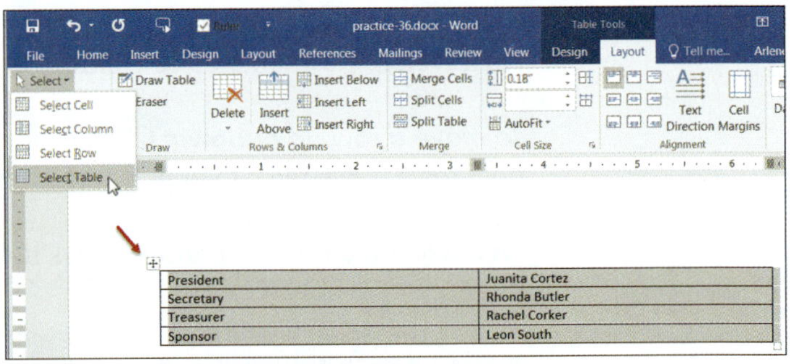

PRACTICE 36 (1 of 2)

1. Insert a table with 2 columns and 3 rows.
2. Insert a 4th row by using all methods discussed in the previous section; undo your insertions until you end up with 4 rows.

PRACTICE (continued)

3. Insert a 3rd column by using all the methods discussed in the previous section.
4. Delete the table and reinsert a table with 2 columns and 2 rows.
5. Click in Cell A1, and type this:

   `President`

6. Press **TAB** to move to Cell B1 and type this:

   `Juanita Cortez`

7. Press **TAB** (*not* **ENTER**) to move to Cell A2 and continue typing the entries as shown next:

   ```
   Secretary    Rhonda Butler
   Treasurer    Rachel Corker
   Sponsor      Leon South
   ```

   If you are in the last cell of a table (Cell B4 in the preceding example) and you press TAB, an additional row is inserted. Press CTRL+Z to remove the unwanted row.

8. Turn on **Show/Hide ¶**. Your finished table should look similar to this:

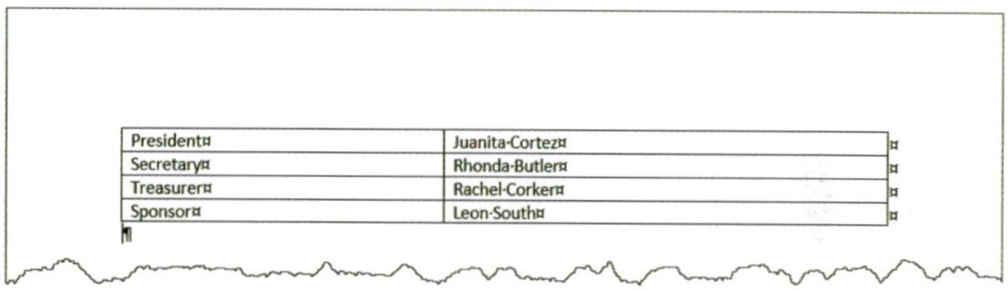

President¤	Juanita·Cortez¤
Secretary¤	Rhonda·Butler¤
Treasurer¤	Rachel·Corker¤
Sponsor¤	Leon·South¤

9. Save changes to *practice-36*.

Note: Keep this document open, and continue reading.

Table—AutoFit to Contents

To resize the width of table columns automatically using AutoFit to Contents:

1. Select the table.
2. From **Table Tools**, **Layout** tab, **Cell Size** group, click the list arrow under **AutoFit**, and click **AutoFit Contents**.

   Or: Select the table; right-click any table cell; click **AutoFit**, **AutoFit to Contents**.

If any of the lines wrap incorrectly when you use the AutoFit feature, point to the cell border to the right of the column until you see a double-sided arrow and double-click.

3. Note that the table has been resized to accommodate the longest word or words in each column.

PRACTICE 36 (2 of 2)

1. Select the table; right-click anywhere inside the selected table.
2. Click **AutoFit**, **AutoFit to Contents**; your finished table should look similar to this:

President¤	Juanita·Cortez¤	¤
Secretary¤	Rhonda·Butler¤	¤
Treasurer¤	Rachel·Corker¤	¤
Sponsor¤	Leon·South¤	¤

¶

3. Save changes to *practice-36*, and return to GDP.

GO TO Textbook

Open Tables

LESSON 37

Table—Merge Cells

REFER TO
R-13A–13D

Table titles and subtitles are typed in the first row of a table in which all cells have been merged to form one continuous cell. Type the title centered, in bold, all-caps, 14-pt. font. Any subtitle is typed on the line below the title centered in bold, upper- and lowercase, 12-pt. font. Press ENTER 1 time below the subtitle (or below the title if no subtitle is used) to insert 1 blank line.

To select table elements using the mouse and keyboard:

To Select		With Mouse	With Mouse and Keyboard
A cell		Click the **table end-of-cell marker.**	
A row	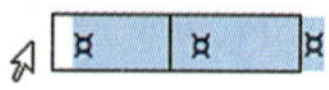	Click just to the left of the row.	
A column	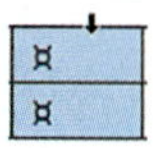	Point to the top border of the column until the black arrow appears, and click.	
Multiple adjoining cells	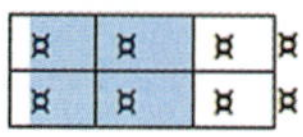	Click inside the first cell; drag across and down as desired. (A1 and B2 in this example)	Click inside the first cell, hold down **SHIFT**, then click in the last desired cell.
A table	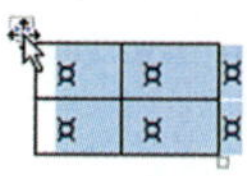	Point to the top corner of Cell A1; click the **Table Move** handle.	Click inside the table; under **Table Tools**, **Layout** tab, **Table** group, click **Select**; **Select Table**; or press **ALT+SHIFT+5** on the numeric keypad (with **NUM LOCK** active).
Text in the next or previous cell	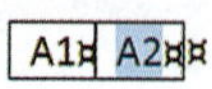		Press **TAB** or **SHIFT+TAB**.

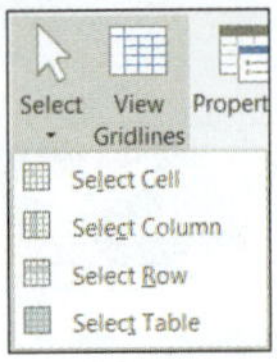

Select button

To select table elements using the Select button: Click inside the table at the desired cell; from the **Table Tools, Layout** tab, **Table** group, click the **Select button**; click **Select Cell**, **Select Column**, **Select Row**, or **Select Table** as desired.

To merge several cells into a single cell:

1. Select the cells you want to merge; for example, click just to the left of the desired row (Row 1 in this example) to select it, or click over the desired column.

¤	¤	¤
Site·Visitation¤	September·13-16¤	Alan·C.·Wingett¤
On-Site·Interviews¤	September·14-15¤	Chad·Spencer¤
Preliminary·Decisions¤	September·23¤	Sherri·Jordan¤
New·York·Visits¤	October·4-7¤	Pedro·Martin¤
Evaluation·Conference¤	October·8¤	Sherri·Jordan¤
Final·Decision¤	October·10¤	Gerald·J.·Pearson¤

¶

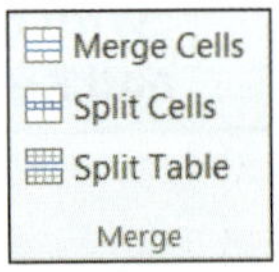

Merge group buttons

2. From the **Table Tools**, **Layout** tab, **Merge** group, click **Merge Cells**, or right-click over the selected row or column, and click **Merge Cells**.
3. Type the desired information in the merged cell with the desired alignment.

VICE-PRESIDENTIAL·SEARCH·SCHEDULE¶ Harry·Wesson,·Coordinator¶ ¤		
Site·Visitation¤	September·13-16¤	Alan·C.·Wingett¤
On-Site·Interviews¤	September·14-15¤	Chad·Spencer¤
Preliminary·Decisions¤	September·23¤	Sherri·Jordan¤
New·York·Visits¤	October·4-7¤	Pedro·Martin¤
Evaluation·Conference¤	October·8¤	Sherri·Jordan¤
Final·Decision¤	October·10¤	Gerald·J.·Pearson¤

¶

To split cells:

1. Click in the desired cell.
2. From **Table Tools**, **Layout** tab, **Merge** group, click **Split Cells**; or right-click over the selected row, and click **Split Cells**.
3. From the **Split Cells** dialog box, in the **Number of columns** box and in the **Number of rows** box, verify that the desired number of columns and rows are entered; click **OK**.

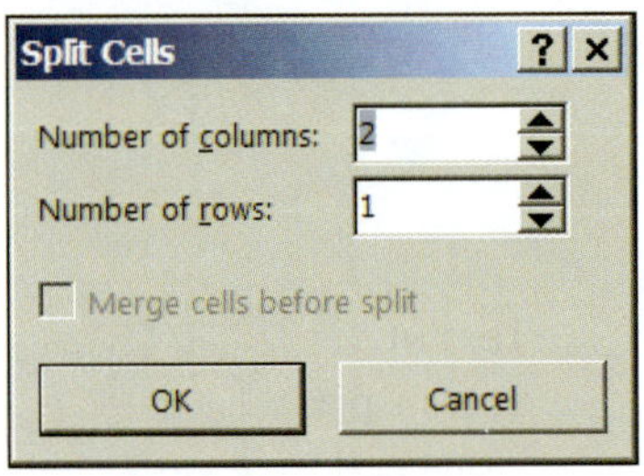

PRACTICE 37 (1 of 2)

1. Select Column 1 and merge the cells; press **CTRL+Z** to undo the merge.
2. Select Row 1 and merge the cells.
3. Select Row 1 and split the cells into 3 columns. (*Hint:* Select the row, right-click, and click **Split Cells**; from the **Split Cells** dialog box, in the **Number of columns** box, type 3; click **OK**.)
4. Select Row 1 and merge the cells again.
5. Change the alignment to center and activate bold.
6. Change to 14-pt. font size, press **CAPS LOCK** on the keyboard, and type this title in all-caps:

   VICE-PRESIDENTIAL SEARCH SCHEDULE

7. Press **ENTER**, change to 12-pt. font size, release **CAPS LOCK**, and type this subtitle in bold:

   Harry Wesson, Coordinator

8. Press **ENTER** 1 time to insert 1 blank line after the subtitle.
9. Select the table, right-click, and click **AutoFit**, **Auto Fit to Contents**; the AutoFit contents of your table should look similar to the illustration in step 3 on page 74.
10. Save changes to *practice-37.*

Note: Keep this document open, and continue reading.

Table—Borders

Borders are the lines that surround all cells in a table. When a new table is inserted, Word applies borders to all cells by default to create a *boxed* table. To create an *open* table, remove all the borders from the table.

REFER TO
WM L. 28, View Gridlines

When borders are removed, click the Borders button list arrow, and activate View Gridlines to display nonprinting gridlines for easier text entry. Gridlines are displayed in this illustration of an open table:

VICE-PRESIDENTIAL·SEARCH·SCHEDULE¶ **Harry·Wesson,·Coordinator¶** ¤		
Site·Visitation¤	September·13-16¤	Alan·C.·Wingett¤
On-Site·Interviews¤	September·14-15¤	Chad·Spencer¤
Preliminary·Decisions¤	September·23¤	Sherri·Jordan¤
New·York·Visits¤	October·4-7¤	Pedro·Martin¤
Evaluation·Conference¤	October·8¤	Sherri·Jordan¤
Final·Decision¤	October·10¤	Gerald·J.·Pearson¤

¶

To remove all borders and to view gridlines: Select the table; from the **Table Tools**, **Design** tab, **Borders** group, click the list arrow under the **Borders** button, and click **No Border**. To view gridlines, from the **Table Tools**, **Layout** tab, **Table** group, click **View Gridlines**.

To apply borders to all cells: Select the table; from the **Table Tools**, **Design** tab, **Borders** group, **Borders** button list arrow, activate **All Borders**.

To apply/remove borders from selected table cells:

1. Select a range of cells, or click in a desired cell.
2. From the **Table Tools**, **Design** tab, **Borders** group, **Borders** button list arrow, click the desired border to apply or remove it in selected cells.

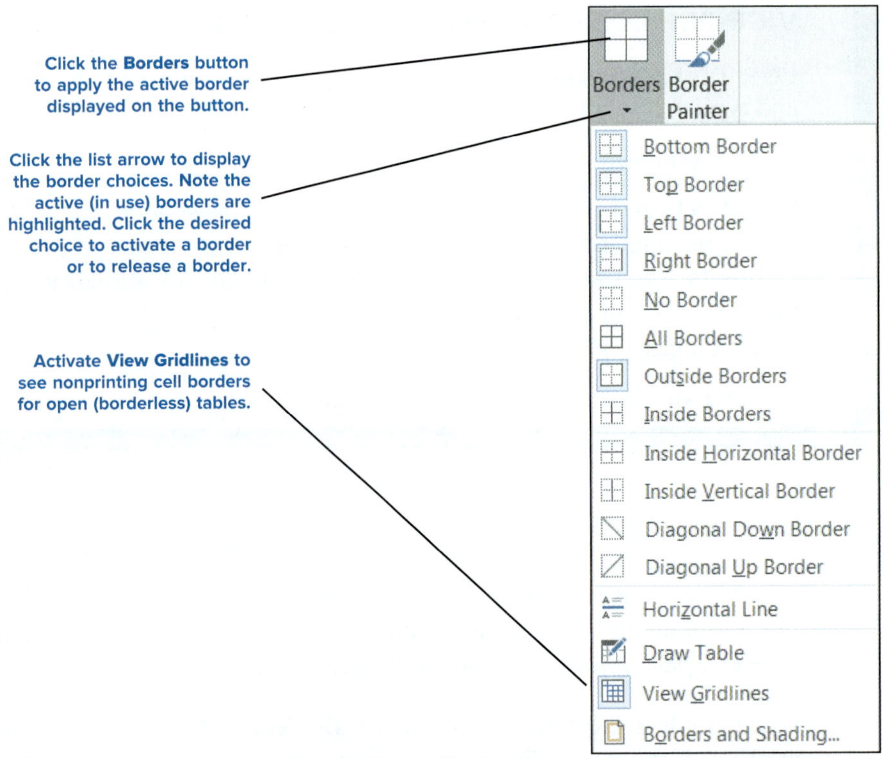

The Borders button displays the most recently used border. If you are inside a table and click the Borders button rather than the list arrow, any active borders will be applied.

3. Repeat this process until the desired borders have been applied or removed.

PRACTICE 37-2 (2 of 2)

1. Remove borders from the table.
2. Hide gridlines. (*Hint:* From the **Table Tools**, **Design** tab, **Borders** group, click the list arrow under the **Borders** button; deselect **View Gridlines**.) Note the change in the table's appearance.
3. Display gridlines, and press **CTRL+P**; your table should look similar to this:

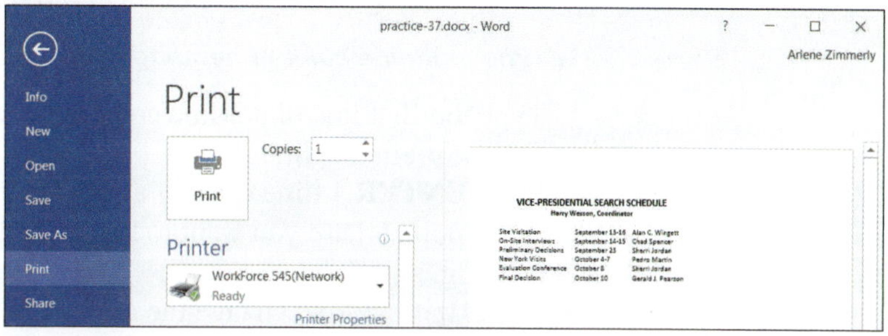

4. Save changes to *practice-37*, and return to GDP.

GO TO Textbook

Open Tables With Column Headings

LESSON **38**

Table—Align Bottom

Column headings are centered using bold upper- and lowercase letters.

To type multiline column headings:

1. Type the first line of a 2-line column heading—do <u>not</u> space after the final word in this line.
2. Press **ENTER** 1 time directly after the last character in the final word at the point where you want to break the line; type the remainder of the heading.
3. Select the row, and change the alignment to **Align Bottom Center**.

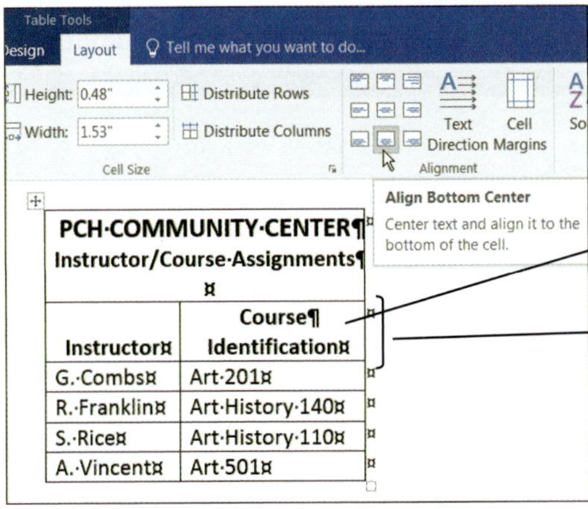

Press ENTER 1 time (do <u>not</u> add a trailing space) at the end of the last word in the first line.

Select the entire row; set Align Bottom Center.

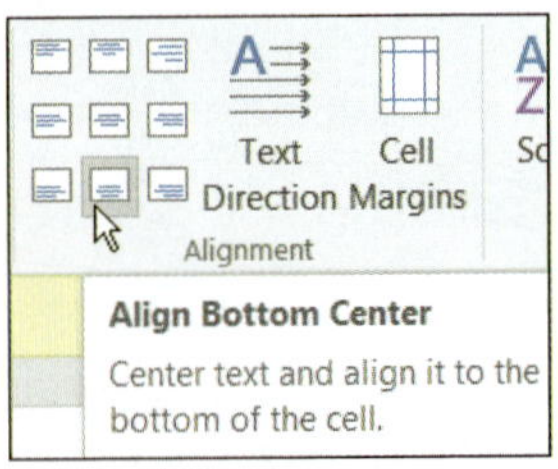

Alignment group
Align Bottom Center active

To center and anchor column headings at the bottom of a row:

1. Click inside the desired cell or select the desired row or column.
2. From the **Table Tools**, **Layout** tab, **Alignment** group, click **Align Bottom Center** to center and anchor cell contents at the bottom of the cell.

PRACTICE 38 (1 of 3)

1. Select Row 1, merge the cells; apply center alignment and activate bold.
2. Click in Row 1, change to 14-pt. font size, and type the title `TYPES OF MORTGAGES` in all-caps.
3. Press **ENTER** 1 time to insert 1 blank line below the title.
4. In the first cell in Row 2, delete the space between "Conventional" and "Mortgages"; then press **ENTER** 1 time to create a 2-line column heading; note in the illustration that a trailing space does not follow "Conventional."
5. Select Row 2; from the **Table Tools**, **Layout** tab, **Alignment** group, click the **Align Bottom Center** button to align cells at the bottom, centered; activate bold.
6. Select the table, right-click over the selected table, and click **AutoFit**, **AutoFit to Contents**. Your AutoFit table should look similar to this:

TYPES·OF·MORTGAGES¶ ¤		¤
Conventional¶ Mortgages¤	**Alternative·Mortgages¤**	¤
Fixed¤	Graduated·payment¤	¤
Adjustable¤	Federal·Housing·Administration¤	¤
Balloon¤	Veterans·Administration¤	¤

Note: Keep this document open, and continue reading.

Table—Center Horizontally

A newly inserted table extends from the left margin to the right margin. After typing the table data, use AutoFit to Contents to adjust to the width of the longest item in the column. The table appears at the left margin. Horizontally center the table as shown in the illustration on the right.

An inserted table appears at the left margin by default.

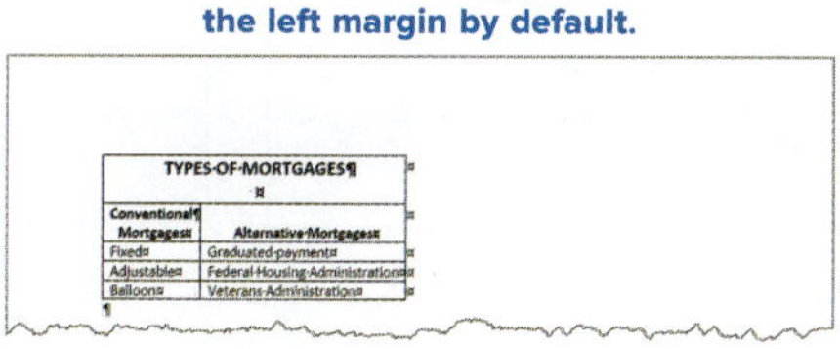

Set alignment to Center to position the table at the horizontal center of the page.

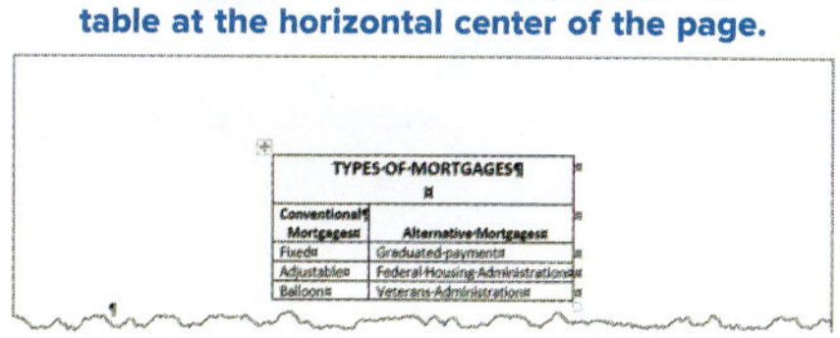

To center a table horizontally:

1. Select the table (click the **Table Move** handle just above the top corner of Cell A1).
2. Press **CTRL+E**; or from the **Home** tab, **Paragraph** group, click the **Center** button.

PRACTICE 38 (2 of 3)

1. Select the table (click the **Table Move** handle just above the top corner of Cell A1).
2. Press **CTRL+E** to center the table horizontally. Your table should look similar to the horizontally centered table in the previous illustration.

Note: Keep this document open, and continue reading.

Table—Center Page

A table (or any in-line content on a page) can be centered vertically between the top and bottom document margins.

Before vertical centering, the table is anchored at the top of the page.

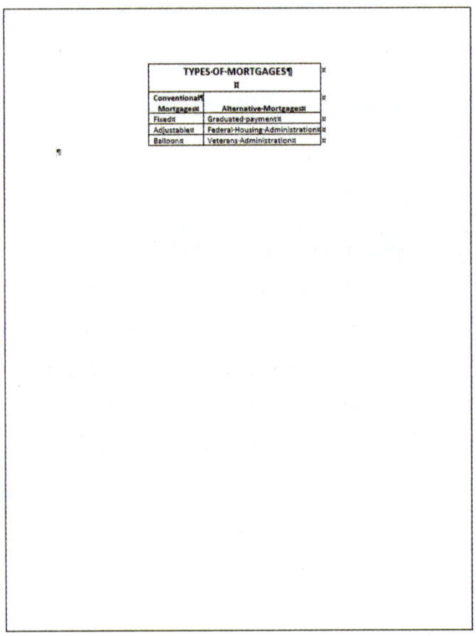

After vertical centering, the table is centered between the top and bottom margins.

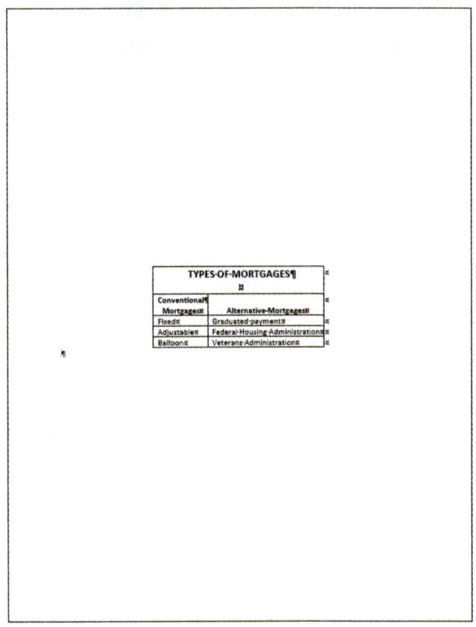

To center a table (or text) vertically on a page:

1. Position the insertion point anywhere on the page you want centered—the insertion point should not be inside the table.
2. From the **Layout** tab, **Page Setup** group, click the **Dialog Box Launcher** to display the **Page Setup** dialog box.

   Or: Display the **Ruler**; double-click on any shaded part of the **Ruler** to the right or left of the white portion of the **Ruler** to display the **Page Setup** dialog box.

3. From the **Page Setup** dialog box, **Layout** tab, **Page** group, **Vertical alignment**, click the list arrow; click **Center**, **OK**.

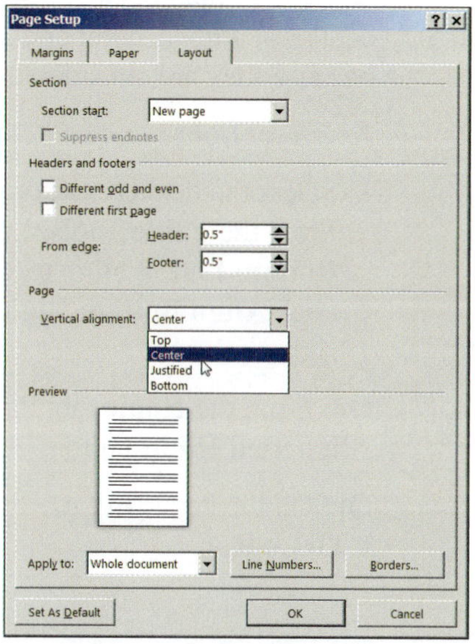

REFER TO

WM L. 45, Tab Set—Ruler Tabs

PRACTICE 38 (3 of 3)

1. Center the table vertically on the page.
2. Change the zoom to **Whole Page** to view the table, which is now centered both horizontally and vertically.
3. Save changes to *practice-38*, and return to GDP.

GO TO Textbook

Ruled Tables With Number Columns

LESSON 39

Table—Align Text Right

REFER TO

WM L. 38, Table—Align Bottom | Table—Center Horizontally | Table—Center Page
WM L. 37, Table—Borders

To improve the readability of a table, change the alignment of column entries. Left-align text column entries. Right-align number column entries that could be used in mathematical calculations—for example, dollar amounts or percentages. Phone numbers, account numbers, and so forth are left aligned because they are considered text entries.

To left- or right-align selected text in column entries:

1. Select the desired text or group of cells or click inside the desired cell.
2. From the **Table Tools**, **Layout** tab, **Alignment** group, click **Align Bottom Left** to align text column entries at the bottom left of the cell, or click **Align Bottom Right** to align number column entries at the bottom right of the cell.

Or: From the **Home** tab, Paragraph group, click the **Align Text Left** or **Align Text Right** button.

Or: On the keyboard, use one of the keyboard shortcuts **CTRL+L** or **CTRL+R**.

PRACTICE 39 (1 of 2)

1. Select Row 1 and merge the cells.
2. Click in Row 1, change to 14-pt. bold font, center alignment, and type the title `PRICE COMPARISONS` in all-caps; press **ENTER** 1 time.
3. Change to a 12-pt. font, type the subtitle `New Cars` in bold, capitalize it as shown, and press **ENTER** 1 time to insert a blank line below the subtitle.
4. In Cell A2, delete the space between "Vehicle" and "Category"; press **ENTER** 1 time to create a 2-line column heading.
5. Select Row 2; use **Align Bottom Center** to align cells at the bottom, center; bold the row.
6. Select the column entries under the column headings for Columns B, C, and D; right-align these number entries.

PRACTICE (continued)

7. Select the table, right-click over the table, and click **AutoFit**, **AutoFit to Contents**.
8. Center the table horizontally. (*Hint:* Select the table with the **Table Move Handle**; press **CTRL+E**.)
9. Center the table vertically. (*Hint:* From the **Layout** tab, **Page Setup** group, click the **Dialog Box Launcher**. From the **Layout** tab, under **Page**, **Vertical alignment**, click **Center**, **OK**.) Your table should look similar to this:

PRICE·COMPARISONS¶ New·Cars¶ ¤			
Vehicle¶ Category¤	**AutoMart¤**	**SmartBuy¤**	**Dealer¤**
Sedan¤	$20,861¤	$21,216¤	$23,743¤
SUV¤	28,700¤	29,562¤	32,270¤
Truck¤	18,600¤	20,247¤	21,983¤

Note: Keep this document open, and continue reading.

Table—Borders, Ruled

REFER TO
R-13C
WM L. 28, View Gridlines

Ruled tables are formatted with a border on the top and bottom of Row 2 and any total row and the bottom of the last row only. To create a ruled table, remove borders from the entire table, and then reapply them to the top and bottom border of Row 2 and any total row, and the bottom border of the last row. When borders are removed, use View Gridlines to see the individual table cell gridlines to guide you as you enter text. Advanced borders and shading features are covered in these lessons:

- Lesson 51: Apply a bottom border to the first row of a resume.
- Lesson 86: Apply a border to the bottom of a header.
- Lesson 111: Apply advanced customized borders and shading.

To remove and apply borders in a ruled table:

1. With **View Gridlines** activated, select the table; from the **Home** tab, **Paragraph** group, click the list arrow for the **Borders** button, and click **No Border**.

2. Select Row 2; from the **Home** tab, **Paragraph** group, click the list arrow for the **Borders** button; then click the **Top Border** button to apply a border to the top of Row 2.
3. With Row 2 still selected, from the **Home** tab, **Paragraph** group, click the list arrow for the **Borders** button; then click the **Bottom Border** button to apply a border to the bottom of Row 2.
4. Select the bottom row of the table.
5. From the **Home** tab, **Paragraph** group, click the **Bottom Border** button to apply a border to the bottom of the last row.

Because a bottom border was just applied, the Bottom Border is the active button—there is no need to click the list arrow to find it. Simply click the Borders button directly.

PRACTICE 39 (2 of 2)

1. With **View Gridlines** activated, remove all borders from the table.
2. Select Row 2, and apply a top and bottom border.
3. Select the last row and apply a bottom border.
4. Press **CTRL+P** to view your table—it should look similar to this.

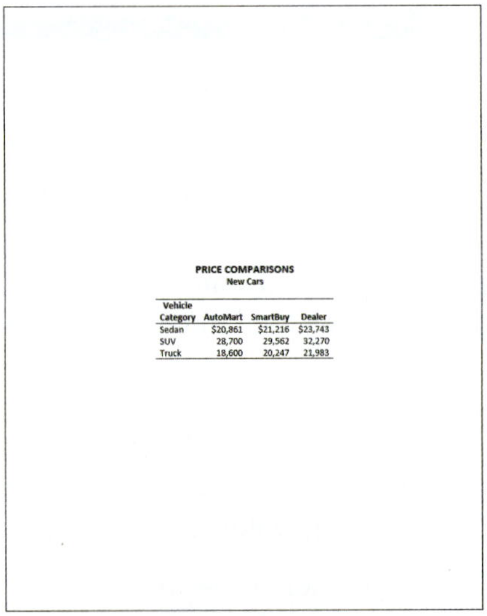

PRICE COMPARISONS
New Cars

Vehicle Category	AutoMart	SmartBuy	Dealer
Sedan	$20,861	$21,216	$23,743
SUV	28,700	29,562	32,270
Truck	18,600	20,247	21,983

5. Save changes to *practice-39*, and return to GDP.

GO TO Textbook

Letters With Indented Displays and Copy Notations and E-Mail With Copies

LESSON 44

Indentation

REFER TO
R-3A

To format an indented display in a single-spaced document:

1. Type the paragraph preceding the indented display, the indented display, and the paragraph after it without any special formatting.
2. Click anywhere inside the long quote that will be formatted as a displayed paragraph or select the desired lines.
3. Display the **Ruler**; from the **Layout** tab, **Paragraph** group, under **Indent**, click the up arrow next to the **Left** and **Right** boxes to increase the paragraph indentation to 0.5" on both sides; note the indent markers on the horizontal ruler.

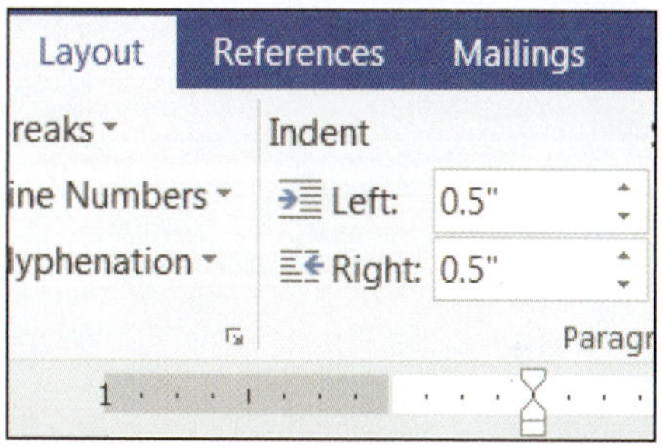

4. Note that both sides of the long quote in the indented display are indented by 0.5"; note the indent markers on both sides of the horizontal ruler.

I·understand·you·have·a·question·pertaining·to·a·proposal·approved·by·the·board·at·the·April· meeting·that·included·guidelines·regarding·paint·colors.·Specifically,·your·concern·focused·on· the·following·segment·from·that·proposal:¶

¶

> Every·owner·shall·maintain·in·good·condition·and·repair·those·portions·of·the· exterior·of·the·residence·which·are·visible·from·the·street·which·fronts·the· residence,·including·without·limitation,·the·walls,·fences,·and·roof·of·such· residence.·When·painting·these·areas,·the·paint·color·must·match·the·current· paint·color·of·the·attached·neighbor.¶

¶

To·clarify·any·future·misunderstandings·with·the·interpretation·of·this·paragraph,·please·call· the·association·office·at·661-555-1212.¶

E-Mail—Copies

This feature is no longer in use in the 11th Edition. Please continue to the Practice exercise.

PRACTICE 44 (1 of 1)

1. Select the second paragraph ("Every owner shall . . .").
2. Format the selected paragraph as an indented display with a 0.5" indent on the left and right sides of the paragraph; your display should look similar to the illustration in the Indentation section in the first part of this lesson.
3. Save and close the file; return to GDP.

GO TO Textbook

Letters in Modified-Block Style

Tab Set—Ruler Tabs

Each time you press TAB to indent text, the insertion point moves in 0.5" increments to Word's default tab settings. If you set a custom tab, it is in effect from the point it was set forward. If you set a custom tab and press TAB 1 time, Word moves directly to that custom tab stop. For existing text, select the desired text and set the tabs, or press CTRL+A to select the entire document and then set tabs.

Use the horizontal ruler to quickly view, set, move, or delete left, center, right, and decimal tabs via the Ruler's Tab Selector button. Each type of custom tab is represented by a unique symbol on the horizontal ruler.

To display the Ruler: From the **View** tab, **Show** group, check **Ruler**; uncheck **Ruler** to hide it.

Check/uncheck **Ruler** from the **Quick Access Toolbar** or from the **View** tab to display/hide the **Ruler**.

Double-click any shaded part of the **Ruler** to open the **Page Setup** dialog box.

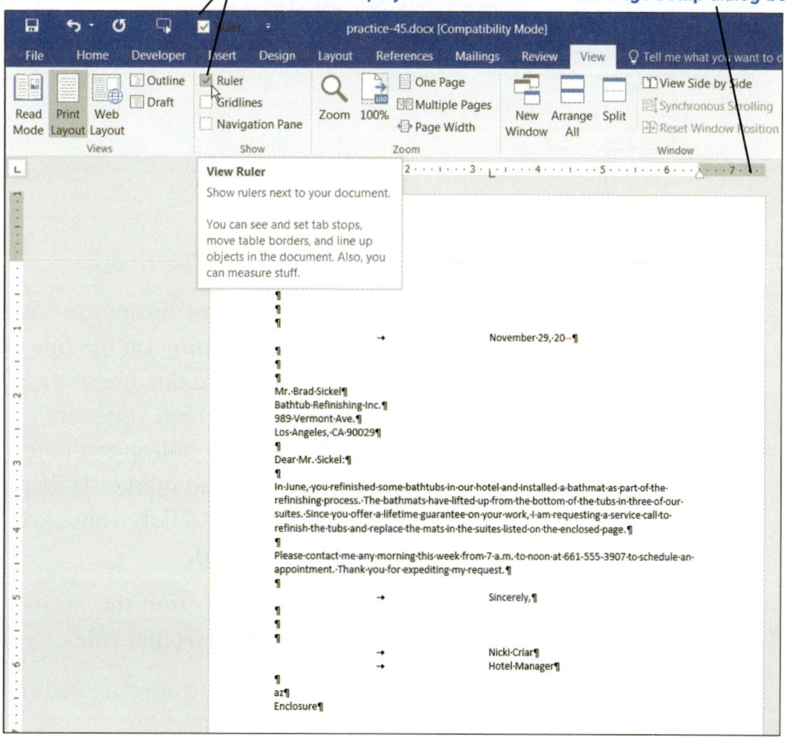

To add the Ruler to the Quick Access Toolbar: Click the list arrow to the right of the **Quick Access Toolbar**; click **More Commands**; from the **Choose commands from** box list arrow, click **Ruler**; click the **Add >>** button in the center, **OK**. Note that the **View Ruler** button is now displayed in the **Quick Access Toolbar**. Check it to display the **Ruler** and uncheck it to hide it.

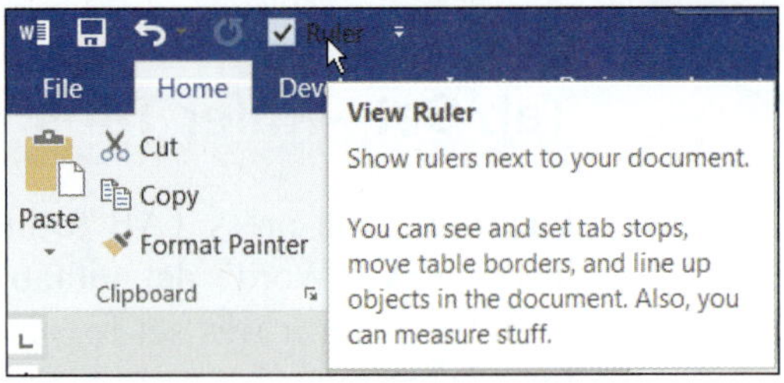

To access the Page Setup dialog box from the ruler: Display the **Ruler**, and double-click the shaded part of the **Ruler**.

To use the Tab Selector buttons to change tab types:

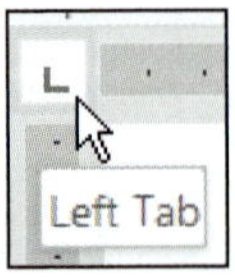

Tab Selector button
Left Tab marker displayed

Right Tab marker displayed

1. Point to the **Tab Selector** button; read the **ScreenTip** to identify type of tab marker in effect.
2. Click the **Tab Selector** button until the desired tab marker is displayed.

Note the Left Tab marker and Right Tab marker on the horizontal ruler in this illustration. Text typed at the left tab position is left aligned. Text typed at the right tab ends at the right tab.

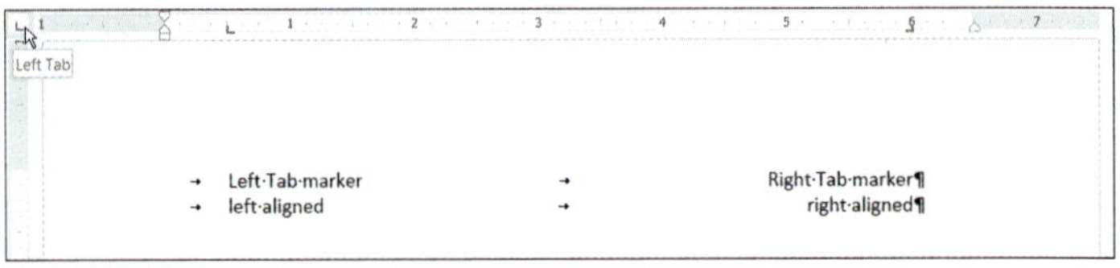

To set custom tabs using the Ruler:

1. Display the **Ruler**. (*Hint:* From the **View** tab, **Show** group, check **Ruler**.)
2. Position the insertion point on the line where you want the new tab to start, or select the entire document to set tabs throughout, or select the desired paragraph(s) where you want to change the tabs.
3. Click the **Tab Selector** button to the left of the horizontal ruler repeatedly until the desired tab marker is displayed.
4. On the horizontal ruler, click where you want the new tab to appear; drag it left or right as needed.

To clear tab settings: Position the insertion point on the desired line; drag the tab marker off the horizontal ruler.

To move tab settings: Position the insertion point on the desired line; drag the tab marker left or right.

REFER TO
R-3B

To set a tab to position the date, complimentary closing, and writer's identification in a modified-block style letter:

1. Click on the **Tab Selector** button until the **Left Tab** marker appears.
2. Click on the horizontal ruler at 3.25".
3. Click immediately in front of the date in the letter, and press **TAB** 1 time to begin the date at the 3.25" tab.
4. Click in front of the complimentary closing and writer's identification lines, and press **TAB** 1 time to begin these lines at the 3.25" tab.

PRACTICE 45 (1 of 1)

1. Display the **Ruler**; press **CTRL+A** to select all lines of the letter; use the horizontal ruler to set a 3.25" left tab. (If you were starting the letter from a blank screen, you would set the tab as the first step and it would be in effect from that point on.)
2. Note the **Left Tab** marker on the horizontal ruler at 3.25".
3. Click in front of the date and each of the closing lines as shown in the illustration, and press **TAB** 1 time to begin each line at 3.25". Your finished job should look similar to this:

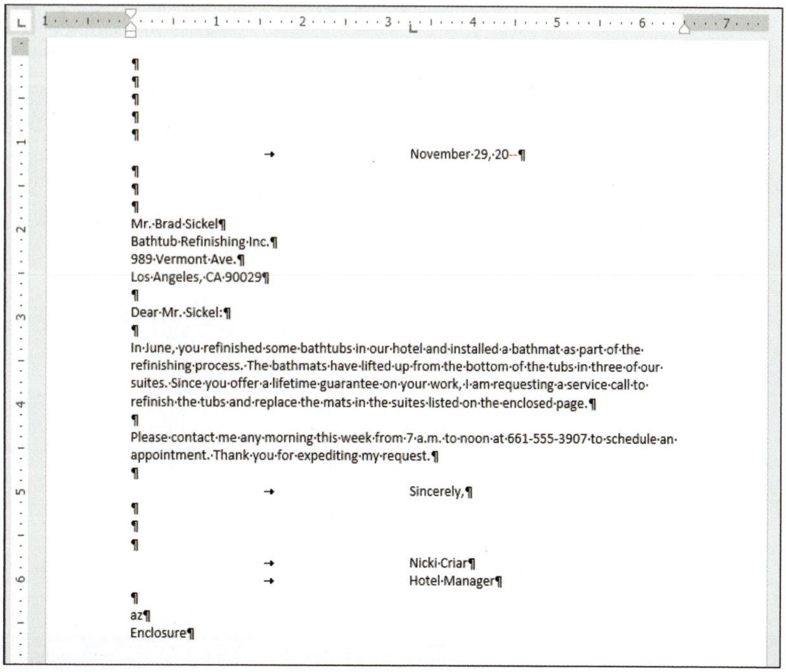

November 29, 20--

Mr. Brad Sickel
Bathtub Refinishing Inc.
989 Vermont Ave.
Los Angeles, CA 90029

Dear Mr. Sickel:

In June, you refinished some bathtubs in our hotel and installed a bathmat as part of the refinishing process. The bathmats have lifted up from the bottom of the tubs in three of our suites. Since you offer a lifetime guarantee on your work, I am requesting a service call to refinish the tubs and replace the mats in the suites listed on the enclosed page.

Please contact me any morning this week from 7 a.m. to noon at 661-555-3907 to schedule an appointment. Thank you for expediting my request.

Sincerely,

Nicki Criar
Hotel Manager

az
Enclosure

4. Save changes to *practice-45*, and return to GDP.

GO TO
Textbook

Left-Bound Business Reports With Indented Displays and Footnotes

LESSON 46

Margins

REFER TO
R-9A

Margins represent the blank space between the edge of the paper and the typed text on all sides of a document. Word uses 1" default margins all around. If you change margins, the new settings affect the entire document, not just the current page. Left-bound reports require a 1.5" left margin to accommodate the loss of visual space when the printed document is placed into a binder or is literally bound like a book.

To change the left margin:

1. From the **Layout** tab, **Page Setup** group, click **Margins**, **Custom Margins**, to display the **Page Setup** dialog box.

   Or: Display the **Ruler**; then double-click on the shaded part of the **Ruler** to display the **Page Setup** dialog box.

2. From the **Margins** tab, click in the **Left** box, and type 1.5, or click the arrows to increase or decrease margins as desired; click **OK**.

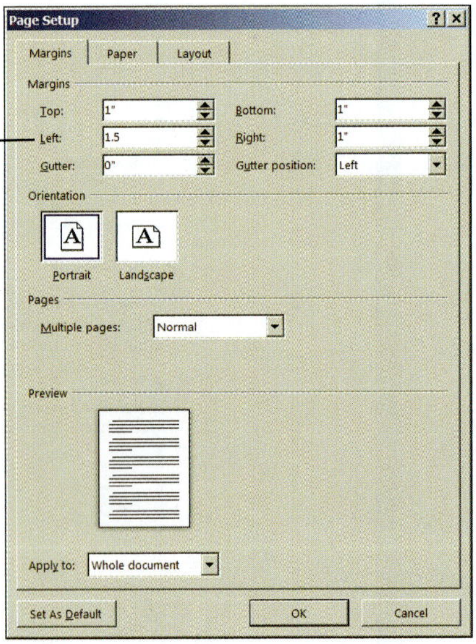

Type 1.5" in the Left box to set the left margin for a left-bound report.

PRACTICE 46 (1 of 2)

1. Display the **Ruler**.
2. Note the line endings in each line before margins are changed.
3. Note the shaded part of the ruler indicates 1" left and right margins.

Before margins are changed, 1" side margins are in use on the horizontal ruler.

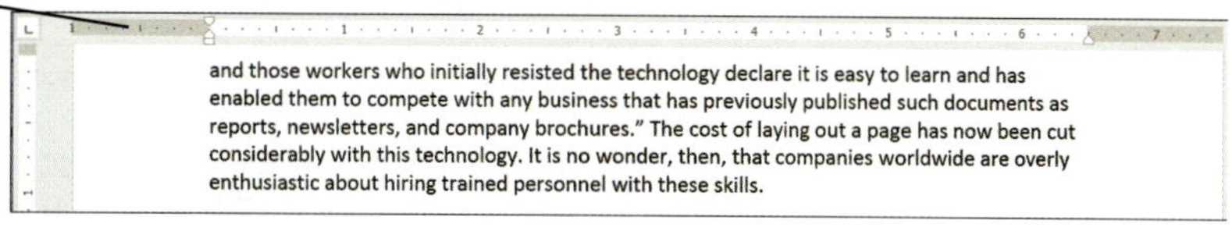
and those workers who initially resisted the technology declare it is easy to learn and has enabled them to compete with any business that has previously published such documents as reports, newsletters, and company brochures." The cost of laying out a page has now been cut considerably with this technology. It is no wonder, then, that companies worldwide are overly enthusiastic about hiring trained personnel with these skills.

4. Change the left margin to 1.5".
5. Note that the ruler now indicates a 1.5" left margin, and the line endings in each line after margins are changed.

After margins are changed, a 1.5" left margin is in use on the horizontal ruler.

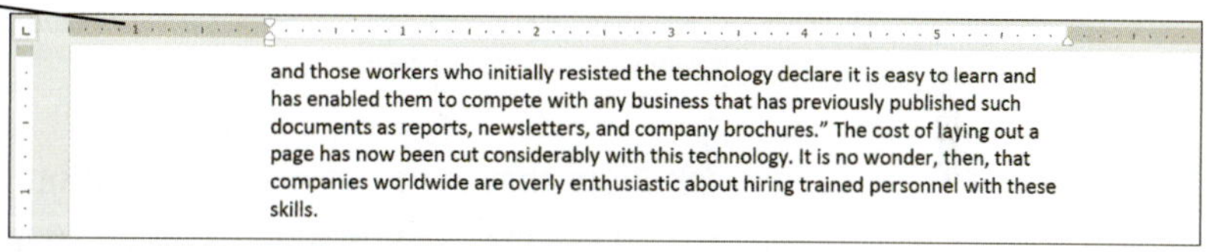
and those workers who initially resisted the technology declare it is easy to learn and has enabled them to compete with any business that has previously published such documents as reports, newsletters, and company brochures." The cost of laying out a page has now been cut considerably with this technology. It is no wonder, then, that companies worldwide are overly enthusiastic about hiring trained personnel with these skills.

6. Save changes to *practice-46.*

Note: Keep this document open, and continue reading.

Footnotes

When you insert a footnote via the Insert Footnote button, Word automatically numbers, positions, and formats the footnote for you. The superscript number will appear in both places automatically.

To insert a footnote:

1. Click directly *after* the character where you want the sequential superscript footnote number to appear. Do <u>not</u> insert a space between the last character in the text and the footnote number.

Position the insertion point exactly where the footnote will be inserted.

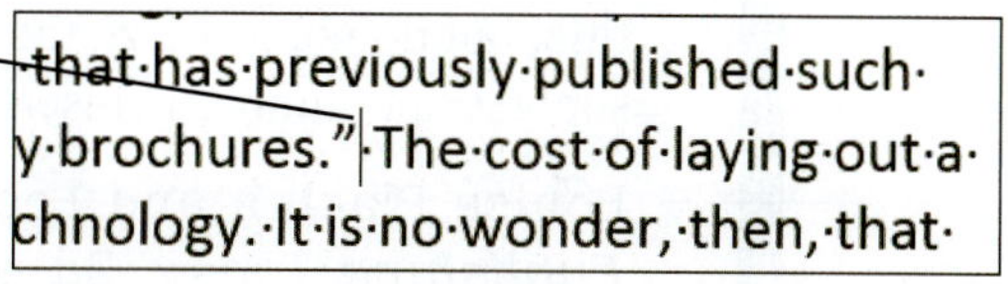
that·has·previously·published·such·
y·brochures."·The·cost·of·laying·out·a·
chnology.·It·is·no·wonder,·then,·that·

Insert Footnote button

2. From the **References** tab, in the **Footnotes** group, click the **Insert Footnote** button. Or on the keyboard, press **CTRL+ALT+F**.

3. Note that a footnote superscript number appears automatically in the document body, the insertion point moves to the bottom of the page, and a divider line and sequential footnote number appear at the bottom of the page.
4. Type the footnote entry at the bottom of the page where the insertion point appears—do <u>not</u> add or remove any spaces after the superscript. (This illustration depicts a split screen for this document.)

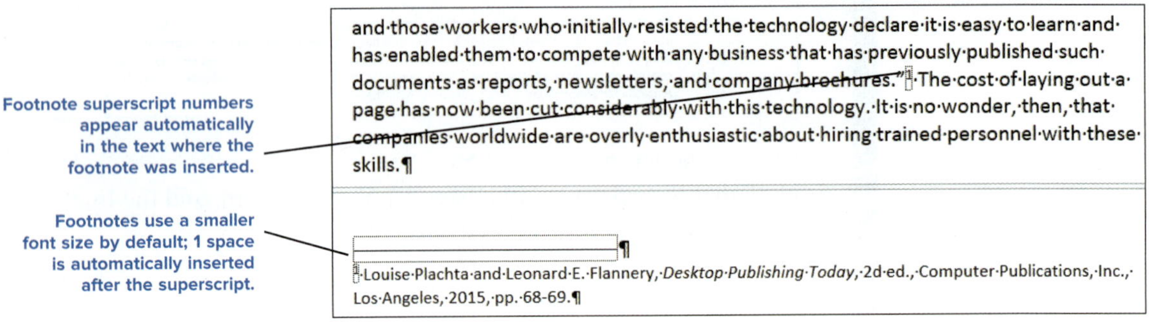
and·those·workers·who·initially·resisted·the·technology·declare·it·is·easy·to·learn·and· has·enabled·them·to·compete·with·any·business·that·has·previously·published·such· documents·as·reports,·newsletters,·and·company·brochures."[1]·The·cost·of·laying·out·a· page·has·now·been·cut·considerably·with·this·technology.·It·is·no·wonder,·then,·that· companies·worldwide·are·overly·enthusiastic·about·hiring·trained·personnel·with·these· skills.¶

¶

[1]·Louise·Plachta·and·Leonard·E.·Flannery,·*Desktop·Publishing·Today*,·2d·ed.,·Computer·Publications,·Inc.,· Los·Angeles,·2015,·pp.·68-69.¶

Note that the font size for the footnote entry is smaller than the text size in the body. Remember to italicize titles of major works, such as titles of books and magazines, in footnote entries.

5. When you finish typing the footnote, do <u>not</u> press **ENTER**; instead, click back inside the main text and continue typing.
6. Repeat these steps for additional footnotes. Word will automatically adjust footnote numbers when entries are added or deleted.

To edit a footnote: Click inside the footnote entry; make any desired changes. Click outside the footnote.

To delete a footnote: Select the footnote number in the document (not in the footnote entry at the bottom of the page). Press **DELETE**. Note that all footnotes are renumbered to reflect the deletion.

PRACTICE 46 (2 of 2)

1. Click immediately after the ending quotation mark in the first sentence, and insert this footnote—remember to italicize the book title, but do <u>not</u> italicize the comma following it; note the footnote superscript number is inserted automatically:

   Louise Plachta and Leonard E. Flannery, *Desktop Publishing Today*, 2d ed., Computer Publications, Inc., Los Angeles, 2015, pp. 68–69.

PRACTICE (continued)

2. Click immediately after the period in the second sentence in the body of the document, and insert this footnote—remember to italicize the magazine title, but do not italicize the comma following it; note the footnote superscript number is inserted automatically and is sequential:

   Terry Denton, "Newspaper Cuts Costs, Increases Quality," *The Monthly Press*, October 2015, p. 160.

3. Edit Footnote 1 by changing the page references from 68–69 to 71–72.
4. Delete Footnote 1, and note that Footnote 2 is renumbered.
5. Undo this action to restore Footnote 1.
6. Press **CTRL+P** to view your document; it should look similar to this:

Note the wider 1.5" left margin.

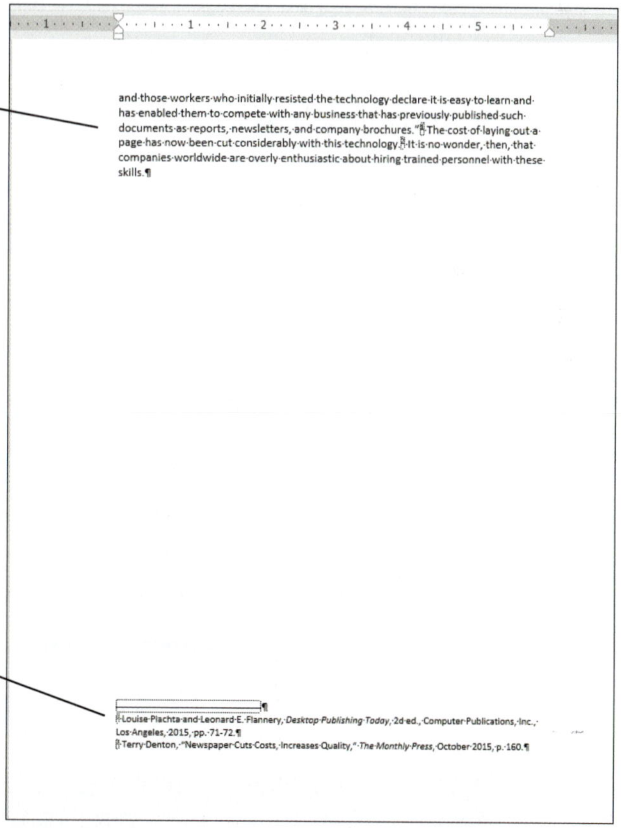

and those workers who initially resisted the technology declare it is easy to learn and has enabled them to compete with any business that has previously published such documents as reports, newsletters, and company brochures."[1] The cost of laying out a page has now been cut considerably with this technology.[2] It is no wonder, then, that companies worldwide are overly enthusiastic about hiring trained personnel with these skills.

[1] Louise Plachta and Leonard E. Flannery, *Desktop Publishing Today*, 2d ed., Computer Publications, Inc., Los Angeles, 2015, pp. 71-72.

[2] Terry Denton, "Newspaper Cuts Costs, Increases Quality," *The Monthly Press*, October 2015, p. 160.

Note the footnotes are positioned automatically at the bottom of the page.

GO TO Textbook

7. Save the changes to *practice-46*, and return to GDP.

Reports in APA Style

47 LESSON

Headers

REFER TO
L. 48D, Reports in MLA Style
R-10A–10B
R-10C–10D

APA-style reports (and MLA-style reports in Lesson 48) require the following throughout:

- Double spacing with equal spacing (0 pt.) between paragraphs.
- Indented paragraphs.

APA-style report headers display on all pages and include a right-aligned shortened report title followed by 1 space and an automatic page number set to start at 3. MLA-style report headers display on all pages and include a right-aligned author's last name followed 1 space and an automatic page number.

PAGE NUMBER—CURRENT POSITION, DIFFERENT NUMBER

To insert a right-aligned header for an APA-style report with text and an automatic page number set to start at 3:

REFER TO
WM L. 32, Page Number

1. Display the **Ruler**; right-click over the header area on the first page, and click **Edit Header**.
2. From **Header & Footer Tools**, **Design** tab, **Header & Footer** group, click **Page Number**, **Top of Page**, **Plain Number 3** from the gallery of designs to insert a page number at the right margin.
3. From the **Header & Footer Tools**, **Design** tab, **Header & Footer** group, click **Page Number**, **Format Page Numbers** to display the **Page Number Format** dialog box.

   For an MLA report header, skip steps 3 and 4.

4. From the **Page Number Format** dialog box, under **Page numbering**, click **Start at** and type 3 in the **Start at** box; click **OK**.

5. Type the shortened report title, and press the **SPACE BAR** 1 time to insert 1 space between the report title and the page number.

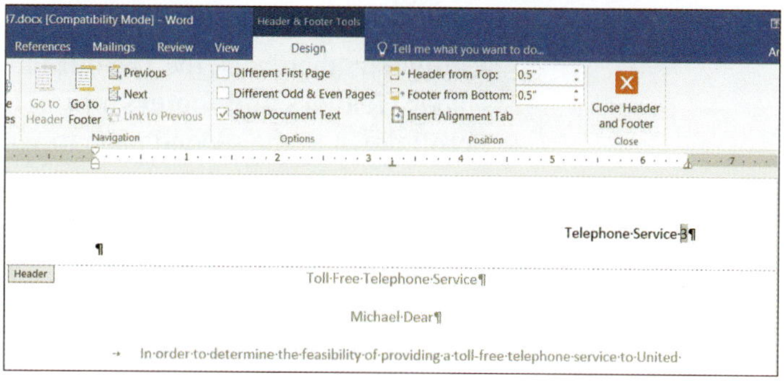

For an MLA report header, type the author's last name rather than the shortened report title.

6. Double-click anywhere outside the **First Page Header** area over the document area to close the header.
7. Note that the header information appears on all pages with the page number starting at 3 on the first page and continuing to 4 on the second page.

HEADERS—MISCELLANEOUS

Some of these header features will be used in future lessons. Remember to refer to this lesson when you have any questions regarding header format.

To start page numbering with a different number:

1. Right-click over the header area, and click Edit Header.
2. From the **Header & Footer Tools**, **Design** tab, **Header & Footer** group, click **Page Number**, **Format Page Numbers**, to display the **Page Number Format** dialog box.
3. From the **Page Number Format** dialog box, under **Page numbering**, click **Start at**; type the desired number in the **Start at** box; click **OK**.

To close a header and return to the document body:

1. Double-click anywhere outside the First Page Header area inside the document area, or from the **Header & Footer Tools**, **Design** tab, **Close** group, click the **Close Header and Footer** button.
2. Note that the header is now dimmed, the document is active, and the **Header & Footer Tools**, **Design** tab disappears.

To edit a header: Double-click anywhere over the header area, or right-click over the header area and click **Edit Header**. (The document should now be dimmed and the header should be active.)

To suppress a header only on the first page of a multipage document (subsequent pages will still include a header):

1. From the **Layout** tab, **Page Setup** group, click the **Dialog Box Launcher**; then click the **Layout** tab.
2. Under **Headers and footers**, check **Different first page**; click **OK**.
3. Scroll down to the second page to view the header.

To remove a header: From the **Insert** tab, **Header & Footer** group, click **Header**, **Remove Header**. Repeat this on the second page if you have suppressed the header on the first page.

To italicize the header or make any font changes: Click inside the header; press **CTRL+A** to select all text; then make any desired font changes.

To add a bottom border to a header: Click inside the header; from the **Home** tab, **Paragraph** group, click the list arrow on the **Borders** button, and click the **Bottom Border** button.

PRACTICE 47 (1 of 1)

In this exercise, you will format an existing report in APA style that already has double spacing set. Under normal circumstances, you would begin from a blank screen and change line spacing to double as your first step.

1. Type the title `Toll Free Telephone Service` at the top of the first page.
2. Press **ENTER** 1 time, type `Michael Dear` as the byline, and press **ENTER** again; center the title and byline.
3. Click at the end of the period in the first sentence, press **ENTER** twice, and delete the extra space at the start of the new paragraph.
4. Press **TAB** to indent the new paragraph, click the up arrow to move up one line, and type the main heading `Analysis of Costs and Benefits`; center the heading.
5. Click after the period in the fourth paragraph ending in "800-number calls"; then press **ENTER**.
6. Change to italic, and type `SmartToll Benefits` as a subheading at the left margin.
7. Click at the end of the next paragraph, press **ENTER**, change to italic, and type `SmartToll Fees` as a subheading at the left margin.

PRACTICE (continued)

8. Click anywhere inside the first page; insert a right-aligned header with a page number that starts at 3.
9. Verify that the insertion point is positioned directly before the page number and type `Telephone Service`; space once.
10. Double-click outside the header in the document body.
11. Press **CTRL+P** to view your document:

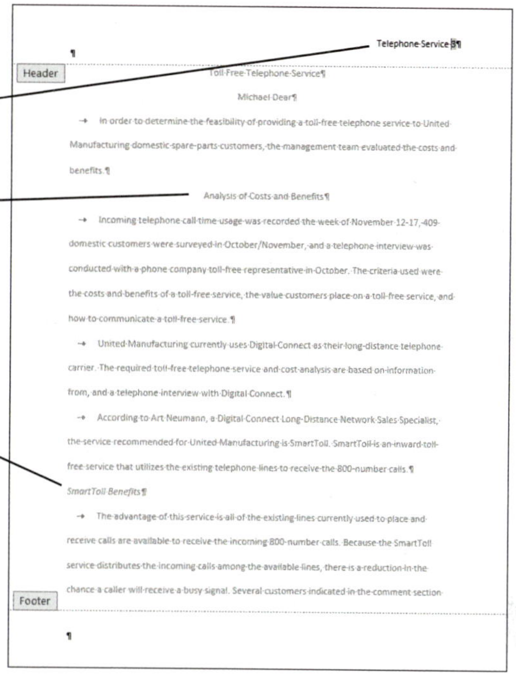

Telephone Service 3

Toll-Free Telephone Service

Michael Dear

In order to determine the feasibility of providing a toll-free telephone service to United Manufacturing domestic spare-parts customers, the management team evaluated the costs and benefits.

Analysis of Costs and Benefits

Incoming telephone call time usage was recorded the week of November 12-17, 409 domestic customers were surveyed in October/November, and a telephone interview was conducted with a phone company toll-free representative in October. The criteria used were the costs and benefits of a toll-free service, the value customers place on a toll-free service, and how to communicate a toll-free service.

United Manufacturing currently uses Digital Connect as their long-distance telephone carrier. The required toll-free telephone service and cost analysis are based on information from, and a telephone interview with Digital Connect.

According to Art Neumann, a Digital Connect Long-Distance Network Sales Specialist, the service recommended for United Manufacturing is SmartToll. SmartToll is an inward toll-free service that utilizes the existing telephone lines to receive the 800-number calls.

SmartToll Benefits

The advantage of this service is all of the existing lines currently used to place and receive calls are available to receive the incoming 800-number calls. Because the SmartToll service distributes the incoming calls among the available lines, there is a reduction in the chance a caller will receive a busy signal. Several customers indicated in the comment section

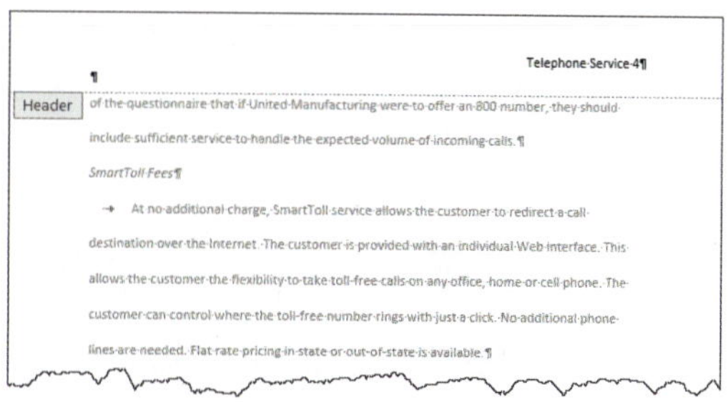

Telephone Service 4

of the questionnaire that if United Manufacturing were to offer an 800 number, they should include sufficient service to handle the expected volume of incoming calls.

SmartToll Fees

At no additional charge, SmartToll service allows the customer to redirect a call destination over the Internet. The customer is provided with an individual Web interface. This allows the customer the flexibility to take toll-free calls on any office, home or cell phone. The customer can control where the toll-free number rings with just a click. No additional phone lines are needed. Flat rate pricing in state or out-of-state is available.

12. Save changes to *practice-47*, and return to GDP.

GO TO Textbook

Report Citations

LESSON 49

Indentation—Hanging

REFER TO
R-9B, 10B, & 10D
WM L. 45, Tab Set—Ruler Tabs

The entries in report bibliographies, APA-style report reference lists, and MLA-style report Works Cited pages are formatted with hanging indents. The first line is positioned at the left margin, and carryover lines are automatically indented by 0.5" as shown in this illustration:

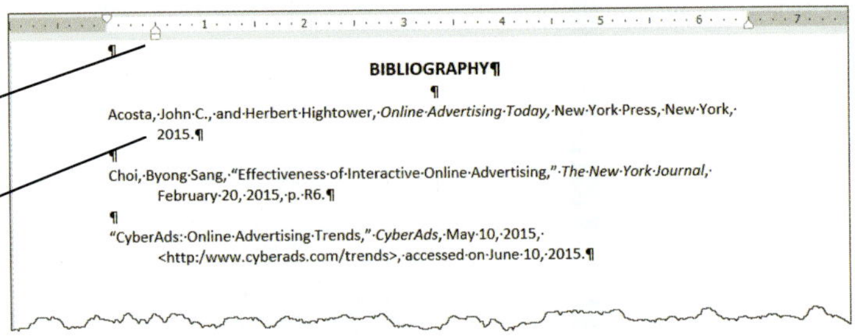
BIBLIOGRAPHY¶

¶

Acosta,·John·C.,·and·Herbert·Hightower,·*Online·Advertising·Today*,·New·York·Press,·New·York,· 2015.¶

¶

Choi,·Byong·Sang,·"Effectiveness·of·Interactive·Online·Advertising,"·*The·New·York·Journal*,· February·20,·2015,·p.·R6.¶

¶

"CyberAds:·Online·Advertising·Trends,"·*CyberAds*,·May·10,·2015,· <http:/www.cyberads.com/trends>,·accessed·on·June·10,·2015.¶

Hanging indent marker

Hanging indent

If you set a hanging indent at the point of the first entry and continue typing all remaining entries, that hanging indent is in effect automatically for all the entries. If you set a hanging indent after a document is finished, you must select the desired lines and then set the hanging indent.

To set a hanging indent: Click in the desired line or select the desired lines; press **CTRL+T**.

To remove a hanging indent: Click in the desired line or select the desired lines; press **CTRL+SHIFT+T**.

AutoCorrect—Hyperlink

REFER TO
WM L. 89, Bookmarks and Hyperlinks

A *hyperlink* is a linked object (usually text or a picture) you click on to jump from one place to another (either within a document or perhaps to an external Web page). Hyperlinked text is underlined, and the mouse pointer displays a hand icon when you point to the hyperlinked element.

When you type an e-mail or Internet address and press the SPACE BAR or press ENTER, that address is automatically converted to a hyperlink. When you type an Internet address in a bibliography or footnote with angle brackets (< >) and type a punctuation mark, press the SPACE BAR, or press ENTER, that address is automatically converted to a hyperlink, and angle brackets are automatically deleted. Follow these steps to remove the hyperlink and replace any missing angle brackets:

REFER TO

WM Appendix A, Using Microsoft Word in the Workplace, GDP—Word Settings, AutoFormat As You Type Options, Hyperlinks

If hyperlinks are not behaving as expected, See Appendix A to verify your Word settings for AutoFormat.

To remove an automatic hyperlink immediately after it appears and revert to the original angle brackets: Press **BACKSPACE** or **CTRL+Z** or click **Undo**. Or if the **AutoCorrect Options** lightning bolt button appears, click the list arrow, and click **Undo Hyperlink**.

To remove a hyperlink later: Right-click the hyperlink; click **Remove Hyperlink**. If angle brackets surrounding the original electronic reference were removed, retype the angle brackets after removing the hyperlink.

To remove a trailing space, but still retain the hyperlink: Press the left directional arrow on the keyboard 1 time; then press **DELETE**.

PRACTICE 49 (1 of 1)

REFER TO

R-10B & R-10D

Note: In this Practice exercise, you will format a bibliography page. Refer to the Reference Manual for an example of an APA reference list page (R-10B) and for an example of an MLA works-cited page (R-10D).

1. In the first entry change the year from 2009 to 2015. Select the comma after "*Today*," and remove the italics.
2. Click at the end of the first reference, press **ENTER** 2 times, and type this entry—remember to italicize the journal title.

   Choi, Byong Sang, "Effectiveness of Interactive Online Advertising," *The New York Journal,* February 20, 2015, p. R6.

3. Select the first two entries, and format them with a hanging indent. (*Hint:* Press **CTRL+T**.) Your document should look similar to this:

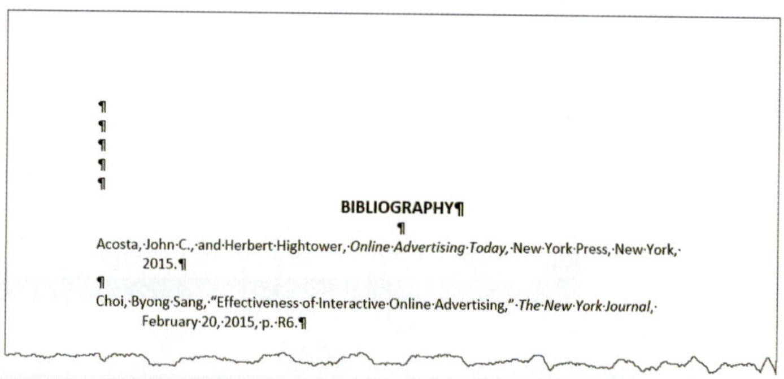

¶
¶
¶
¶
¶

BIBLIOGRAPHY¶

¶

Acosta, John C., and Herbert Hightower, *Online Advertising Today,* New York Press, New York, 2015.¶

¶

Choi, Byong Sang, "Effectiveness of Interactive Online Advertising," *The New York Journal,* February 20, 2015, p. R6.¶

PRACTICE (continued)

4. Click at the end of the last reference, and press **ENTER** 2 times.
5. Type this entry—remember to italicize the journal title, but do not italicize the comma following it. Note that when you type the opening angle bracket, the Internet address, the closing angle bracket, and the comma, the Internet address is converted to a hyperlink as shown in the illustration:

   "CyberAds: Online Advertising Trends," *CyberAds*, May 10, 2015, <http://www.cyberads.com/trends>, accessed on June 10, 2015.

   "CyberAds:·Online·Advertising·Trends,·*CyberAds*,·May·10,·2015,·
   http://www.cyberads.com/trends,¶

6. Press **CTRL+Z** to undo the hyperlink if you notice the hyperlink immediately after it appears.

   Or: If you notice the hyperlink later, right-click over the Internet address, and click **Remove Hyperlink**. Then replace the angle brackets at the beginning and end of the Internet address.

7. Verify that your final entry looks like this, including the access information that follows the Internet address:

   "CyberAds:·Online·Advertising·Trends,"·*CyberAds*,·May·10,·2015,·
   <http:/www.cyberads.com/trends>,·accessed·on·June·10,·2015.¶

8. Your finished document should look similar to this:

   ¶
   ¶
   ¶
   ¶
   ¶

   BIBLIOGRAPHY¶

   ¶

   Acosta,·John·C.,·and·Herbert·Hightower,·*Online·Advertising·Today,*·New·York·Press,·New·York,·2015.¶

   ¶

   Choi,·Byong·Sang,·"Effectiveness·of·Interactive·Online·Advertising,"·*The·New·York·Journal*,·February·20,·2015,·p.·R6.¶

   ¶

   "CyberAds:·Online·Advertising·Trends,"·*CyberAds*,·May·10,·2015,·<http:/www.cyberads.com/trends>,·accessed·on·June·10,·2015.¶

9. Save changes to *practice-49*, and return to GDP.

GO TO Textbook

Preliminary Report Pages

LESSON 50

Tab Set—Dot Leaders

REFER TO
WM L. 45, Tab Set—Ruler Tabs

REFER TO
R-7D

In this lesson, you will use the Paragraph dialog box to set custom left tabs and custom dot leader tabs and use the Ruler to verify tab settings as you manually format a table of contents. *Dot leaders* are a series of dots that lead the eye from a heading to a page number in a table of contents.

To format a table of contents with custom tabs: Set a 0.5" left tab to position the report subheadings; set a 6.5" right dot leader tab to insert dot leaders and position the corresponding page number at the right margin.

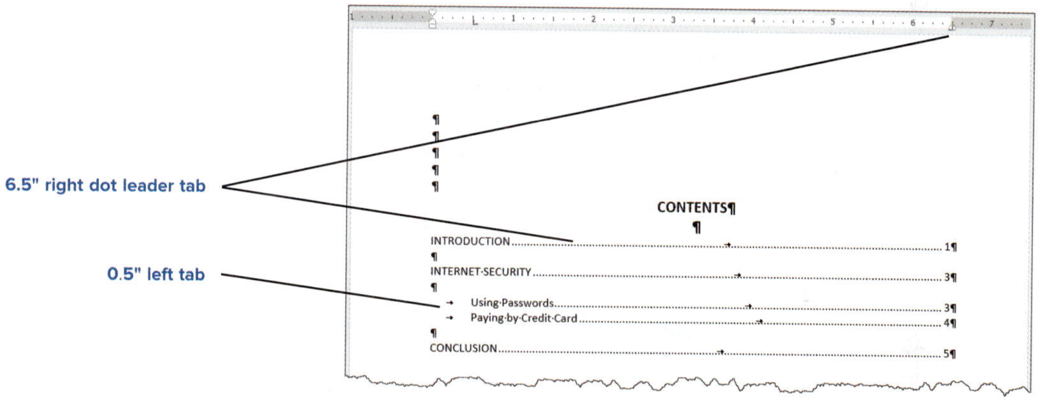

To set custom tabs for a table of contents using the menu:

If you have already typed the table of contents, select the entire document (press CTRL+A), and then set custom tabs.

1. From the **Home** or **Layout** tab, **Paragraph** group, click the **Dialog Box Launcher**.
2. From the **Paragraph** dialog box, **Indents and Spacing** tab, click the **Tabs** button at the bottom of the dialog box.
3. From the **Tabs** dialog box, set a tab to position the subheadings as follows: In the **Tab stop position** box, type .5 and in the **Alignment** section, select **Left**; click **Set**.

4. From the **Tabs** dialog box, set a tab to position the page as follows: In the **Tab stop position** box, type 6.5; in the **Alignment** section, select **Right**; in the **Leader** section, select **2** for dot leaders; click **Set**.

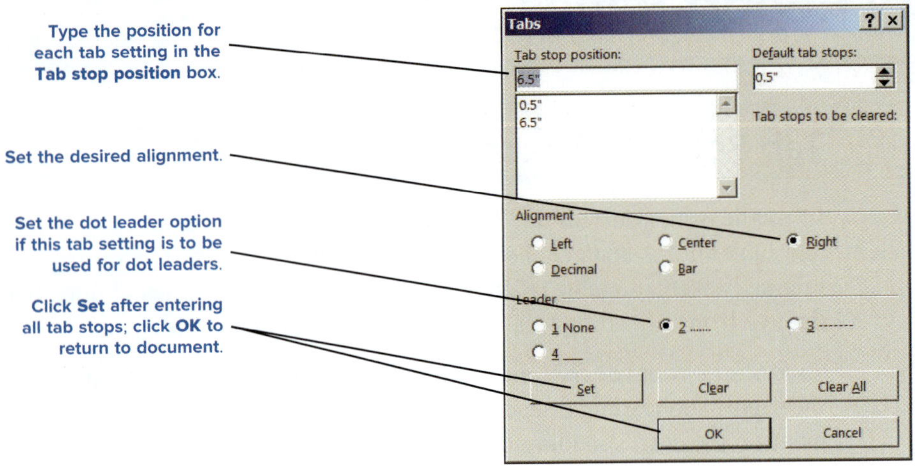

5. Note that both custom tab stops appear below the **Tab stop position** box; click **OK**.

To type a table of contents main heading with dot leaders and a page number:

1. Type the main heading.
2. Press **TAB** to insert dot leaders automatically from the heading to the right margin and to move to the right margin; type the page number.

To type a table of contents subheading with dot leaders and a page number:

1. Press **TAB** to indent the line 0.5", and type the subheading.
2. Press **TAB** again to insert dot leaders automatically from the heading to the right margin and to move to the right margin; type the page number.

PRACTICE 50 (1 of 1)

1. Set a left tab at 0.5" and a right dot-leader tab at 6.5".
2. Display the **Ruler** to verify tab settings.
3. Press **ENTER** 5 times.
4. Change to 14-pt. bold font, center alignment; type this: CONTENTS.
5. Press **ENTER** 2 times, change to left alignment, change the font size to 12, and release the **Bold** button.
6. Type INTRODUCTION (the first heading); press **TAB** (displays dot leaders extending to the right margin); type 1 (the page number); press **ENTER** 2 times.

PRACTICE (continued)

7. Type `INTERNET SECURITY`; press **TAB**; type `3`; press **ENTER** 2 times.
8. Press **TAB** to indent the first subheading by 0.5"; type `Using Passwords` (the first subheading); press **TAB**; type `3`; press **ENTER**.
9. Press **TAB**; type `Paying by Credit Card`; press **TAB**; type `4`; press **ENTER** 2 times.
10. Type `CONCLUSION`; press **TAB**; type `5`. Your document should look similar to this:

¶
¶
¶
¶
¶

CONTENTS¶

¶

INTRODUCTION ....→........................ 1¶
¶
INTERNET·SECURITY ....→........................ 3¶
¶
→ Using·Passwords ....→........................ 3¶
→ Paying·by·Credit·Card ....→........................ 4¶
¶
CONCLUSION ....→........................ 5¶

11. Save changes to *practice-50*, and return to GDP.

GO TO Textbook

Resumes

Font

Font refers to the general *typeface* (design) of a typed character. Common typefaces are Calibri (Word's default typeface) and Times New Roman. You learned to apply bold and change font sizes. In this lesson, you will learn to change font typefaces.

To change fonts:

1. Position the insertion point where you want to begin using the new font or select the desired text.
2. From the **Home** tab, **Font** group, click the down arrow to the right of the **Font** box.
3. Click the desired font—scroll down the list if necessary.

As you change fonts, the most recent choice is added to the font drop-down list under **Recently Used Fonts**.

Font box.

Recently Used Fonts list with the most recently used fonts.

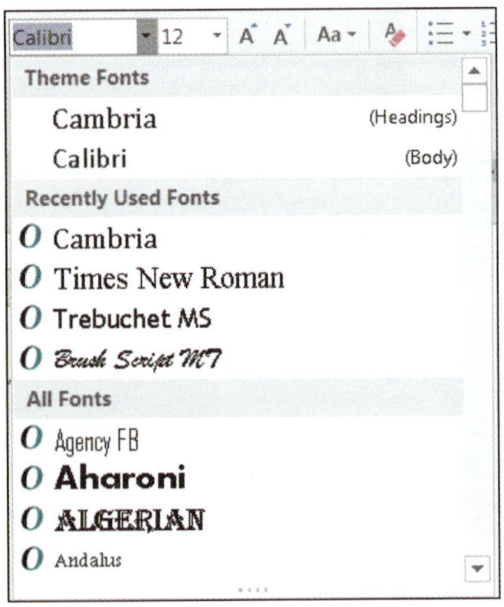

Or: Press **CTRL+D**, and make the desired choices in the **Font** dialog box:

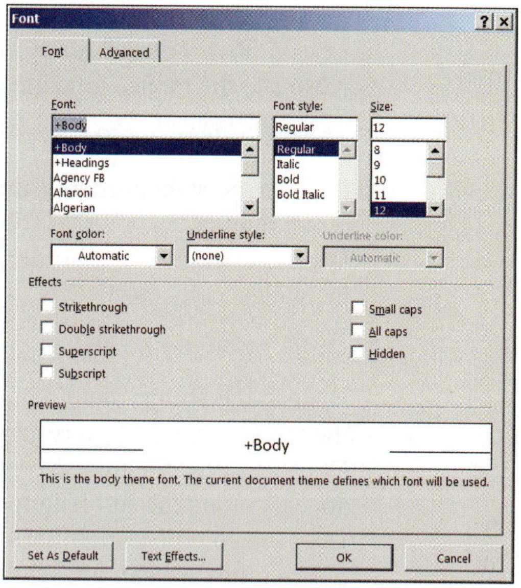

To change the font or font style, size, and effect:

1. From the **Font** dialog box, **Font** tab, under **Font**, click the desired font.
2. Under **Font style**, **Size**, and **Effects**, click the desired choices; click **OK**.

PRACTICE 51 (1 of 2)

1. Select the table, right-click over the table, and click **AutoFit, AutoFit to Window**, to ensure that the table extends the full width of the page margins.
2. In Row 1, center the name, and change the font to Cambria 14 pt. Bold.
3. Center both lines below the name; change the font to Cambria 12 pt. Bold. (Row 1 should look similar to the illustration at the end of this lesson.)
4. Save changes to *practice-51*.

Note: Keep this document open, and continue reading.

Table—Change Column Width

In Lesson 36, you used AutoFit to Contents to change column widths. You can also use the mouse to manually change column widths.

To change column widths by double-clicking the right border:

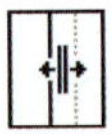

Resize pointer

1. Point to the right border of the table column until the mouse changes to a resize pointer.
2. Double-click the right border of the desired column to adjust the width to the widest cell entry.

To change column widths by dragging on the right border:

1. Display the **Ruler**, and point to the right border of the table column until the mouse changes to a resize pointer.
2. Click and hold the mouse button; note the dotted vertical line that appears along the full length of the border extending up to the ruler.
3. Drag the column border until the dotted vertical line points to the desired position on the ruler above.

As long as the cell is not selected, dragging the right border adjusts the entire column width, not just the selected cell's width. Hold down ALT as you drag to see the exact ruler measurements.

PRACTICE 51 (2 of 2)

1. Press **CTRL+HOME**, and press **ENTER** 5 times.
2. Remove all table borders. (*Hint:* Select the table; from the **Table Tools**, **Design** tab, **Borders** group, click the list arrow under the **Borders** button, and click **No Border**.)
3. If necessary, display table gridlines. (*Hint:* From the **Table Tools**, **Layout** tab, **Table** group, click **View Gridlines**.)
4. Select Row 1, and apply a bottom border. (*Hint:* From the **Table Tools**, **Design** tab, **Borders** group, click the list arrow under the **Borders** button; then click **Bottom Border**.)

If you apply a border and get unexpected results, such as an extra thick border or colored border, close all Word files, and restart Word to return to border default settings.

PRACTICE (continued)

5. Bold all the headings in Column A.
6. In the EXPERIENCE section in Column B, italicize the job titles and business names. Do <u>not</u> italicize the comma after the job title.
7. Increase the indent for the job description paragraphs by 0.5". (*Hint:* With the insertion point in the desired paragraph, from the **Home** tab, **Paragraph** group, click the **Increase Indent** button 1 time.)
8. Drag the right border of Column A to accommodate the widest entry without wrapping. Your document should look similar to this:

ANGELICA P. JUAREZ

1842 Amber Road, Germantown, TN 38139
Phone: 901-555-5102; e-mail: ajuarez@netcast.com

OBJECTIVE	To obtain a position in admissions counseling in a post-secondary school setting, preferably in Tennessee.
EDUCATION	Delta State University, Cleveland, Mississippi B.A. degree in psychology Graduated: May 2009 Cleveland High School, Cleveland, Mississippi Graduated: May 2004
EXPERIENCE	*School Counselor*, *Germantown Elementary* Germantown, Tennessee, 2009 to Present Provide individual and group counseling services to meet the developmental, preventive, and remedial needs of students. Assist teachers with the educational placement of students by using appropriate educational assessment strategies. *Administrative Assistant*, *Shaw Industries* Cleveland, Mississippi, 2008 to 2009 Prepared reports for section supervisor. Maintained budget using Excel software. Planned and prepared itinerary for section supervisor. Supervised area secretaries and office clerks. Worked in customer service.
ACTIVITIES	Activities pursued while attending college: • Volunteer reading tutor, Cleveland Youth Literacy, 2005 • Special Olympics volunteer, 2006
REFERENCES	Available upon request.

9. Save changes to *practice-51*, and return to GDP.

GO TO Textbook

Special Correspondence Features

LESSON 67

Sort

You can sort text alphabetically, numerically, or by date within a document in ascending order (A to Z or 0 to 9, for example). You can also sort in descending order (Z to A or 9 to 0).

To perform a paragraph sort:

Sort button

1. Select only the paragraphs to be sorted.
2. From the **Home** tab, **Paragraph** group, click the **Sort** button.
3. From the **Sort Text** dialog box, **Sort by** box, click **Paragraphs** if necessary; in the **Type** box, click **Text** if necessary; then click **Ascending** if necessary.

To sort a bulleted list alphabetically in ascending order (A to Z), use these settings.

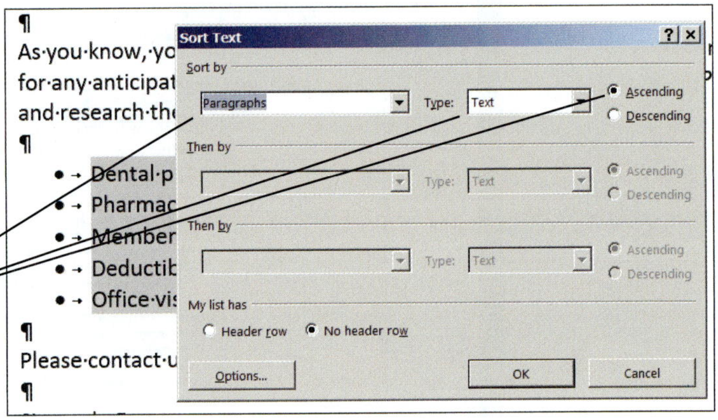

4. Click **OK**. The list is sorted alphabetically from A to Z.

To undo a sort: Click **Undo**, or press **CTRL+Z** immediately after sorting.

PRACTICE 67 (1 of 1)

1. Select the list; from the **Home** tab, **Paragraph** group, click the **Bullets** button to remove the bullets; click the **Bullets** button again to reapply bullets; note the default list indent is in effect.

PRACTICE (continued)

2. Note the random alphabetical order of information in the list:

   As·you·know,·your·health·care·plan·will·
   for·any·anticipated·future·expenses,·you
   and·research·the·following·topics:¶
   ¶
   - → Dental·plan·program¶
   - → Pharmacy·co-pay·structure¶
   - → Member-managed·care¶
   - → Deductibles¶
   - → Office·visits¶

   ¶
   Please·contact·us·if·you·have·any·questi

3. Sort the list in ascending order; note the list is now sorted in alphabetical ascending order (A to Z):

   As·you·know,·your·health·care·plan·will·
   for·any·anticipated·future·expenses,·you
   and·research·the·following·topics:¶
   ¶
   - → Deductibles¶
   - → Dental·plan·program¶
   - → Member-managed·care¶
   - → Office·visits¶
   - → Pharmacy·co-pay·structure¶

   ¶
   Please·contact·us·if·you·have·any·questi

4. Save changes to *practice-67*, and return to GDP.

GO TO Textbook

More Special Correspondence Features

LESSON 68

Table—Shading

To give your table a polished look and to increase readability, add shading to desired rows, columns, or cells. Shading is a design element—don't overuse it. Shading choices should be purposeful and attractive.

To add shading:

1. Select the desired cells, rows, or columns.
2. From the **Home** tab, **Paragraph** group, click the list arrow to the right of the **Borders** button; click **Borders and Shading**.

   Or: Click inside the table; from the **Table Tools**, **Design** tab, **Borders** group, click the list arrow at the bottom of the **Borders** button; click **Borders and Shading**.

3. From the **Borders and Shading** dialog box, click the **Shading** tab.
4. Under **Patterns**, click the down arrow in the **Style** box, and click the desired shading option; click **OK**.
   - **Clear** (the default setting) provides no shading.
   - **Solid** (**100%**) provides solid black shading with white text.
   - **10%**, **20%**, or **25%** shading provides gradient gray shading with black text.

E-Mail—Blind Copies

This feature is no longer in use in the 11th Edition. Please continue to the Practice exercise.

PRACTICE 68 (1 of 1)

1. If necessary, activate **View Gridlines**. (*Hint:* From the **Home** tab, **Paragraph** group, click the list arrow on the **Borders** button. From the drop-down menu, click **View Gridlines**.)
2. Click after the colon following the last word in the first paragraph, and press **ENTER** 1 time to insert 1 blank line before the table.

PRACTICE (continued)

3. Click before the first word in the second paragraph, and press **ENTER** 1 time to insert 1 blank line after the table.
4. Select Row 1.
5. From the **Home** tab, **Paragraph** group, click the list arrow on the **Borders** button; click **Borders and Shading** at the bottom.
6. From the **Borders and Shading** dialog box, click the **Shading** tab; from the **Patterns** group, click the **Style** list arrow; click **Solid (100%)** shading; click **OK**; note that Row 1 now has 100% shading applied and the font is white.
7. Select Row 2, and apply a 25% shading style; note that Row 2 now has 25% shading applied, and the font is still black.
8. Apply an outside border to the entire table. (*Hint:* Select the table; from the **Home** tab, **Paragraph** group, click the list arrow on the **Borders** button; click **Outside Borders**.) Your table should now look similar to this illustration.

eks,·we·will·submit·to·you·and·your·committee·sever
:e·list·for·the·printed·stationery:¶

AMERICAN·LANDSCAPE·LOGO¶ ¤	
Stationery¤	**Cost¤**
Letterhead·(500·sheets)¤	$··80.00¤
Business·cards·(1,000·cards)¤	39.50¤
Coated·brochures·(1,000·sheets)¤	219.30¤
Envelopes¤	92.00¤

you·need·any·further·details.¶

9. Save changes to *practice-68*, and return to GDP.

GO TO Textbook

Multipage Memos With Tables

LESSON 69

Find and Replace

REFER TO

WM L. 24, Navigation Pane—Search

In Lesson 24, you used the Navigation Pane to search for and find designated keystrokes in a document. In this lesson, you will use Find and Replace to perform an advanced search.

To use Find and Replace for an advanced search:

1. Press **CTRL+H**.
2. From the **Replace** tab, **Find what** box, delete any existing text, and type the desired search text.
3. In the **Replace with** box, type the desired replacement text.
4. Click **Find Next**; note that the next occurrence of the text is highlighted; click **Replace** to replace that single instance, or click **Replace All** to replace all instances without reviewing each replacement.

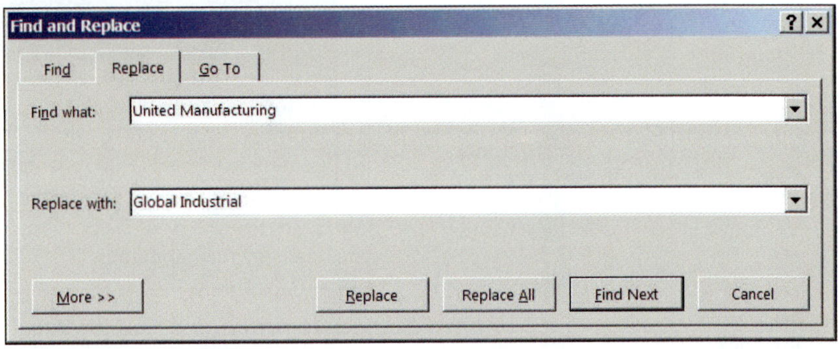

Use Find Next to verify each replacement individually if you are unsure about accurate replacements if you use Replace All.

5. Click the **Close** (**X**) button to resume work on the document.

PRACTICE 69 (1 of 1)

1. Press **CTRL+H** to open the **Find and Replace** dialog box.
2. From the **Replace** tab, type `United Manufacturing` in the **Find what** box.
3. From the **Replace** tab, type `Global Industrial` in the **Replace with** box.
4. Click **Find Next**; note that you are moved to the first result—drag the **Find and Replace** dialog box out of the way if it is obstructing your view of the highlighted words.
5. Click **Replace**; note that *Global Industrial* replaced *United Manufacturing* and the next result is highlighted.
6. Click **Replace All**; note the prompt that states 3 replacements were made—click **OK**; close the **Find and Replace** window.
7. If necessary, press **CTRL+F** to display the **Navigation Pane** if it is not already displayed; in the **Navigation Pane Search document** box, type `United Manufacturing`; note that "No matches" displays confirming that all replacements were made.
8. Save changes to *practice-69*, and return to GDP.

GO TO Textbook

LESSON 73

Procedures Manual

Footers

A *footer* is any information (such as text and a page number) that appears at the bottom of every page in a document. For example:

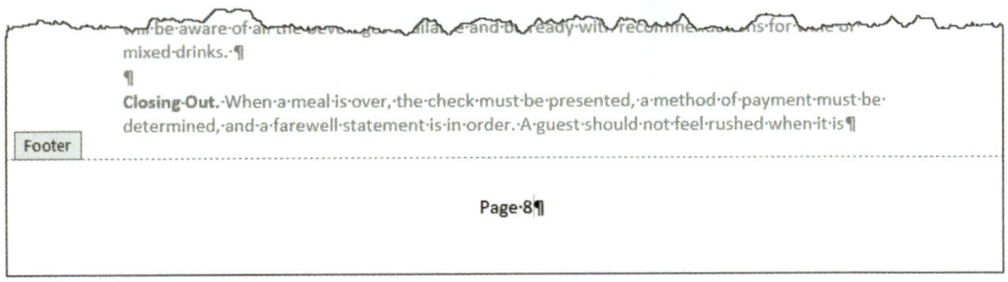

To insert a centered footer with "Page" and a plain page number into all pages of a document:

1. Right-click over the footer area, and click **Edit Footer**.
2. Press **CTRL+E** to change to center alignment.
3. Type Page and press the **SPACE BAR** 1 time.
4. From the **Header & Footer Tools**, **Design** tab, **Header & Footer** group, click **Page Number**, **Current Position**, **Plain Number**, from the gallery of designs to insert a centered, plain page number.

To set a page number to start at a particular number:

1. From the **Header & Footer Tools**, **Design** tab, **Header & Footer** group, click **Page Number**, **Current Position**, **Plain Number**.
2. From the **Header & Footer Tools**, **Design** tab, **Header & Footer** group, click **Page Number**, **Format Page Numbers**.
3. From the **Page Number Format** dialog box, under **Page numbering**, click **Start at**, and type the desired starting page number; click **OK**.

To close a footer and return to the document body: Double-click anywhere outside the **Footer** area. Or from the **Header & Footer Tools, Design** tab, **Close** group, click **Close Header and Footer**.

To edit a footer: Double-click anywhere over the footer area. Or right-click over the footer area and click **Edit Footer**; edit and close the footer.

To remove a footer: From the **Insert** tab, **Header & Footer** group, click **Footer**; from the menu at the bottom of the gallery, click **Remove Footer**. (If you have suppressed the footer on the first page, click anywhere inside the body of the second page before taking the preceding steps.)

REFER TO

WM L. 32, Page Number
WM L. 47, Headers

HEADERS—LEFT/RIGHT ALIGNED

Headers include two default tabs—one center tab and one right tab. Review the next illustration for a header in a procedures manual, which includes left-aligned text as well as right-aligned text positioned via the Right Tab setting as shown on the horizontal ruler.

To insert a header with left- and right-aligned content:

1. Display the **Ruler**; activate **Show/Hide ¶**.
2. Right-click over the header area, and click **Edit Header**.
3. Note the default header tab settings—a **Center Tab** at 3.25" and a **Right Tab** at 6.5".
4. At the left margin, type the desired text.
5. Press **TAB** 2 times to move to the **Right Tab** setting, activate any desired formatting (such as **CTRL+I** for italics), and type the desired text; for example:

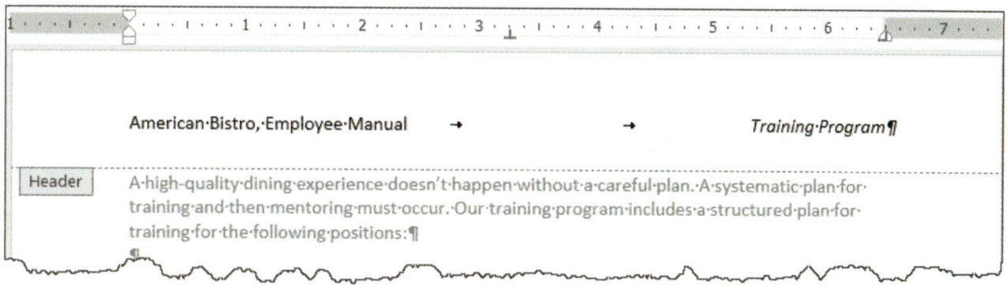

PRACTICE 73 (1 of 1)

The Start Work file simulates a continuation page in a procedures manual for American Bistro (a chain of restaurants). The title of the manual is "Employee Manual" and the report section name is "Training Program."

1. Right-click over the header area, and click **Edit Header**.
2. Display the **Ruler**, and note the default header tabs—a center tab at 3.25" and a right tab at 6.5".
3. At the left margin inside the header, type this:

   `American Bistro, Employee Manual`

4. Press **TAB** 2 times to move to the to the right tab position; press **CTRL+I**, type these words in italics, and close the header.

   `Training Program`

   The header should look similar to the illustration at the end of the Practice exercise.

PRACTICE (continued)

5. Right-click anywhere over the footer area, and click **Edit Footer**; press **CTRL+E** to change to center alignment.
6. Type `Page` and press the **SPACE BAR** 1 time.
7. Insert a centered, plain page number set to start at 8 for this continuation page.
8. Close the footer. The continuation page of this report should look similar to this:

American Bistro, Employee Manual → → *Training Program*

A high-quality dining experience doesn't happen without a careful plan. A systematic plan for training and then mentoring must occur. Our training program includes a structured plan for training for the following positions:

- Server
- Dishwasher
- Line Cook
- Prep Cook
- Bus Person
- Host or Hostess
- Bartender

Each of these positions will be discussed in detail and many constructive suggestions will be outlined.

SERVER

The functions and the responsibilities of the server are many and varied. General job guidelines and responsibilities and opening and closing procedures are critical. Guest service is the goal for all restaurant employees, but is particularly important for those who deal with the customer directly.

Quality Control and Ordering. A server must be aware of quality control in terms of the food being served. Is it fresh, properly prepared, and promptly served? Ordering procedures must be in place so that the guest feels confident that the order will arrive promptly, accurately, and as expected.

Personal Appearance. Guests will make a direct correlation between a server's personal appearance and the overall quality of the dining experience. If the server is not dressed appropriately, the guest will begin the dining experience with a negative impression. If the server creates a good first impression in appearance and attitude, the guest will anticipate a wonderful and very pleasant dining experience.

Suggestive Selling. Suggestive selling as a guest is ordering and reviewing the menu is a fine art that must be practiced and rehearsed. The specials and features of the day must sound enticing and attractive but the guest must not feel pressured to order.

Beverage Service. Most guests begin their dining service by ordering a beverage. A good server will be aware of all the beverages available and be ready with recommendations for wine or mixed drinks.

Closing Out. When a meal is over, the check must be presented, a method of payment must be determined, and a farewell statement is in order. A guest should not feel rushed when it is

Page 8

9. Save changes to *practice-73*, and return to GDP.

GO TO Textbook

Reports Formatted in Columns

LESSON 74

Columns

Use newspaper-style columns to flow text from the bottom of one column to the top of the next. Use justified alignment to avoid jagged line endings. Enable automatic hyphenation to reduce large gaps of white space. See the illustrations at the end of this lesson for examples. Use the Columns feature to create multiple columns and customize column settings.

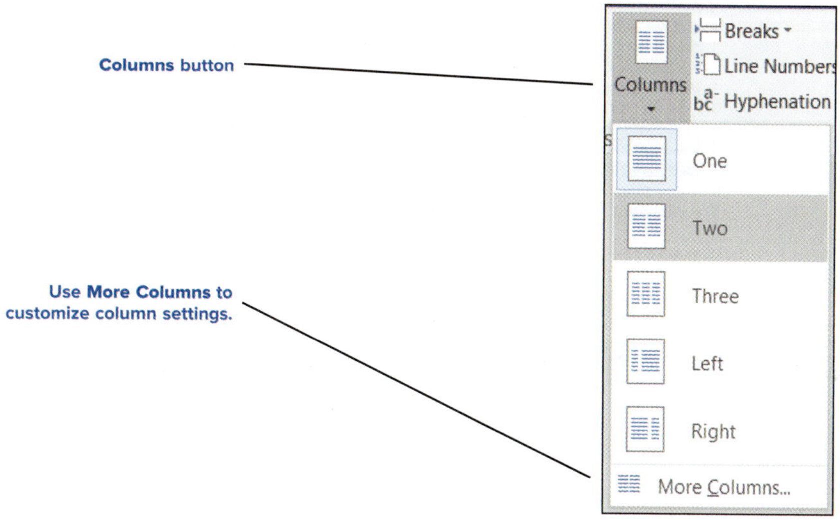

To add balanced columns to an existing document:

1. With **Show/Hide ¶** active, click where you want the columns to begin at the start of the body in your completed document; carefully select the text in the body that will be arranged in columns:
   - Position the insertion point just *before* the first character in the desired text.
   - Scroll to the end of the document, press and hold **SHIFT**, and click just *after* the last typed character in the document but just *before* the Paragraph formatting mark.

   You must exclude the Paragraph formatting mark (¶) in your selection to create a continuous section break and to create balanced columns that are evenly divided. If the mark is accidentally selected, hold down the SHIFT key, and press the left keyboard directional arrow once to move to the left and deselect the Paragraph formatting mark.

Study this illustration carefully noting in particular the exact position where the selection begins and ends.

TIME AND PERCEPTION¶

¶

Shannon Jones¶

¶

Time is a method human beings use to measure and sequence events, to compare the durations of events, and to measure the intervals between events. Time is a hot topic in terms of religion, philosophy, and science. However, defining time in an objective, accepted way has been nearly impossible amongst scholarly types. How, in fact, do you compare one moment to the next?¶

¶

Our perception of time as human beings has grown out of a natural series of rhythms that are linked to daily, monthly, and yearly cycles. No matter how much we live by our wristwatches, our bodies and our lives will always be somewhat influenced by an internal clock. What is of even greater interest, though, are the many uses and perceptions of time based on individuals and their cultures.¶

¶

RHYTHM AND TEMPO¶

¶

Rhythm and tempo are ways we relate to time and are discerning features of a culture. In some cultures, people move very slowly; in others, moving quickly is the norm. Mixing the two types may create feelings of discomfort. People may have trouble relating to each other because they are not synchronized. To be synchronized is to subtly move in union with another person; it is vital to a strong partnership.¶

¶

In general, Americans move at a fast tempo, although there are regional departures. In meetings, Americans tend to be impatient and want to "get down to business" right away. They have been taught that it is best to come to the point quickly and avoid vagueness. Because American business operates in a short time frame, prompt results are often of more interest than the building of long-term relationships.¶

¶

PERCEPTION AND MEMORY¶

¶

Picture yourself in a room watching someone enter, walk across the room, and sit down. By the time the person sits down, your brain must remember the actions that happened previous to the act of sitting down. All these memories and perceptions are filed as bits of data in the brain. The perception of the passing of time from the first event of entering the room to the last event of sitting down occurs only if the observer is aware and comparing the events.¶

¶

What would happen if the observer could not remember one or more of the events from the time the person entered the room to the time that person was seated? The brain might interpret the scene and assign a time frame, but unless the observer remembers, the perception of time passing would not exist.¶

¶

LIVING IN THE MOMENT¶

¶

If a human being perceives himself to be of a certain age, this is because he has accumulated data, remembers that data, and has a basis for a comparison. If a person cannot remember his past, such as a person with dementia, then he would not be aware of the existence of such a past. He would only be experiencing the single "moment" he was living in.¶

2. From the **Layout** tab, in the **Page Setup** group, click the **Columns** button; click **Two** (or click the desired number of columns).
3. Note that a *Section Break (Continuous)* formatting code appears, and the columns are automatically balanced.

TIME AND PERCEPTION¶

¶

Shannon Jones¶

¶:::::::::::::::::::::::::::::::Section Break (Continuous):::::::::::::::::::::::::::::::

Time is a method human beings use to measure and sequence events, to compare the durations of events, and to measure the intervals between events. Time is a hot topic in terms of religion, philosophy, and science. However, defining time in an objective, accepted way has been nearly impossible amongst scholarly types. How, in fact, do you compare one moment to the next?¶

¶

Our perception of time as human beings has grown out of a natural series of rhythms that are linked to daily, monthly, and yearly cycles. No matter how much we live by our wristwatches, our bodies and our lives will always be somewhat influenced by an internal clock. What is of even greater interest, though, are the many uses and perceptions of time based on individuals and their cultures.¶

¶

RHYTHM AND TEMPO¶

¶

Rhythm and tempo are ways we relate to time and are discerning features of a culture. In some cultures, people move very slowly; in others, moving quickly is the norm. Mixing the two types may create feelings of discomfort. People may have trouble relating to each other because they are not synchronized. To be synchronized is to subtly move in union with another person; it is vital to a strong partnership.¶

¶

In general, Americans move at a fast tempo, although there are regional departures. In meetings, Americans tend to be impatient and want to "get down to business" right away. They have been taught that it is best to come to the point quickly and avoid vagueness. Because American business operates in a short time frame, prompt results are often of more interest than the building of long-term relationships.¶

¶

PERCEPTION AND MEMORY¶

¶

Picture yourself in a room watching someone enter, walk across the room, and sit down. By the time the person sits down, your brain must remember the actions that happened previous to the act of sitting down. All these memories and perceptions are filed as bits of data in the brain. The perception of the passing of time from the first event of entering the room to the last event of sitting down occurs only if the observer is aware and comparing the events.¶

¶

What would happen if the observer could not remember one or more of the events from the time the person entered the room to the time that person was seated? The brain might interpret the scene and assign a time frame, but unless the observer remembers, the perception of time passing would not exist.¶

¶

LIVING IN THE MOMENT¶

¶

If a human being perceives himself to be of a certain age, this is because he has accumulated data, remembers that data, and has a basis for a comparison. If a person cannot remember his past, such as a person with dementia, then he would not be aware of the existence of such a past. He would only be experiencing the single "moment" he was living in.:::::::::::::::::::::::::::::::

¶

PRACTICE 74 (1 of 2)

1. With **Show/Hide ¶** active, click in front of "Time" in the first paragraph; scroll to the end of the document, press and hold **SHIFT**, and click just *after* the last typed character in the document but just *before* the Paragraph formatting mark.
2. From the **Layout** tab, in the **Page Setup** group, click the **Columns** button; click **Two**.
3. Note that a *Section Break (Continuous)* formatting code appears at the end of the document, and the columns are automatically balanced.
4. Note that the line endings are very jagged—automatic hyphenation will resolve that.

Note: Keep this document open, and continue reading.

Hyphenation

Automatic hyphenation is off by default—use it only for text formatted in narrow columns to reduce the ragged appearance of line endings. It also reduces large gaps of white space in justified text. *Soft hyphens* are inserted automatically via the Hyphenation feature, and they appear and disappear as text is entered or deleted.

To hyphenate words automatically:

1. From the **Layout** tab, in the **Page Setup** group, click the **Hyphenation** button, **Hyphenation Options**.
2. In the **Hyphenation** dialog box, check **Automatically hyphenate document** if it is not already checked.
3. In the **Limit consecutive hyphens to**: box, click the up arrow until **2** is displayed; click **OK**.

PRACTICE 74 (2 of 2)

1. Press **CTRL+A** to select the entire document.

   If you are typing a new document from a blank screen formatted with hyphenation and newspaper columns, you would start at step 2.

2. From the **Layout** tab, **Page Setup** group, click the **Hyphenation** button, **Hyphenation Options**.

PRACTICE (continued)

3. From the **Hyphenation** dialog box, check **Automatically hyphenate document**. In the **Limit consecutive hyphens to**: box, click the up arrow until **2** is displayed; click **OK**.
4. Click before "Time" in the first paragraph; press **CTRL+SHIFT+END** to select the body; press **CTRL+J** to justify the lines.
5. Note the large gaps between the words in the last line of the document; click just after the period at the end of the document; press **ENTER**; note the gaps are gone.
6. Note the one-liner heading under the second column on the first page; to fix it, select that heading, the blank line below it, and the first line of the following paragraph; from the **Home** tab, **Paragraph** group, click the **Paragraph Dialog Box Launcher**; from the **Paragraph** window, **Line and Page Breaks** tab, under **Pagination**, check **Keep with next**, **OK**.
7. Insert a right-aligned header on the second page. Right-click over the header area on the first page, and click **Edit Header**; from **Header & Footer Tools**, **Design** tab, **Header & Footer** group, click **Page Number**, **Top of Page**, **Plain Number 3**; verify that the insertion point is positioned directly before the page number, type `Jones`, and press the **SPACE BAR** 1 time; from the **Header & Footer Tools**, **Design** tab, **Options** group, check **Different First Page**; close the header. Your finished document should look similar to this:

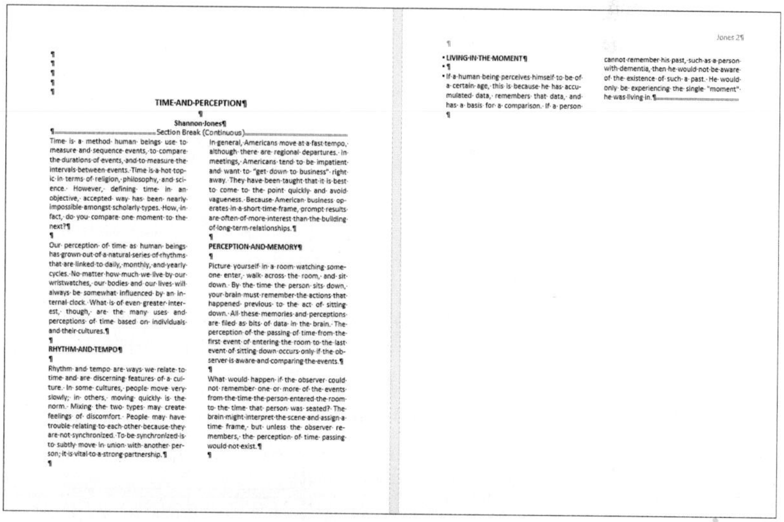

TIME AND PERCEPTION

Shannon Jones

Section Break (Continuous)

Time is a method human beings use to measure and sequence events, to compare the durations of events, and to measure the intervals between events. Time is a hot topic in terms of religion, philosophy, and science. However, defining time in an objective, accepted way has been nearly impossible amongst scholarly types. How, in fact, do you compare one moment to the next?

Our perception of time as human beings has grown out of a natural series of rhythms that are linked to daily, monthly, and yearly cycles. No matter how much we live by our wristwatches, our bodies and our lives will always be somewhat influenced by an internal clock. What is of even greater interest, though, are the many uses and perceptions of time based on individuals and their cultures.

RHYTHM AND TEMPO

Rhythm and tempo are ways we relate to time and are discerning features of a culture. In some cultures, people move very slowly; in others, moving quickly is the norm. Mixing the two types may create feelings of discomfort. People may have trouble relating to each other because they are not synchronized. To be synchronized is to subtly move in union with another person; it is vital to a strong partnership.

In general, Americans move at a fast tempo, although there are regional departures. In meetings, Americans tend to be impatient and want to "get down to business" right away. They have been taught that it is best to come to the point quickly and avoid vagueness. Because American business operates in a short time frame, prompt results are often of more interest than the building of long-term relationships.

PERCEPTION AND MEMORY

Picture yourself in a room watching someone enter, walk across the room, and sit down. By the time the person sits down, your brain must remember the actions that happened previous to the act of sitting down. All these memories and perceptions are filed as bits of data in the brain. The perception of the passing of time from the first event of entering the room to the last event of sitting down occurs only if the observer is aware and comparing the events.

What would happen if the observer could not remember one or more of the events from the time the person entered the room to the time that person was seated? The brain might interpret the scene and assign a time frame, but unless the observer remembers, the perception of time passing would not exist.

Jones 2

LIVING IN THE MOMENT

If a human being perceives himself to be of a certain age, this is because he has accumulated data, remembers that data, and has a basis for a comparison. If a person cannot remember his past, such as a person with dementia, then he would not be aware of the existence of such a past. He would only be experiencing the single "moment" he was living in.

8. Save changes to *practice-74*, and return to GDP.

REFER TO
WM L. 31, Alignment

REFER TO
WM L. 47, Headers

GO TO
Textbook

Tables With Footnotes or Source Notes

LESSON 76

Table—Text Direction

The default orientation for text in a table is horizontal. If a table includes long column headings with short column content, use vertical orientation.

To change the text direction or orientation of text in a table:

Text Direction button

Text Direction vertical button

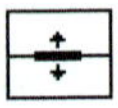
Resize pointer

REFER TO
R-8B & R-13A

1. Click the cell or select the row that contains the text to be changed.
2. From the **Table Tools**, **Layout** tab, **Alignment** group, click the **Text Direction** button repeatedly until you see the desired text direction; note that the **Text Direction** button image changes to give you a preview of the alignment.
3. Click the **Align Bottom Center** button.
4. Point to the bottom border of the row containing the vertical text until you see the table **Resize** pointer—zoom in if necessary to find the pointer more easily.
5. Drag down using the table **Resize** pointer until the vertical text appears in one continuous line without wrapping.

A *table note* is typed in the last row of a table. Merge the last row as your final step to ensure expected results when formatting a table.

Table—Insert, Delete, and Move Rows or Columns

To insert an additional row: Click in the last cell, and press **TAB**.

Or: Turn on **Show/Hide ¶**, click immediately to the right of any row just before the **table end-of-cell marker**, and press **ENTER**.

Or: Click inside the table anywhere; point to the selection area just to the left of an outside border of a cell until the **Insert Control** button appears—it looks like a plus sign with extended space between rows. Click the **Insert Control** button as many times as desired.

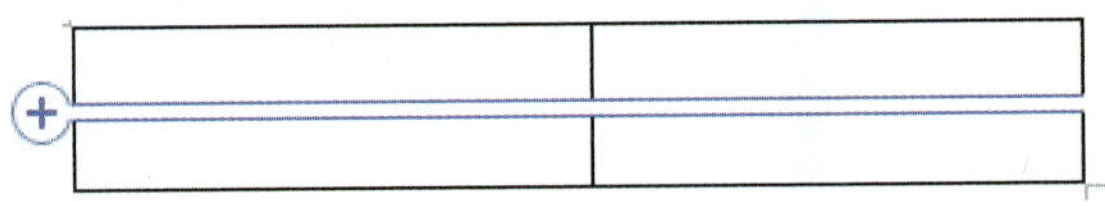

To insert an additional column: Click inside the desired column; from the **Table Tools, Layout** tab, **Rows & Columns** group, click **Insert Left** or **Insert Right**.

Or: Click inside the table anywhere; point to the selection area just above a column until the **Insert Control** button appears—it looks like a plus sign with extended space between columns; click the **Insert Control** button as many times as desired.

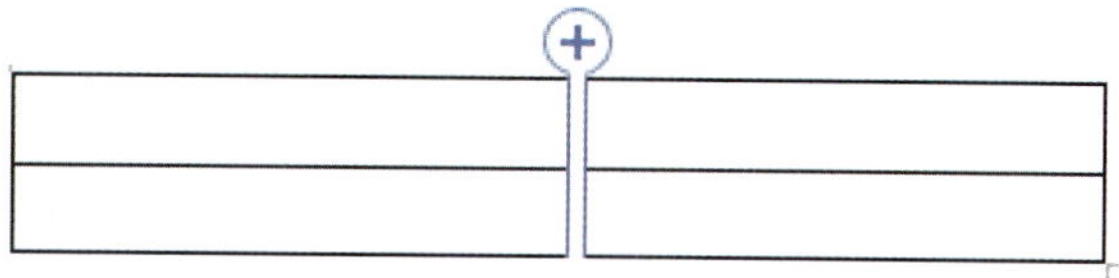

To delete a row or column: Select the desired row or column; right-click and click **Delete Rows** or **Delete Columns**, or press **CTRL+X**.

To move a row up or down: Click inside the row to be moved; then press **ALT+SHIFT+↑** or **ALT+SHIFT+↓**.

Or: Select the row and drag and drop it into place.

To move a column left or right: Select the column by holding the mouse over the top of the column until you see the black down arrow; click the column to select it, hold the mouse pointer over the column, and then drag and drop the column into place.

PRACTICE 76 (1 of 1)

1. Select Row 1.
2. From the **Table Tools**, **Layout** tab, **Alignment** group, click the **Text Direction** button until the "A" appears at the bottom left of the button; then click the **Align Bottom Center** button as shown in the illustration:

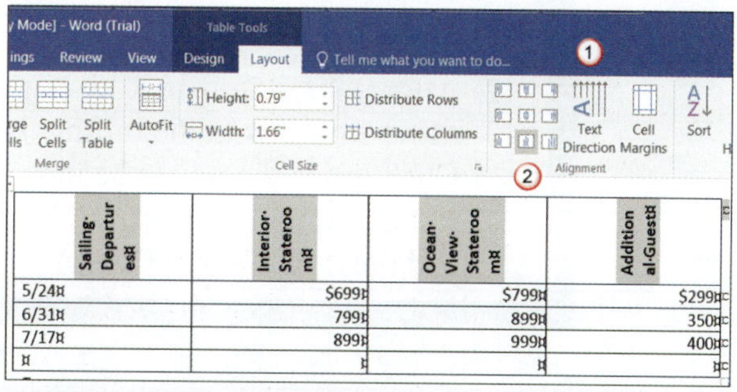

PRACTICE (continued)

3. Drag the bottom border of Row 1 down until the column headings appear in one continuous line (without wrapping text) and without leaving too much blank space above the longest item.
4. Select the table; right-click over the selected table, and apply the **AutoFit to Contents** feature.
5. Center the table horizontally. (*Hint:* With the table still selected, press **CTRL+E**.) Your table should appear similar to this:

Sailing·Departures¤	Interior·Stateroom¤	Ocean·View·Stateroom¤	Additional·Guest¤
5/24¤	$699¤	$799¤	$299¤
6/31¤	799¤	899¤	350¤
7/17¤	899¤	999¤	400¤
¤	¤	¤	¤

REFER TO
WM L. 36, Table—AutoFit to Contents

6. Center the table vertically on the page. (*Hint:* Double-click on any shaded part of the **Ruler**; from the **Page Setup** dialog box, **Layout** tab, **Page** group, **Vertical alignment**, click the list arrow; click **Center**, **OK**.)
7. Insert a new row below Row 2.
8. Type the following information in the cells of the new row.

   6/29 | 759 | 859 | 325

9. Cut the next row with the sailing departure date of "6/31."
10. Insert a new column to the right of Column C.
11. Type the following information in the cells of the new column.

   Junior Suite | $899 | 959 | 1,099

12. Align *Junior Suite* in Row 1 at the bottom center.
13. Move Row 3 with the sailing date of 6/29 down one row. (*Hint:* Click inside the row to be moved, and press **ALT+SHIFT+↓**.)
14. Move that row back up. (*Hint:* Click inside the row to be moved, and press **ALT+SHIFT+↑**.)

REFER TO
WM L. 38, Table—Center Horizontally | Table—Center Page

PRACTICE (continued)

15. Merge the cells in the last row; type this note left aligned:

    `Note: Prices subject to change.`

16. Your table should look similar to this:

Sailing·Departures¤	Interior·Stateroom¤	Ocean·View·Stateroom¤	Junior·Suite¤	Additional·Guest¤
5/24¤	$699¤	$799¤	$899¤	$299¤
6/29¤	759¤	859¤	959¤	325¤
7/17¤	899¤	999¤	1,099¤	400¤
Note:·Prices·subject·to·change.¤				

17. Save changes to *practice-76*, and return to GDP.

GO TO Textbook

Tables in Landscape Orientation

LESSON **78**

Page Orientation

Wide tables usually look better on a page with landscape orientation. Use Landscape Orientation to change the default page orientation from *portrait* (vertical) to *landscape* (horizontal). Use Portrait Orientation to change the page orientation back to vertical.

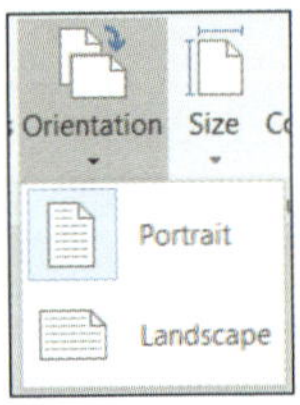

Orientation button

To change the page orientation: From the **Layout** tab, in the **Page Setup** group, click the **Orientation** button, and click either **Portrait** or **Landscape**.

Or: Press **CTRL+P**; under **Settings**, **Pages**, click **Portrait Orientation** or **Landscape Orientation** to change the desired orientation.

PRACTICE 78 (1 of 1)

1. Change the page orientation to **Landscape**.
2. Use **Zoom** to display **Whole Page**. Your document should look similar to this:

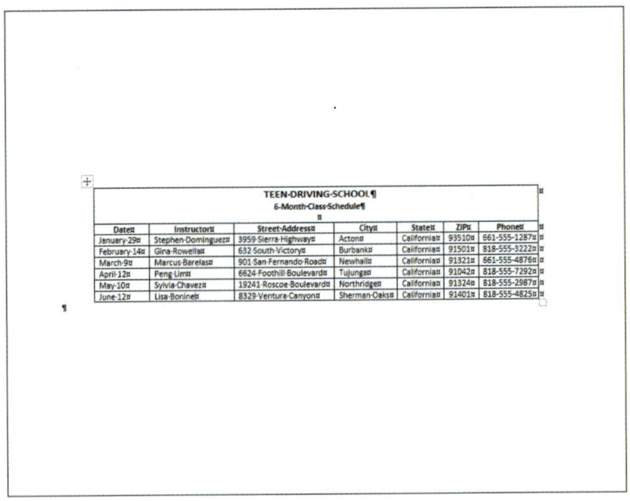

TEEN DRIVING SCHOOL 6-Month Class Schedule						
Date	Instructor	Street Address	City	State	ZIP	Phone
January 29	Stephen Dominguez	3959 Sierra Highway	Acton	California	93510	661-555-1287
February 14	Gina Rowella	632 South Victory	Burbank	California	91501	818-555-3222
March 9	Marcus Barelas	901 San Fernando Road	Newhall	California	91321	661-555-4876
April 12	Peng Lim	6624 Foothill Boulevard	Tujunga	California	91042	818-555-7292
May 10	Sylvia Chavez	19241 Roscoe Boulevard	Northridge	California	91324	818-555-2987
June 12	Lisa Bonine	8329 Ventura Canyon	Sherman Oaks	California	91401	818-555-4825

3. Save changes to *practice-78*, and return to GDP.

GO TO Textbook

Multipage Tables

79 LESSON

Table—Repeating Table Heading Rows

To repeat a table row on subsequent pages:

1. Select the rows of text that you want to use as a repeated table header row.

MANUSCRIPT·PROCESSING¶ McGraw-Hill·Higher·Education¶ ¤				
	Rejected¤		Accepted¤	
Short·Title¤	Editorial¤	Reviewer¤	Editorial¤	Reviewer¤

2. From the **Table Tools**, **Layout** tab, **Data** group, click **Repeat Header Rows**.
3. Scroll to the second page of the table, and note that the header rows are now repeated on each page.

PRACTICE 79 (1 of 1)

REFER TO
WM L. 47, Headers

1. Insert a page number to display at the top right of the second page only. (*Hint:* Right-click over the header area, and click **Edit Header**; from the **Header & Footer Tools**, **Design** tab, **Header & Footer** group, click **Page Number**, **Top of Page**, **Plain Number 3**; from the **Options** group, check **Different First Page**; close the header.)
2. Select the first three rows of the table on the first page.

   You may need to click and drag all the way across the rows to select all cells because some cells are merged.

3. From the **Table Tools**, **Layout** tab, **Data** group, click **Repeat Header Rows**.
4. Scroll to the second page; note that the three header rows are now repeated on page 2 and the second page includes a page number.
5. Select Row 1; from the **Table Tools**, **Design** tab, **Borders** group, **Borders** button, click the list arrow below the **Borders** button, and click **Borders and Shading**.
6. From the **Borders and Shading** dialog box, **Shading** tab, under **Patterns**, click the **Style** box list arrow, **Solid (100%)**, **OK**.

REFER TO
WM L. 68, Table—Shading

PRACTICE (continued)

7. Note that Row 1 has a solid black shading, and the text font color has automatically changed to white.
8. Select the rows with the column headings (Rows 2–3), repeat steps 5 and 6, except click **25%**. (*Hint:* You may need to drag all the way across the Rows 2 and 3 to select all cells because some cells are merged.)
9. From the **View** tab, **Zoom** group, click **Multiple Pages**.
10. Compare your table with this illustration—your table should look similar to this:

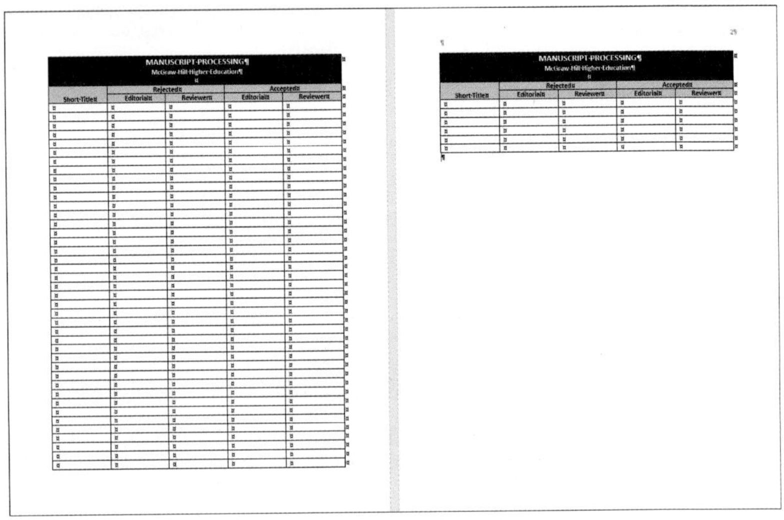

11. Save changes to *practice-79*, and return to GDP.

GO TO Textbook

Tables with Predesigned Formats

LESSON 80

Table—Styles

REFER TO

WM L. 38, Table—Align Bottom | Table—Center Horizontally | Table—Center Page
WM L. 37, Table—Borders
WM L. 89, Bookmarks and Hyperlinks

Use Word's Table Styles feature to format a table using predesigned formatting elements such as headings, borders, and shading. Use Live Preview to choose the formatting that enhances the table's design and readability. Use Table Style Options to format different parts of the table in unique ways to distinguish them.

An applied table style overrides a few manual formatting choices (for example, table and cell alignment, font size, and bolding) you might have set before applying the style. Therefore, apply a table style and desired options first and manual formatting last.

To apply a table style:

1. Scroll down and increase your **Zoom** level so that your table is enlarged and positioned at the bottom of the window; the **Live Preview** should now be easier to see.
2. Click anywhere in the table.
3. From the **Table Tools**, **Design** tab, **Table Styles** group, click the **More** list arrow button to the right of the **Table Styles** group to expand the gallery.

   Your gallery choices will vary from the illustrations depending upon Table Style Options that are in effect and theme choices. These differences are not cause for concern.

   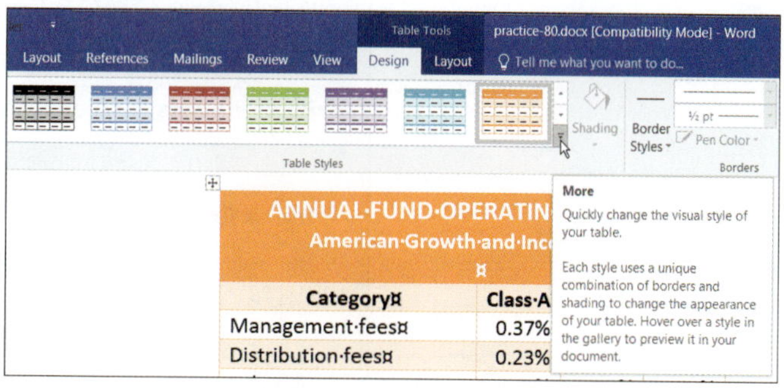

4. Point to each table style, and pause to read the **ScreenTip** displaying the style name. (See step 4 in the Practice exercise for an illustration.)

   The GDP screen for jobs with table styles will specify the table style you should choose for accurate format scoring.

5. Check and uncheck **Header Row**, **Total Row**, **Banded Rows**, **First Column**, **Last Column**, and **Banded Columns** in **Table Style Options**, and note the effect on the table. Note also that the design gallery sample icons change dramatically depending upon which options are checked in the **Style Options** group.

If the Live Preview is blocked by the gallery, point to the lower right-hand corner until you see a diagonal 2-sided arrow; drag to resize the list temporarily so it does not block your view of the table.

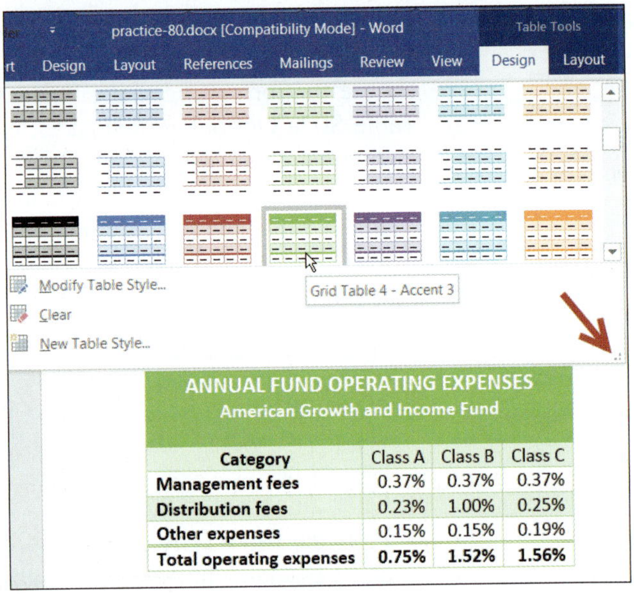

6. Under the **Table Tools**, **Design** tab, in the **Table Style Options** group, point to each button, and read the descriptive **ScreenTip** for details about that design option.

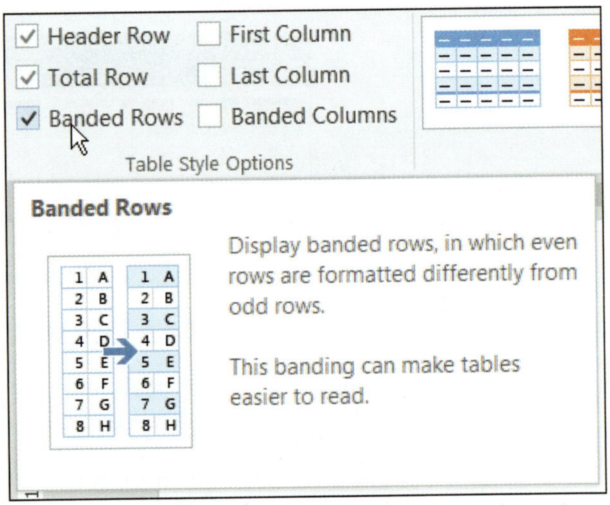

7. When you have settled on a style, click the desired style in the **Table Styles** group, and check the desired boxes in the **Table Style Options** group.
8. Center the table horizontally; adjust any fonts (color, size, and bolding), spacing, and alignment as needed.

To apply a table style followed by manual formatting:

1. Create a table, and type the table contents in plain text without any manual formatting—no centering, bolding, or font size changes.
2. Apply a table style.
3. Remove any hyperlinks in e-mail addresses or Web addresses because hyperlink styles often clash with table styles—right-click the hyperlinked text; click **Remove Hyperlink**.

   A *hyperlink* is a linked object (usually text or a picture) you click on to jump from one place to another within a document. Hyperlinked text is underlined and displayed in a distinct color, and the mouse pointer displays as a hand icon when you point to it.

4. Manually format content as desired.

To distinguish a table title in Row 1: From the **Table Tools**, **Design** tab, **Table Style Options**, check **Header Row**. Note the effect on the text.

To distinguish text in Column A: Check **First Column**. Note the effect on the text.

To distinguish a bottom row that includes a total line: Check **Total Row**. Uncheck other options if they are not appropriate for the table content.

To clear a table style:

1. Click anywhere inside the table; from the **Table Tools**, **Design** tab, **Table Styles** group, click the **More** list arrow.
2. Click **Clear** at the bottom of the style list.

PRACTICE 80 (1 of 1)

1. Click inside the table; from the **Table Tools**, **Design** tab, **Table Styles** group, click the **More** list arrow; point to the various table styles and note the **Live Preview**.
2. Click the **More** list arrow; apply the **Grid Table 5 Dark – Accent 5** table style.

PRACTICE (continued)

3. Clear the table style; apply the **Grid Table 4 – Accent 6** table style. (Your color choices may vary from this illustration.)

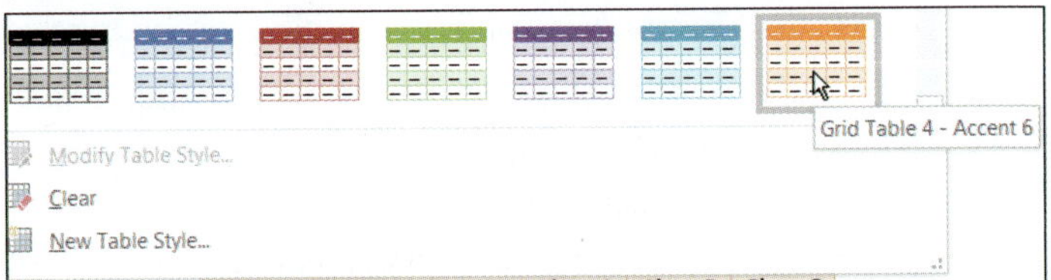

Category	Class A	Class B	Class C
Management fees	0.37%	0.37%	0.37%
Distribution fees	0.23%	1.00%	0.25%
Other expenses	0.15%	0.15%	0.19%
Total operating expenses	0.75%	1.52%	1.56%

4. From the **Table Tools, Design** tab, **Table Style Options** group, check **Header Row**, **Total Row**, and **Banded Rows**; uncheck all other options.
5. Verify the following: The title should be 14-pt., centered, and in bold. The column headings should be centered and in bold. The entries in Columns B, C, and D should be right aligned. The total row should be in bold.
6. Select the table, right-click, **AutoFit**, **AutoFit to Contents**.
7. Select the table; center it horizontally. (*Hint:* Press **CTRL+E**.)
8. Verify that the table is vertically aligned. (*Hint:* Display the **Ruler**; double-click the shaded part of the **Ruler**; from the **Page Setup** dialog box, **Layout** tab, **Page** group, **Vertical Alignment**, change to **Center**; click **OK**.) Your table should appear similar to this:

ANNUAL FUND OPERATING EXPENSES **American Growth and Income Fund**			
Category	**Class A**	**Class B**	**Class C**
Management fees	0.37%	0.37%	0.37%
Distribution fees	0.23%	1.00%	0.25%
Other expenses	0.15%	0.15%	0.19%
Total operating expenses	**0.75%**	**1.52%**	**1.56%**

9. Save changes to *practice-80*, and return to GDP.

GO TO Textbook

International Formatting—Canada

81

LESSON

Paper Size

Standard paper size is 8.5" by 11". You can, however, change paper size electronically in Word and change paper in your printer to the desired paper size if you need to print. You can print nonstandard paper sizes only if your printer can handle different paper sizes.

To change the paper size:

1. From the **Layout** tab, **Page Setup** group, click the **Size** button.

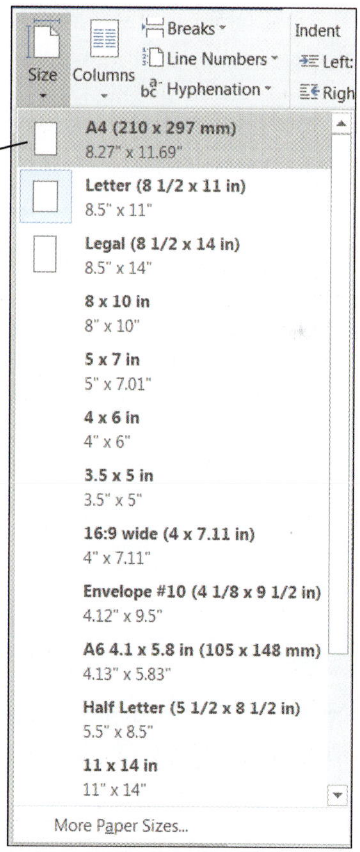

A4 metric size paper is slightly narrower and longer than **Letter** size.

Look at the **Ruler** carefully to verify the **A4** dimensions.

The order of paper sizes in your drop-down list might vary.

2. From the expanded list, click the desired paper size.

PRACTICE 81 (1 of 1)

REFER TO
WM L. 45, Tab Set—Ruler Tabs

GO TO
Textbook

1. Zoom to a whole page view; display the **Ruler**; note the right margin is set at 6.5".
2. Note the line ending of the first line in the first paragraph.
3. Change the paper size to **A4**. Note the right margin is now set at 6.25" and the line ending of the first line has changed.
4. Save changes to *practice-81*, and return to GDP.

International Formatting—Mexico

LESSON 82

Symbol—Insert

Many international words include diacritical marks to designate phonetic sounds and to distinguish words for understanding. Use the Symbol feature to insert these specialized characters.

To insert a symbol via the Ribbon:

1. Click where you want to insert a symbol, or select an existing letter.
2. From the **Insert** tab, **Symbols** group, click the **Symbol** button, **More Symbols**.
3. If **(normal text)** is not selected in the **Font** box, click the list arrow and click **(normal text)**, the first choice directly under the **Font** box.
4. In the **Subset** box, click **Latin-1 Supplement** to move to a character code subset for the desired symbol.
5. Click the down arrow under the scroll bar (not the scroll box) repeatedly until you see the desired symbol with the desired lowercase letter.
6. Click a symbol to see a highlighted view.
7. Click **Insert** to insert the symbol.
8. Note that the **Symbol** dialog box remains open, and the inserted symbol is automatically added to the **Recently used symbols** area under the **Symbols** button for easy insertion next time; click **Close** to return to the document.

   If the inserted symbol appears in the document with an unexpected font, select the inserted symbol and apply the desired font.

Select the desired subset; then use the directional down and up arrows on the keyboard to navigate through the list.

The **Recently used symbols** list changes dynamically as you insert symbols.

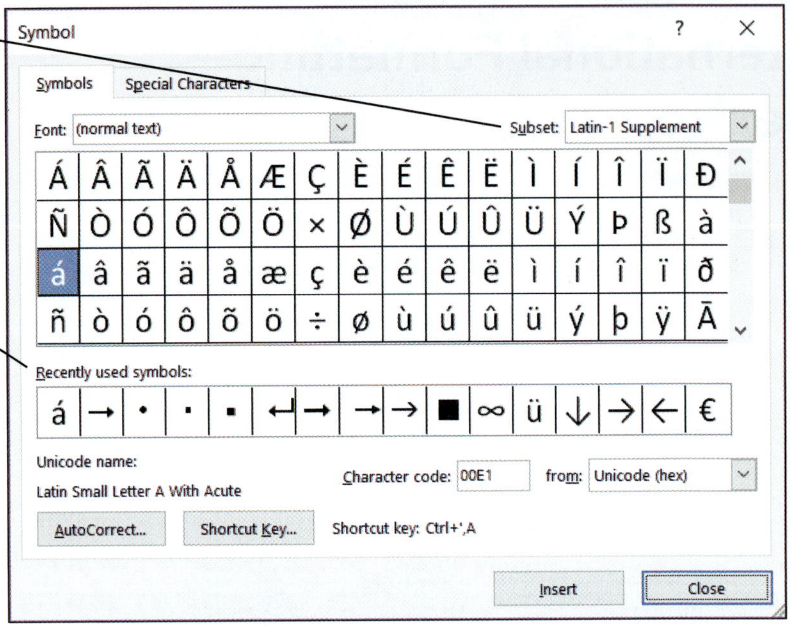

9. The newly inserted character should match the selected symbol from the **Symbols** tab.
10. Verify the capitalization of the symbol—you might need to change capitalization from uppercase to lowercase.

To insert a symbol via the numeric keypad and keyboard:

1. Select the desired letter to be replaced.
2. Press the relevant shortcut keys—use **ALT** plus the number code using the numeric keypad with **NUM LOCK** active—do not use the numbers on the top row of the keyboard.

If you are unsure if NUM LOCK is active, press CTRL+N to open a blank word document, and tap any number key on the numeric keypad. If a number does not appear, you know that NUM LOCK is not active.

Symbol	Name	Example	Numeric Keypad Shortcut
á	a acute	Yucatán	ALT+160
é	e acute	Querétaro	ALT+130
í	i acute	García	ALT+161
ñ	n tilde	Señor	ALT+164
ó	o acute	Torreón	ALT+162
ú	u acute	Cancún	ALT+163
ü	u umlaut	Nürnberg	ALT+129

PRACTICE 82 (1 of 1)

1. Note that the examples in Column C don't include any special symbols:

Symbol	Name	Example	Shortcut
á	a acute	Yucatan	Alt + 160
é	e acute	Queretaro	Alt + 130
í	i acute	Garcia	Alt + 161
ñ	n tilde	Senor	Alt + 164
ó	o acute	Torreon	Alt + 162
ú	u acute	Cancun	Alt + 163
ü	u umlaut	Nurnberg	Alt + 129

2. Insert symbols in the words in Column C as shown using either the **Ribbon** or the keyboard shortcuts shown in this illustration; when you are finished, Column C should look similar to this illustration:

Symbol	Name	Example	Shortcut
á	a acute	Yucatán	Alt + 160
é	e acute	Querétaro	Alt + 130
í	i acute	García	Alt + 161
ñ	n tilde	Señor	Alt + 164
ó	o acute	Torreón	Alt + 162
ú	u acute	Cancún	Alt + 163
ü	u umlaut	Nürnberg	Alt + 129

3. Save changes to *practice-82*, and return to GDP.

GO TO Textbook

Formal Report Project—A

LESSON **86**

REFER TO

WM Appendix A, Using Microsoft Word in the Workplace, GDP—Word Settings, Normal Style

Styles are powerful formatting tools used to apply consistent, automatic formatting to titles, headings, and other text in a single click. When you edit an existing style, all text formatted previously with that style is updated automatically throughout the document.

Styles are categorized as either *paragraph* styles, *character* styles, or *linked* styles. Explore Word Help for details. In this lesson, you will apply the *Title*, *Subtitle*, *Heading 1*, and *Heading 2* styles to different parts of a business report. The Quick Style gallery includes a variety of preset styles and changes dynamically—your gallery list might differ.

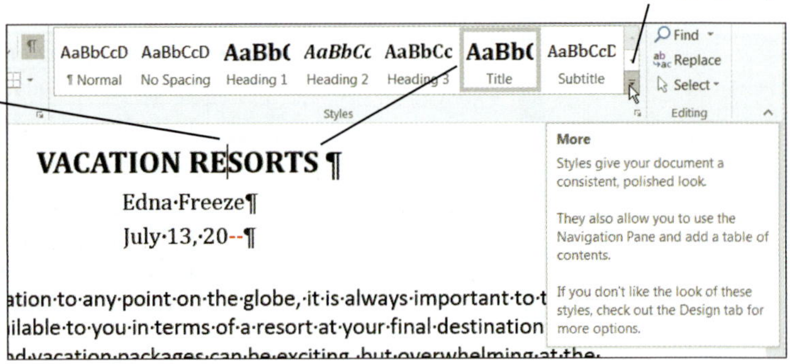

Styles

To apply an individual style to selected text:

1. Select the desired text.
2. From the **Home** tab, **Styles** group, click the desired style; click the **More** list arrow to see all styles in the **Quick Styles** gallery.
3. Point to each style to see a **Live Preview** in the selected text or in the entire paragraph; then click the desired style.

To remove a style:

1. Select the desired text; from the **Home** tab, **Styles** group, click the **Styles Diagonal Box Launcher**.
2. From the **Styles** box, click **Normal** from the style list; then close the **Styles** box.

PARAGRAPH—BOTTOM BORDER

To insert a header with content at the left margin, content at the right tab, and a bottom border:

REFER TO

WM L. 32, Page Number
WM L. 47, Headers
WM L. 37, Table—Borders

1. Move to the first page of the document; right-click over the header area; click **Edit Header**.
2. Activate any desired text formatting, such as **CTRL+I** for italics when you want it to be in effect throughout the header content.
3. Type the desired text (for example, type *Vacation Resorts*) at the left margin, and press **TAB** 2 times to position the insertion point at the Right Tab setting; type *Page* and press the **SPACE BAR** 1 time.
4. From the **Header & Footer Tools**, **Design** tab, **Header & Footer** group, click **Page Number**, **Current Position**, **Plain Number**, from the gallery of designs.
5. From the **Home** tab, **Paragraph** group, click the list arrow on the **Borders** button, and click the **Bottom Border** button.
6. To suppress the header on the first page, from the **Header & Footer Tools**, **Design** tab, **Options** group, check **Different First Page**. Note that the **First Page Header** section is now blank—if any content remains in the **First Page Header** section, press **CTRL+A** to select everything in the header, and press **CTRL+X** to cut it.
7. From the **Header & Footer Tools**, **Design** tab, **Close** group, click the **Close Header and Footer** button to close the header.
8. Scroll down to the second page of the document—the header you just created in steps 2–6 should appear at the top of the second page. (See the illustration in the next Practice exercise.)

PRACTICE 86 (1 of 1)

1. Apply the **Title** style to the report title.
2. Apply the **Subtitle** style to the author's name and date; bold both lines.
3. If necessary, center the report title, author's name, and date.
4. Apply the **Heading 2** style to the three side headings
5. Right-click over the header area, and click **Edit Header**.
6. From the **Home** tab, **Font** group, change to Cambria 10-pt. italic.
7. Type *Vacation Resorts* at the left margin and press **TAB** 2 times; type *Page* and press the **SPACE BAR** 1 time.
8. From the **Header & Footer Tools**, **Design** tab, **Header & Footer** group, click **Page Number**, **Current Position**, **Plain Number**, from the gallery of designs to insert a page number.

PRACTICE (continued)

9. From the **Home** tab, **Paragraph** group, click the list arrow on the **Borders** button, and click the **Bottom Border** button.
10. From the **Header & Footer Tools**, **Design** tab, **Options** group, click **Different First Page.** The header on page 2 should look similar to this:

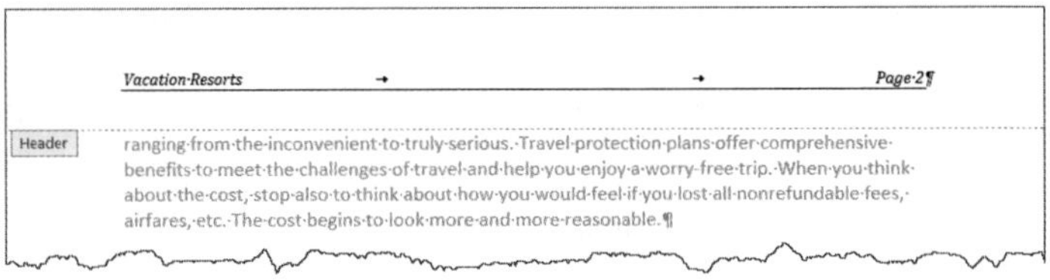

Vacation Resorts *Page 2*

Header

ranging from the inconvenient to truly serious. Travel protection plans offer comprehensive benefits to meet the challenges of travel and help you enjoy a worry-free trip. When you think about the cost, stop also to think about how you would feel if you lost all nonrefundable fees, airfares, etc. The cost begins to look more and more reasonable.

11. Close the header. (*Hint:* From the **Header & Footer Tools**, **Design** tab, **Close** group, click the **Close Header and Footer** button.) Your report should look similar to this:

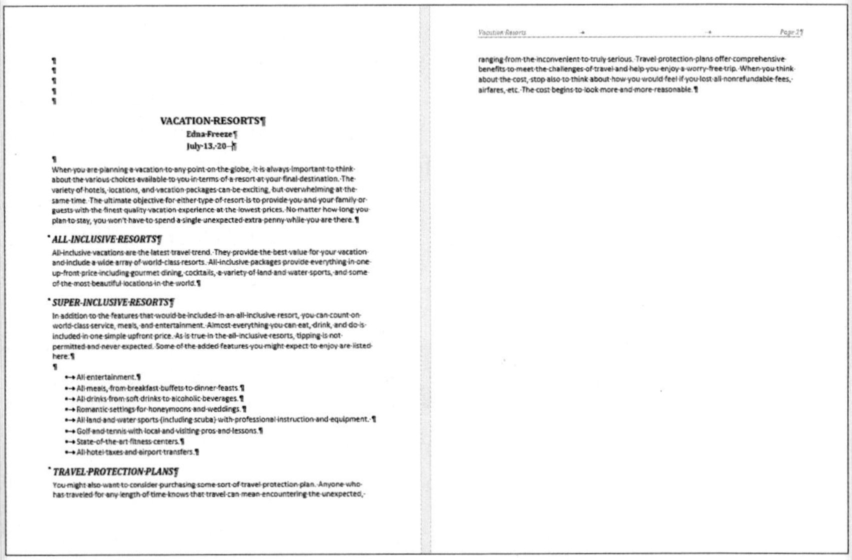

VACATION RESORTS
Edna Freeze
July 13, 20--

When you are planning a vacation to any point on the globe, it is always important to think about the various choices available to you in terms of a resort at your final destination. The variety of hotels, locations, and vacation packages can be exciting, but overwhelming at the same time. The ultimate objective for either type of resort is to provide you and your family or guests with the finest quality vacation experience at the lowest prices. No matter how long you plan to stay, you won't have to spend a single unexpected extra penny while you are there.

ALL-INCLUSIVE RESORTS

All-inclusive vacations are the latest travel trend. They provide the best value for your vacation and include a wide array of world-class resorts. All-inclusive packages provide everything in one up-front price including gourmet dining, cocktails, a variety of land and water sports, and some of the most beautiful locations in the world.

SUPER-INCLUSIVE RESORTS

In addition to the features that would be included in an all-inclusive resort, you can count on world-class service, meals, and entertainment. Almost everything you can eat, drink, and do is included in one simple upfront price. As is true in the all-inclusive resorts, tipping is not permitted and never expected. Some of the added features you might expect to enjoy are listed here:

- All entertainment.
- All meals, from breakfast buffets to dinner feasts.
- All drinks from soft drinks to alcoholic beverages.
- Romantic settings for honeymoons and weddings.
- All land and water sports (including scuba) with professional instruction and equipment.
- Golf and tennis with local and visiting pros and lessons.
- State-of-the-art fitness centers.
- All hotel taxes and airport transfers.

TRAVEL PROTECTION PLANS

You might also want to consider purchasing some sort of travel protection plan. Anyone who has traveled for any length of time knows that travel can mean encountering the unexpected,

Vacation Resorts *Page 2*

ranging from the inconvenient to truly serious. Travel protection plans offer comprehensive benefits to meet the challenges of travel and help you enjoy a worry-free trip. When you think about the cost, stop also to think about how you would feel if you lost all nonrefundable fees, airfares, etc. The cost begins to look more and more reasonable.

12. Save changes to *practice-86*, and return to GDP.

GO TO Textbook

Formal Report Project—C

88

Clip Art—Insert (Online Pictures—Insert)

Since the 11th Edition was published, Clip Art has been retired as a Word feature and has been replaced by Online Pictures. When you see references in your textbook to clip art, use the Online Pictures feature. Microsoft controls this dynamic feature and could change or update it any time.

Adding a picture (*picture* and *image* are used interchangeably) makes a document interesting and memorable. Word uses Microsoft's Bing search engine to populate the gallery with pictures related to the search keywords.

To insert an online image:

1. Click in the document where you want to insert an image.
2. From the **Insert** tab, **Illustrations** group, click the **Online Pictures** button; note that an **Insert Pictures** window opens.
3. In the **Bing Image Search** box, type one or more keywords describing the image, and press **ENTER**.
4. Click the desired image in the first gallery, which filters images so that only Creative Commons images are included, or click **Show all web results** to view all images unfiltered.
5. Click the **View Larger** button for a closer look.
6. Click **Insert** to insert the selected image into your document.
7. Note that the image is inserted and selected and an on-demand **Picture Tools**, **Format** tab appears.
8. Resize the image as desired.

To delete the selected image, press **DELETE** or press **CTRL+X** to copy the cut image to the **Clipboard** for possible reuse.

To resize the image proportionally using one exact height or width measurement:

1. Click the image; from the **Picture Tools**, **Format** tab, **Size** group, type the desired size in *either* the **Height** *or* **Width** box.
2. Note that the image is resized in proportion to its original dimensions.

To resize the image using the same exact measurement:

1. Click the image; from the **Picture Tools**, **Format** tab, **Size** group, click the **Dialog Box Launcher** diagonal arrow.
2. From the **Layout** dialog box, **Size** tab, under **Scale**, uncheck **Lock aspect ratio** so the image size and width can be set to any desired measurement; click **OK**.
3. From the **Picture Tools**, **Format** tab, **Size** group, type the desired size in *both* the **Height** *and* **Width** box.

To size an image visually: Click the image to select it; position the mouse pointer over any corner sizing handle until the pointer changes to a double-sided arrow; drag as desired. (Drag on a corner sizing handle—not a handle in the middle—to prevent distortion of the image.)

Crop handles

To crop an image visually:

1. With the image selected, from the **Picture Tools**, **Format** tab, **Size** group, click the **Crop** button.
2. Note that the image includes thick, black crop handles; drag them in using any handle to "cut out" undesired portions of the picture.
3. Note that the dark gray background represents the original dimensions of the image.
4. Click outside the image to deselect it; note the undesired dark gray portions of the original image do not display.

Some pictures include an image background (usually a white background) that is noticeable if you use the image in a document with a page color or inside a table with shading. You can remove the background if desired.

To remove an image background: With the image selected, from the **Picture Tools**, **Format** tab, **Adjust** group, click the **Remove Background** button. Click outside the image to view the image with the background removed.

To reset an image: If the edited image is undesirable, select the image; from the **Picture Tools**, **Format** tab, **Adjust** group, click **Reset Picture** twice.

To change an image's visual style: With the image selected, from the **Picture Tools**, **Format** tab, **Picture Styles** group, point to each different style; note the style name that displays as a **Screen Tip**, and note the **Live Preview** in the document; click the desired style.

Experiment freely with all the buttons and interesting tools in these groups—Adjust, Picture Styles, Arrange, and Size. The Live Preview feature is helpful as you practice using these tools.

To rotate an image visually: Click the image to select it; position the mouse pointer over the rotation handle that appears over the top center of the image; click and hold the rotation handle as you rotate the image in a circle as desired.

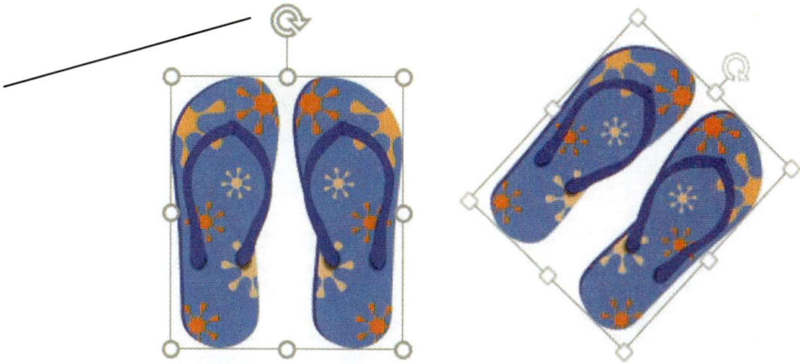

TEXT WRAPPING

To control how text wraps around inserted images, apply one of these **Text Wrapping** options:

- **In Line with Text.** When you first insert an image, text wrapping is set by default to In Line with Text. Text moves around the picture as if the inserted picture were a large typed character within a line of text.
- **Square.** Text wraps in a square shape around all sides of the image.
- **Tight.** Text wraps around the actual shape of the image filling in any white space around the picture shape.
- **Through.** Text wraps around the actual shape of the image filling in any white space around the picture shape. This wrap is even closer than the Tight option.
- **Top and Bottom.** Text is placed above and below the image, but never beside the image.
- **Behind Text.** The image appears behind the text without rearranging the text.
- **In Front of Text.** The image appears on top of the text without rearranging the text.

To set text wrapping and visually position an image:

1. With the picture selected, size it as desired and select a visual style.

   Many inserted images are initially quite large; therefore, size the picture first, set text wrapping, and position the image.

2. Click the **Layout Options** button that appears to the top right of the picture. Change the wrap from the default **In Line with Text** wrapping to the desired text wrapping. Under **With Text Wrapping**, click the desired wrap—usually **Square**.

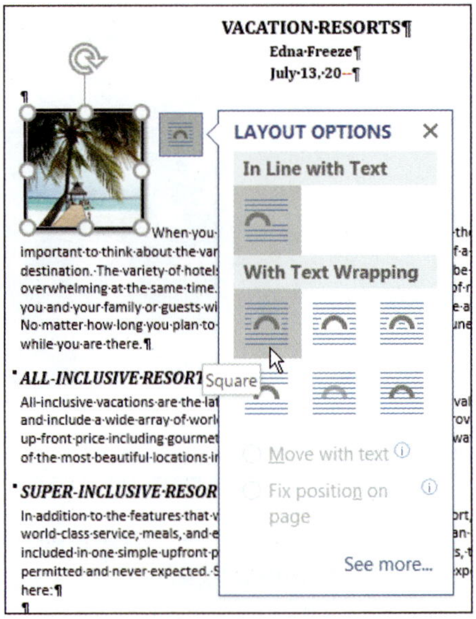

3. Position the mouse pointer over the selected graphic until a 4-headed move pointer displays.
4. Drag the image into position.

To position an image using the green alignment guides:

1. Click the sized image with the desired picture style to select it.
2. Set text wrapping to **Square**.
3. Drag the image to the position as shown in the illustration; note the green horizontal and vertical alignment guides that display as the image reaches the top of the paragraph and the right margin.

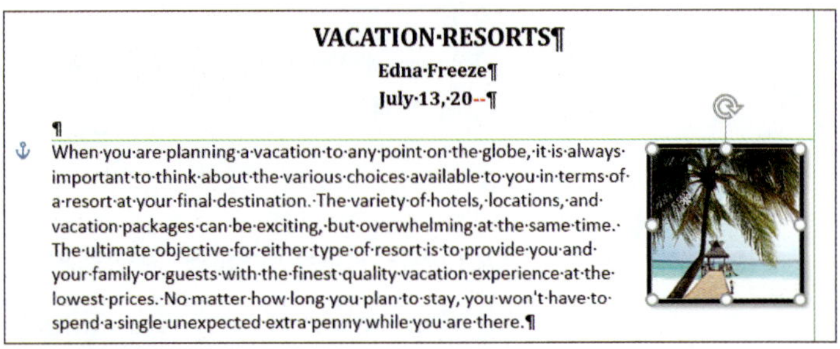

If the green alignment guides do not display, do this: With the picture selected, from the Picture Tools, Format tab, Arrange group, click the Align button. Verify that Use Alignment Guides is checked. Drag the selected image near any margin, the center of the page, or the top of a paragraph, for example, to display the green alignment guides.

OBJECT ANCHOR

Object Anchor

Word anchors and links an inserted object to the paragraph in which the object was inserted. When Show/Hide ¶ is active and an object is selected, an *object anchor* appears in the left margin next to the paragraph—see the previous illustration for an example.

If you delete text and an image is also deleted, press CTRL+Z, drag and drop the object anchor on a different paragraph; repeat the deletion.

REFER TO
WM L. 37, Table—Borders

PRACTICE 88 (1 of 1)

1. If necessary, turn on **Show/Hide ¶**; bold the two lines below the title (author's name and date).
2. On page 2, right-click the header, and click **Edit Header**; delete the blank line below the typed information in the header—note the bottom border disappears when you delete the blank line; replace the bottom border. (*Hint:* From the **Home** tab, **Paragraph** group, click the list arrow on the **Borders** button, and click the **Bottom Border** button; close the header.) Note the bottom border reappears directly under the typed header information.
3. Click directly before the first word in the first paragraph; insert an image related to a tropical beach—choose a square or nearly square image so it won't be noticeably distorted when you set exact dimensions.
4. Resize the image using the exact measurement of 1.25" for both the height and width.
5. Change the wrap style to **Square**.
6. Apply the **Simple Frame**, **Black** picture style.
7. Drag and drop the image in the middle of the text in the first paragraph so that text appears on both sides of the image.
8. Observe changes as you click each text wrapping option; undo each one as you go, and set the final wrap style to **Square**.
9. Drag and drop the image to the top right corner of the first paragraph using the green alignment guides to position it—the image

PRACTICE (continued)

should not extend into the right margin or above the line of type for the first paragraph. Your finished document should look similar to this:

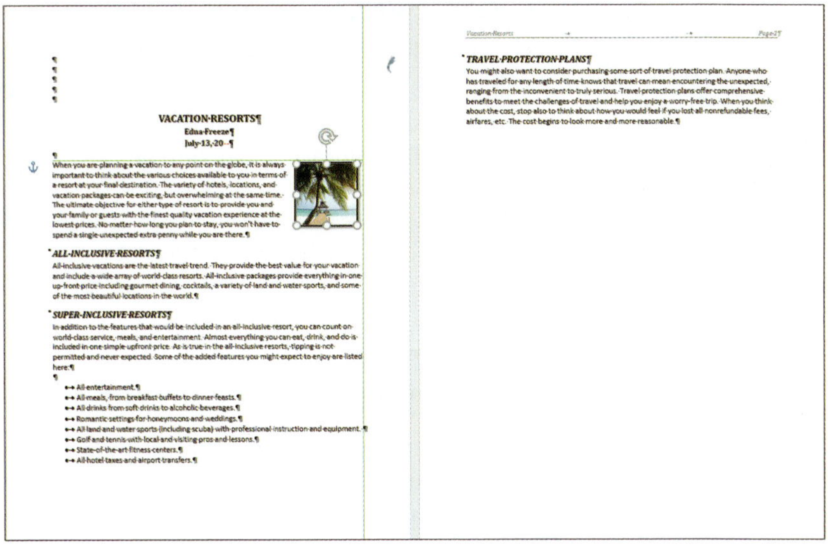

VACATION RESORTS

Edna Freeze

July 13, 20--

When you are planning a vacation to any point on the globe, it is always important to think about the various choices available to you in terms of a resort at your final destination. The variety of hotels, locations, and vacation packages can be exciting, but overwhelming at the same time. The ultimate objective for either type of resort is to provide you and your family or guests with the finest quality vacation experience at the lowest prices. No matter how long you plan to stay, you won't have to spend a single unexpected extra penny while you are there.

ALL-INCLUSIVE RESORTS

All-inclusive vacations are the latest travel trend. They provide the best value for your vacation and include a wide array of world-class resorts. All-inclusive packages provide everything in one up-front price including gourmet dining, cocktails, a variety of land and water sports, and some of the most beautiful locations in the world.

SUPER-INCLUSIVE RESORTS

In addition to the features that would be included in an all-inclusive resort, you can count on world-class service, meals, and entertainment. Almost everything you can eat, drink, and do is included in one simple upfront price. As is true in the all-inclusive resorts, tipping is not permitted and never expected. Some of the added features you might expect to enjoy are listed here:

- All entertainment.
- All meals, from breakfast buffets to dinner feasts.
- All drinks from soft drinks to alcoholic beverages.
- Romantic settings for honeymoons and weddings.
- All land and water sports (including scuba) with professional instruction and equipment.
- Golf and tennis with local and visiting pros and lessons.
- State-of-the-art fitness centers.
- All hotel taxes and airport transfers.

Vacation Resorts Page 2

TRAVEL PROTECTION PLANS

You might also want to consider purchasing some sort of travel protection plan. Anyone who has traveled for any length of time knows that travel can mean encountering the unexpected, ranging from the inconvenient to truly serious. Travel protection plans offer comprehensive benefits to meet the challenges of travel and help you enjoy a worry-free trip. When you think about the cost, stop also to think about how you would feel if you lost all nonrefundable fees, airfares, etc. The cost begins to look more and more reasonable.

The image in the preceding illustration was intentionally selected in order to display the green alignment guides and object anchor.

10. Save changes to *practice-88*, and return to GDP.

GO TO Textbook

Formal Report Project—D

89 LESSON

File—Insert

To insert the contents of a Word document into the current document:

1. Position the insertion point where the inserted contents should appear.
2. From the **Insert** tab, **Text** group, click the list arrow next to the **Object** button (don't click the button itself); then click **Text from File**.
3. Note that the **Insert File** dialog box opens.
4. Browse to the desired location and file. Click the desired file, and click **Insert**.

If the desired file does not display, you likely have a file filter in effect. Consult Windows Help for steps to display All Files (*.*) when you are browsing.

REFER TO
WM L. 37, Table—Borders

PRACTICE 89 (1 of 2)

1. With **Show/Hide ¶** active, bold the two lines below the title (author's name and date).
2. On page 2, right-click the header, and click **Edit Header**; delete the blank line below the typed information—note the bottom border disappears; replace the bottom border. (*Hint:* From the **Home** tab, **Paragraph** group, click the list arrow on the **Borders** button, and click the **Bottom Border** button; close the header.) Note the bottom border now appears directly under the typed header information.
3. Press **CTRL+END**, and press **ENTER** 2 times.
4. From GDP's Lesson 89H screen, click **Download File** to download *practice-89-insert* (a one-paragraph document) following your browser's steps.

PRACTICE (continued)

5. Insert the file named *practice-89-insert*; the paragraph highlighted in the illustration should now appear below your last paragraph:

> **▪*TRAVEL·PROTECTION·PLANS¶***
>
> You·might·also·want·to·consider·purchasing·some·sort·of·travel·protection·plan.·Anyone·who·has·traveled·for·any·length·of·time·knows·that·travel·plans·can·be·interrupted·by·unexpected·events·ranging·from·the·inconvenient·to·truly·serious.·Travel·Insurance·Associates·offers·a·variety·of·insurance·packages·with·comprehensive·benefits·to·meet·the·challenges·of·travel·and·help·you·enjoy·a·worry-free·trip.·When·you·think·about·the·cost,·stop·also·to·think·about·how·you·would·feel·if·you·lost·all·nonrefundable·fees,·airfares,·and·so·forth.·The·cost·begins·to·look·more·and·more·reasonable.·Visit·their·Web·site·at·www.tia.com·for·full·details.¶
>
> ¶
>
> Comprehensive·travel·protection·plans·are·designed·for·the·travelers·who·are·looking·for·things·like·trip·cancellation·and·interruption·benefits·and·other·coverage·benefits·such·as·medical·expenses,·baggage·and·personal·belongings·recovery,·baggage·delay,·travel·delay,·and·emergency·evacuation.¶
>
> ¶

Note: Keep this document open and continue reading.

Bookmarks and Hyperlinks

A *hyperlink* is a linked item (usually text or an image) you click to jump from one place to another. Hyperlinked text is underlined and displayed in color. The mouse pointer displays as a hand icon when you point to any hyperlinked item. A *bookmark* marks the target location for a relevant hyperlink and should be created before the hyperlink. Create electronic bookmarks and manual hyperlinks to move from a hyperlink to a bookmarked location within a document.

REFER TO

WM L. 49, AutoCorrect—Hyperlink
WM Appendix A, Using Microsoft Word in the Workplace GDP—Word Settings, AutoFormat As You Type Options, Hyperlinks

If hyperlinked text does not automatically convert to a hyperlink as expected or if you click the hyperlink and a ScreenTip displays telling you to use CTRL+Click to follow a hyperlink, see Appendix A to adjust your settings.

To create a bookmark:

1. Click at the desired position in the text—this location will become the targeted destination for the hyperlink.
2. From the **Insert** tab, **Links** group, click **Bookmark**.
3. From the **Bookmark** dialog box, click in the **Bookmark** name box; type a descriptive, short bookmark name (no spaces or hyphens); click **Add**.
4. Note that nothing appears visually that point in the document; however, an electronic bookmark has been added at that position.

To remove a bookmark: From the **Insert** tab, **Links** group, click **Bookmark**. From the **Bookmark** dialog box, select the desired bookmark name, and click **Delete**, **Close**.

To create a text hyperlink to an existing bookmark:

1. Select the text (or click an image) to be hyperlinked.
2. From the **Insert** tab, **Links** group, click **Hyperlink**.
3. From the **Insert Hyperlink** dialog box, under **Link to**, click **Place in This Document**.
4. In the **Select a place in this document** box, under **Bookmarks**, click the desired bookmark name; click **OK**.
5. Note that the selected text is converted to a hyperlink.
6. Click the new hyperlink to move the insertion point to the bookmark.

PRACTICE 89 (2 of 2)

1. Move to page 2; under the side heading "TRAVEL PROTECTION PLANS," click just before "Travel Insurance Associates" in the first paragraph.

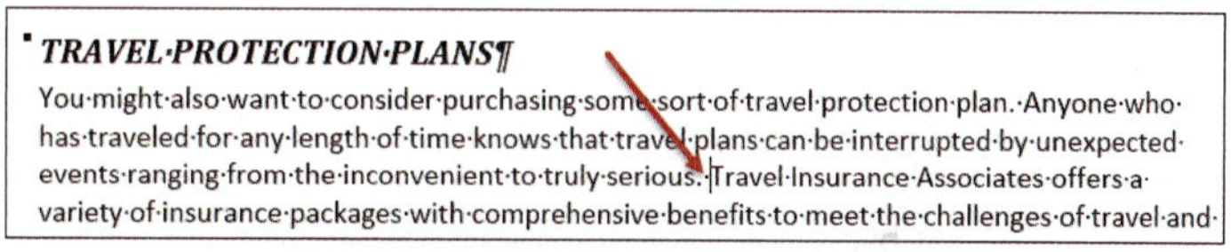

2. Create a bookmark named "TIA" without spaces.
3. Move to page 1, second paragraph, first sentence, and select "Travel Insurance Associates"; create a hyperlink to the "TIA" bookmark.

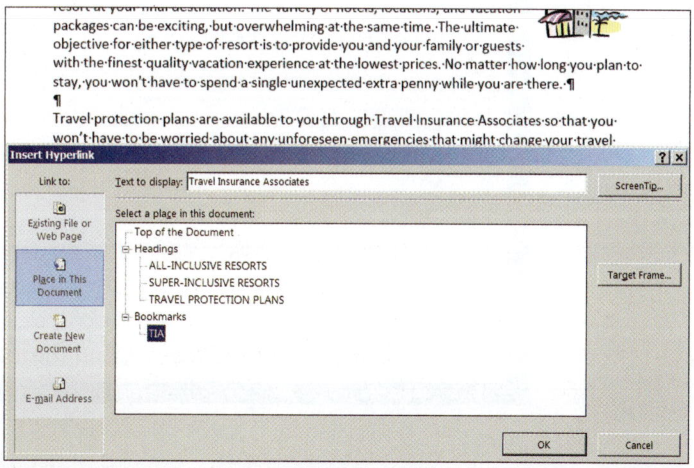

PRACTICE (continued)

4. Click the "Travel Insurance Associates" hyperlink to test it. The insertion point should move automatically to page 2 just before the "T" in "Travel Insurance Associates."

   > stay,·you·won't·have·to·spend·a·single·unexpected·extra·penny·while·you·are·there.·¶
   > ¶
   > Travel·protection·plans·are·available·to·you·through·Travel·Insurance·Associates·so·that·you·
   > won't·have·to·be·worried·about·any·unforeseen·emergencies·that·might·change·your·travel·

   If the hyperlink does not move to the bookmark as expected, follow the previous steps to remove the bookmark. Remove the hyperlink—right-click over the hyperlinked text and click Remove Hyperlink. Repeat the steps to create a bookmark and hyperlink.

   If you click the hyperlink and nothing happens, you need to change a Word Option: From the File tab, click Options; from the Advanced tab, under Editing options, uncheck Use CTRL+Click to follow hyperlink; click OK twice.

REFER TO

WM Appendix A, Using Microsoft Word in the Workplace, GDP—Word Settings, AutoFormat As You Type Options, Hyperlinks

5. Your finished report should look similar to this, but your image will likely be different:

VACATION RESORTS

Edna Freeze

July 13, 20--

When you are planning a vacation to any point on the globe, it is always important to think about the various choices available to you in terms of a resort at your final destination. The variety of hotels, locations, and vacation packages can be exciting, but overwhelming at the same time. The ultimate objective for either type of resort is to provide you and your family or guests with the finest quality vacation experience at the lowest prices. No matter how long you plan to stay, you won't have to spend a single unexpected extra penny while you are there.

Travel protection plans are available to you through Travel Insurance Associates so that you won't have to be worried about any unforeseen emergencies that might change your travel plans unexpectedly. Nothing can ruin the anticipation of a lovely vacation faster than thoughts about losing your money on a cancelled vacation.

ALL-INCLUSIVE RESORTS

All-inclusive vacations are the latest travel trend. They provide the best value for your vacation and include a wide array of world-class resorts. All-inclusive packages provide everything in one up-front price including gourmet dining, cocktails, a variety of land and water sports, and some of the most beautiful locations in the world.

SUPER-INCLUSIVE RESORTS

In addition to the features that would be included in an all-inclusive resort, you can count on world-class service, meals, and entertainment. Almost everything you can eat, drink, and do is included in one simple upfront price. As is true in the all-inclusive resorts, tipping is not permitted and never expected. Some of the added features you might expect to enjoy are listed here:

- All entertainment.
- All meals, from breakfast buffets to dinner feasts.
- All drinks from soft drinks to alcoholic beverages.
- Romantic settings for honeymoons and weddings.
- All land and water sports (including scuba) with professional instruction and equipment.
- Golf and tennis with local and visiting pros and lessons.
- State-of-the-art fitness centers.

Vacation Resorts *Page 2*

- All hotel taxes.
- All airport transfers.

Entertainment. Depending upon the resort you choose, you will find that your entertainment packages will vary. World-class entertainment is often included as part of your vacation package. Many resorts offer several night clubs and junior clubs for the teenagers who might be traveling with you. Small children can sign up for our adventure clubs that will keep them happily entertained in complete safety while you enjoy the luxury vacation you so richly deserve.

Meals and Beverages. All meals, beverages (alcoholic and otherwise), and room service are included in the price of your vacation package. Most resorts offer 24-hour room service, and tipping is not necessary. You can arrange for any special dietary needs you might have in advance of your stay.

Amenities. Excursions for land and water sports may be reserved in advance of your stay or after you arrive. World-class golfing, lighted tennis courts, and all equipment are available at our resorts. Trained pros are there to help you improve your game. All resorts include a world-class spa and fitness training centers. You will have your own personal trainer and can enjoy attending a variety of fitness classes or just use the fitness center on your own.

Hotel Taxes and Airport Transfers. All hotel taxes have been included along with airport transfers. You must make arrangements in advance for your transfers. An agent will be waiting at your destination resort to help you make your return trip to the airport.

TRAVEL PROTECTION PLANS

You might also want to consider purchasing some sort of travel protection plan. Anyone who has traveled for any length of time knows that travel plans can be interrupted by unexpected events ranging from the inconvenient to truly serious. Travel Insurance Associates offers a variety of insurance packages with comprehensive benefits to meet the challenges of travel and help you enjoy a worry-free trip. When you think about the cost, stop also to think about how you would feel if you lost all nonrefundable fees, airfares, and so forth. The cost begins to look more and more reasonable. Visit their Web site at www.tia.com for full details.

Comprehensive travel protection plans are designed for the travelers who are looking for things like trip cancellation and interruption benefits and other coverage benefits such as medical expenses, baggage and personal belongings recovery, baggage delay, travel delay, and emergency evacuation.

6. Save changes to *practice-89*, and return to GDP.

GO TO Textbook

Formal Report Project—E 90

Cover Page—Insert

You could manually create a cover page for a formal report, but Word includes a Cover Page feature that you can use to create a preformatted, professionally designed cover page. This feature can retrieve some content from Microsoft, so the gallery list may vary.

To insert a cover page:

1. Open a blank Word document.
2. From the **Insert** tab, **Pages** group, click the **Cover Page** button.
3. From the gallery of cover pages, click the desired choice.

Depending upon your choice, a cover page will appear with fields to enter information, such as the company name, document title and subtitle, author name, year, and company address. You can click inside these fields to display the field name, to type the desired information, or to select the field and delete it.

PRACTICE 90 (1 of 1)

1. From the **Insert** tab, **Pages** group, click the **Cover Page** button.
2. Scroll down the gallery list, and click **Motion** (or another suitable choice if Motion is unavailable) to insert that cover page.
3. Note that the various fields have placeholder text, such as *Year* and *Document title*, in their respective boxes.
4. Click in the *Year* box, and click the list arrow that appears; click the *Today* button at the bottom of the calendar; note that the current year appears.
5. Click in the *Title* field (the name displayed in the field box is *Document Title*), type the following text, and note that the placeholder text is replaced by the text you type:

   `Vacations by Rail`

PRACTICE (continued)

6. Double-click in the *Author* box to select any text that might already be entered; with the text still selected, type this:

    `Edna Freeze`

7. Double-click in the *Company* box to select any text that might already be entered; type this:

    `EuroTravel`

8. Click inside the *Date* field, point to and click the *Date* tab at the top of the date box to select the entire field; press **DELETE** to the remove the field entirely.
9. Select the text you just typed in the *Author* and *Company* fields, and increase the font size to 24 pt.
10. From the **Design** tab, **Document Formatting** group, click the **Colors** button list arrow; point to the various colors, noting the change in color in the **Live Preview**; click **Grayscale**.
11. Press **CTRL+END** to move to the end of the document, and press **BACKSPACE** twice to remove the blank page. Your document should look similar to this, but the year will likely be different:

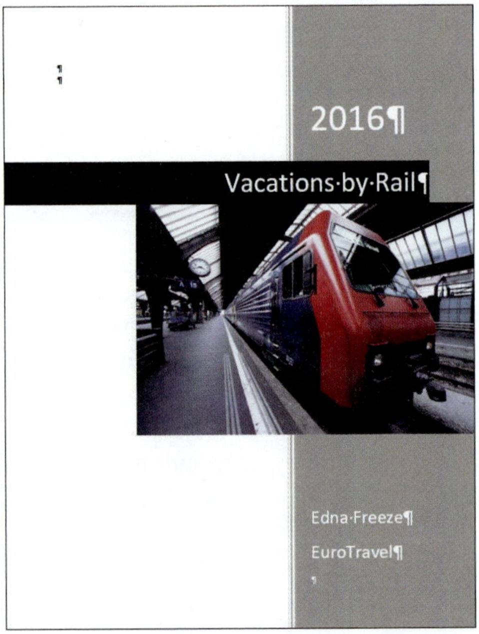

13. Save changes to *practice-90*, and return to GDP.

GO TO Textbook

Medical Office Documents—B 92

Table—Tab

In this lesson, you will design a medical office billing form. You will insert more precise spacing above and below the text in Row 1 via the Paragraph Spacing Before and Spacing After features to produce a form with a refined appearance.

When you click inside a table cell and press TAB, the insertion point moves to the next cell or row and automatically selects any existing text for possible replacement upon the next keystroke. To edit the selected text, click inside the text first to deselect it, then edit as needed.

To indent text inside a table with the TAB key: Press **CTRL+TAB** to move in .5" increments to the default tab settings, or set custom tabs to indent text or to align text.

To set custom tabs inside a table and adjust column widths: Before you set custom tabs, finish typing the table; select the table and use **AutoFit** to adjust column widths automatically; merge any cells as applicable. Move to the desired row, and set any desired tabs to indent text inside that row. (*Hint:* From the **Home** tab, **Paragraph** group, click the **Dialog Box Launcher** arrow; from the **Indents and Spacing** tab, click the **Tabs** button; from the **Tabs** dialog window, **Tab stop position** box, type in the desired position; under **Alignment**, click the desired alignment; click **OK**.)

If custom tabs need to be available throughout the table, select the table first, and then set the tabs.

PRACTICE 92 (1 of 1)

Note: You will begin by using default .5" tab settings to indent text.

1. Display the **Ruler**, and turn on **Show/Hide ¶**.
2. In the last line of Row 1, click after the last digit in the telephone number; then press **CTRL+TAB** once.

PRACTICE (continued)

3. In Row 2, click after the colon in each line, and press **CTRL+TAB** once.
4. In Column A, beginning with Row 4, replace the "--" with the current year (in black).
5. In the last row, click after "Total Due," and press **CTRL+TAB** once.
6. Select the table, right-click anywhere over the table, and click **AutoFit**, **AutoFit to Contents**.
7. Note the effects of the default tab settings on text alignment:
   - Row 1 has an acceptable amount of white space between the telephone and e-mail information.
   - In Row 2, a left tab needs to be set at approximately 1.5" to align the information after the colons.
   - In the last row, a right tab needs to be set at the right margin to adjust the spacing after "Total Due."

Note: Next, set custom tabs to align text attractively.

1. Verify that the **Left Tab** marker to the left of the ruler is displayed. If it is not, click the **Tab Selection** button until it displays.
2. Scroll up so that Row 2 is positioned just under the ruler, zoom in so you can see Row 2 clearly, and select the 3 typed lines in Row 2.

   Do not select the row itself, or you will not be able to set tabs using the ruler.

3. On the white part of the ruler, hold the mouse over the 1.5" position and click to set the left tab. Note that the **Left Tab** marker now appears on the ruler—drag it into place as needed. Your document should look similar to this:

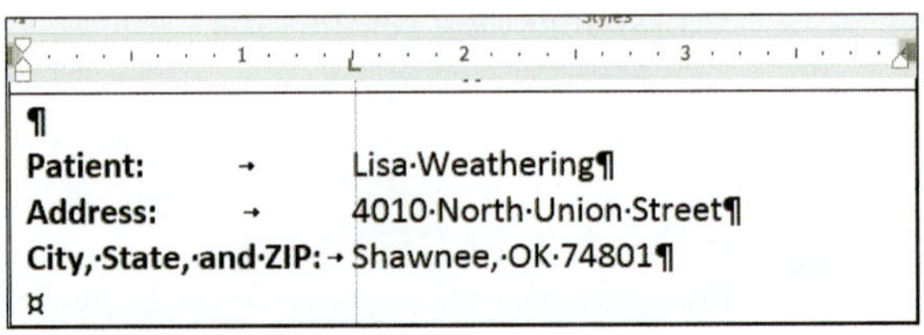

¶
Patient: → Lisa·Weathering¶
Address: → 4010·North·Union·Street¶
City,·State,·and·ZIP: → Shawnee,·OK·74801¶
¤

   If the custom left tab is set incorrectly, with the lines still selected, point carefully to the Left Tab marker until the "Left Tab"

ScreenTip appears; then drag the marker. (Waiting for the ScreenTip assures you that you are not going to set a new tab accidentally.)

4. Click in the last row, and click the **Tab Selection** button until the **Right Tab** marker appears. Scroll up so that Row 2 is positioned just under the ruler.
5. On the white part of the ruler, hold the mouse over the 3.5" position and click to set the right tab. Next, drag the tab marker into position until it stops at the right table border (about 4" on the horizontal ruler). Then release it:

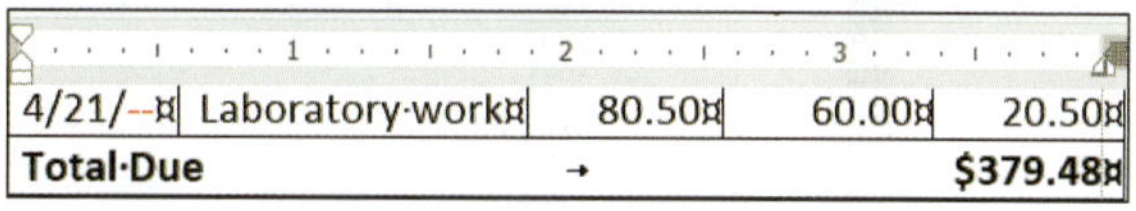

6. Note that after you set the right tab, the last row should be right-aligned and look similar to this:

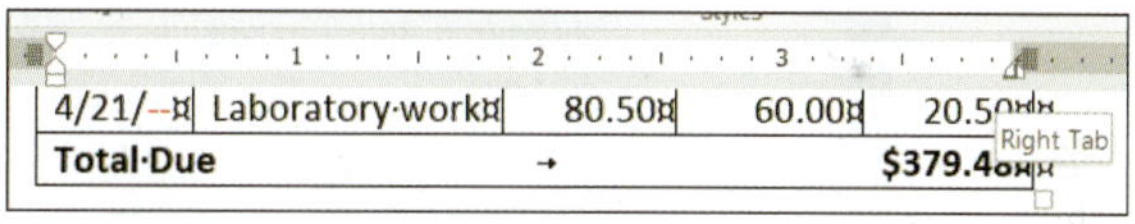

Note: Next, apply a table style to format the table attractively and improve readability.

1. Click inside the table. From the **Table Tools**, **Design** tab, **Table Style Options** group, check only **Header Row**, **Total Row**, and **Banded Columns**.

   If a table includes a bottom row with a total line, that row should be formatted differently to improve readability and comprehension. Thus, under Table Style Options, check Total Row to format the last row in a unique way.

2. From the **Table Tools**, **Design** tab, **Table Styles** group, click the **More** list arrow; scroll down to view the **List Tables** gallery; apply the **List Table 4–Accent 1** style (or any desired style) to this table.
3. Center the table horizontally. (*Hint:* Select the table, and press **CTRL+E**.)

PRACTICE (continued)

4. Verify that all text bolding matches the next illustration, and adjust accordingly.
5. Adjust any other fonts (color and size), spacing, and alignment as desired. Your table should appear similar to this, except you will have changed the year to the current year in black under the Date column, and your color choices may differ:

BILLING STATEMENT

Patricia Wellsman, M.D.
Unity Community Hospital
1120 West MacArthur
Shawnee, OK 74804

Telephone: 405-555-3943 E-Mail: pwellsman@UCH.org

Patient: Lisa Weathering
Address: 4010 North Union Street
City, State, and ZIP: Shawnee, OK 74801

Date	**Description**	**Charge**	**Payment**	**Balance**
3/21/--	Well care	$165.76	$ 50.00	$115.76
3/28/--	Laboratory work	325.50	300.00	25.50
4/10/--	X-ray	150.30	0.00	150.30
4/15/--	Office medical	167.42	100.00	67.42
4/21/--	Laboratory work	80.50	60.00	20.50
Total Due				**$379.48**

6. Save changes to *practice-92*, and return to GDP.

GO TO Textbook

Legal Office Documents—C

98

Line Numbering

Use the Line Numbers feature to number lines in legal documents for ease of reference in a court of law. Automatic line numbers appear on every line in the document and also restart on each page automatically.

To begin automatic line numbering:

REFER TO
WM L. 24, Zoom

1. Position the insertion point at the start of the page where you want line numbering to begin. (*Hint:* Press **CTRL+HOME**.)
2. Change the **Zoom** level to **Page width** to view the line numbers.
3. From the **Layout** tab, **Page Setup** group, click the **Line Numbers** button, **Line Numbering Options**.
4. From the **Page Setup** dialog box, **Layout** tab, click the **Line Numbers** button at the bottom to display the **Line Numbers** dialog box.
5. Check **Add line numbering**; adjust your settings to match those in the illustration (**1**, **Auto**, **1**, **Restart each page**); click **OK** twice.

Check **Add line numbering.**

Under **Numbering, Restart each page** is selected by default; thus, line numbering on multipage legal documents is continued automatically on all pages of the document.

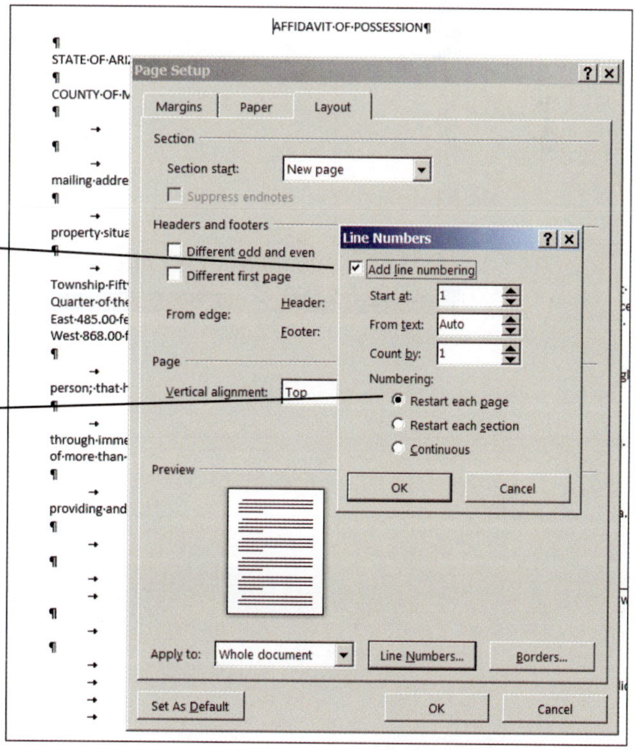

PRACTICE 98 (1 of 1)

1. Change the zoom level to **Page width**.
2. Add line numbering; your document should look similar to this:

AFFIDAVIT OF POSSESSION

STATE OF ARIZONA

COUNTY OF MARICOPA

Robert Burton, being first duly sworn, deposes and says:

That he is an adult person and is a resident of Maricopa County, Arizona, and that his mailing address is 2146 West Jefferson Street, Phoenix, AZ 85003.

That he knows the history, ownership, and occupancy of the following-described property situated in Maricopa County, Arizona, to wit:

All that part of the Northwest Quarter of the Southwest Quarter of Section Eight (8), Township Fifty (50), further described as follows: Beginning at the Southwest corner of said Northwest Quarter of the Southwest Quarter; thence North along the West line of said quarter 800.00 feet; thence East 485.00 feet; thence South 100.00 feet; thence East 103.00 feet; thence South 700.00 feet; thence West 868.00 feet.

That the record title holder in fee simple of the above property is Robert Burton, a single person; that he is presently in possession of the above-described premises;

That ownership of the aforesaid property is based upon an unbroken chain of title through immediate and remote grantors by deed of conveyance which has been recorded for a period of more than eleven (11) years, to wit: Since July 21, 1999, at 4 p.m.;

That the purpose of this Affidavit of Possession is to show proof of ownership by providing and recording evidence of possession for marketable title as required by the State of Arizona.

DATED this _____ day of December 2010, at Phoenix, Arizona.

____
Maria Flores Attorney at Law

Subscribed and sworn to before me this _____ day of December 2010.

____
Gerald Gannon Notary Public
Maricopa County, Arizona
My Commission Expires May 1, 2015

3. Save changes to *practice-98*, and return to GDP.

GO TO Textbook

Using Correspondence Templates

LESSON **101**

Templates—Correspondence

You can create a professionally designed document by using a Word template with formatted content, such as the memo template shown here. You will use a memo and a report template, which will be opened automatically via GDP.

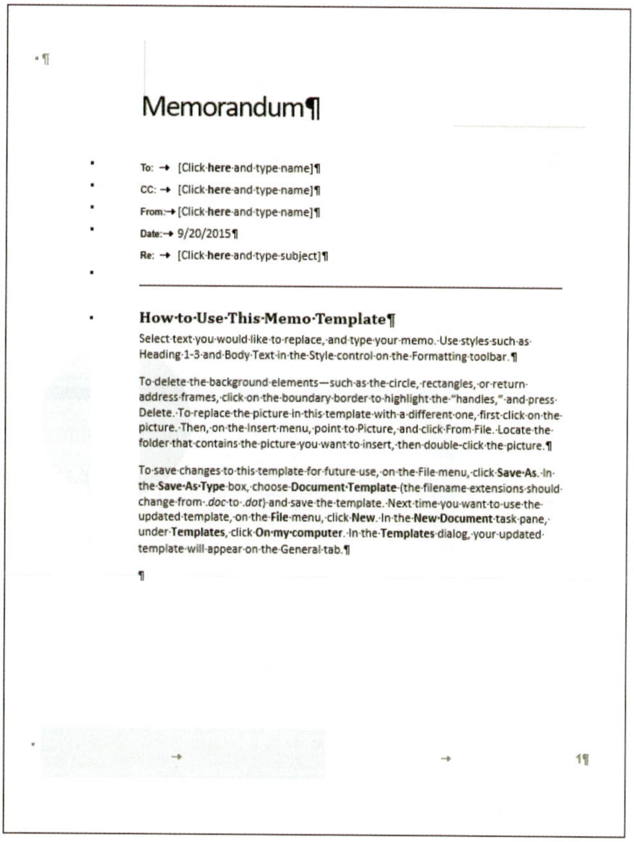

Click any *placeholder* to highlight it. The highlighted placeholder text disappears with the first keystroke of the *replacement text* you type, which adopts any automatic formatting set by the placeholder field. Follow specific directions in the Practice exercise for inserting replacement text.

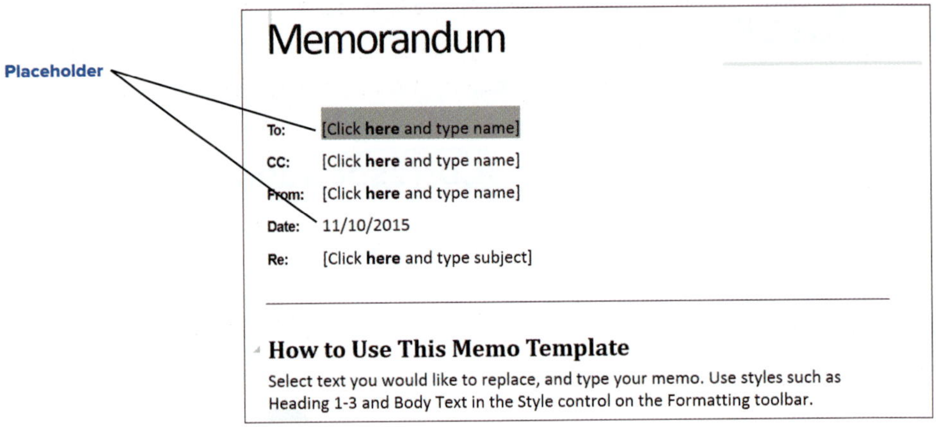

To download and use an Office.com template: You must be online to access Office.com via Word. You will not download templates from Office.com during this course because they change continuously; however, because you will likely use Office.com templates in the workplace, you should consult Word Help for relevant steps.

PRACTICE 101 (1 of 1)

1. Note that the memo template shown in the previous illustration opens automatically ready for input with an assigned name in the title bar. Turn on **Show/Hide ¶** to see formatting marks.
2. Click the placeholder after "To" to select it; with the placeholder still selected, type `Helen Lalin` as the recipient's name.
3. Click the placeholder after "CC" to select it; with the placeholder still selected, type `Jose Limon` as the copy recipient's name.
4. Click the placeholder after "From" to select it; with the placeholder still selected, type `Shannon Newsome` as the sender's name.
5. Click the placeholder after "Date" to select it; drag across the date field from the start to the end, delete it, and type this:

   `February 14, 20--`

6. Click the placeholder after "Re" to select it; with the placeholder still selected, type this:

   `Luncheon Invitation`

PRACTICE (continued)

7. Select the instructions for the body of the memo from the first bold line of the memo template instructions to the end of the last paragraph of instructions. Your selected text should look like this:

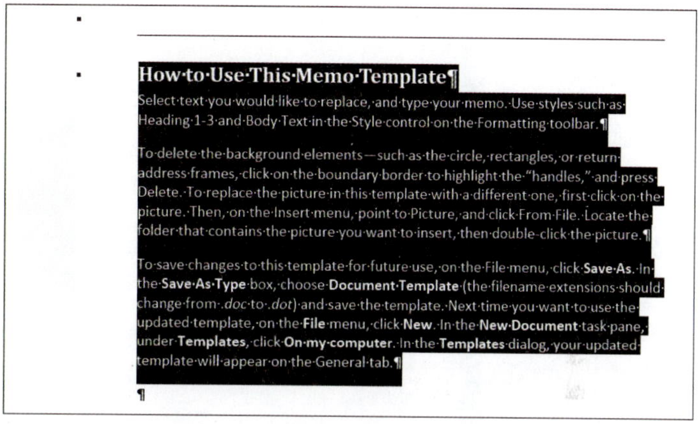
How·to·Use·This·Memo·Template¶

Select·text·you·would·like·to·replace,·and·type·your·memo.·Use·styles·such·as·Heading·1-3·and·Body·Text·in·the·Style·control·on·the·Formatting·toolbar.¶

To·delete·the·background·elements—such·as·the·circle,·rectangles,·or·return·address·frames,·click·on·the·boundary·border·to·highlight·the·"handles,"·and·press·Delete.·To·replace·the·picture·in·this·template·with·a·different·one,·first·click·on·the·picture.·Then,·on·the·Insert·menu,·point·to·Picture,·and·click·From·File.·Locate·the·folder·that·contains·the·picture·you·want·to·insert,·then·double-click·the·picture.¶

To·save·changes·to·this·template·for·future·use,·on·the·File·menu,·click·**Save·As**.·In·the·**Save·As·Type**·box,·choose·**Document·Template**·(the·filename·extensions·should·change·from·*.doc*·to·*.dot*)·and·save·the·template.·Next·time·you·want·to·use·the·updated·template,·on·the·**File**·menu,·click·**New**.·In·the·**New·Document**·task·pane,·under·**Templates**,·click·**On·my·computer**.·In·the·**Templates**·dialog,·your·updated·template·will·appear·on·the·General·tab.¶

¶

8. With the instructions still selected, type this paragraph—do <u>not</u> press DELETE; note that once you begin typing, the selected text is automatically deleted and replaced with your typed keystrokes:

   ```
   I will be happy to attend the luncheon meeting of
   the Purchasing Managers' Association with you next
   Tuesday at the Friar's Club. Since I'll be at a workshop
   until 11:15 that morning, I'll meet you in their lobby at
   12:15 p.m.
   ```

   Do <u>not</u> use DELETE to delete selected text! If you delete the selected text rather than typing the replacement text while the original text is still selected, the embedded paragraph styles will also be removed. Extra space will not be inserted between paragraphs automatically when you press ENTER. If you make this mistake, click Undo to reverse your actions, select the instructions, and begin typing.

9. Press **ENTER** 1 time to begin the next paragraph; note that extra space is inserted automatically below the paragraph you just typed.

   If extra space is not inserted below the paragraph you just typed, undo your actions through step 7 and repeat steps 7 through 9.

10. Type this as the final paragraph:

    ```
    Thanks for thinking of me.
    ```

PRACTICE (continued)

11. Press **ENTER** 1 time, and type your reference initials. Your document should look similar to this:

> # Memorandum
>
> **To:** Helen Lalin
> **CC:** Jose Limon
> **From:** Shannon Newsome
> **Date:** February 14, 20--
> **Re:** Luncheon Invitation
>
> ---
>
> I will be happy to attend the luncheon meeting of the Purchasing Managers' Association with you next Tuesday at the Friar's Club. Since I'll be at a workshop until 11:15 that morning, I'll meet you in their lobby at 12:15 p.m.
>
> Thanks for thinking of me.
>
> urs
>
> 1

12. Save changes to *practice-101*, and return to GDP.

GO TO Textbook

Using Report Templates

102

LESSON

Templates—Report

You will use this multipage report template, which will be opened via GDP, in this lesson. This template includes an *Address* field and several preformatted sections with instructions. Follow specific directions in the Practice exercise for inserting replacement text.

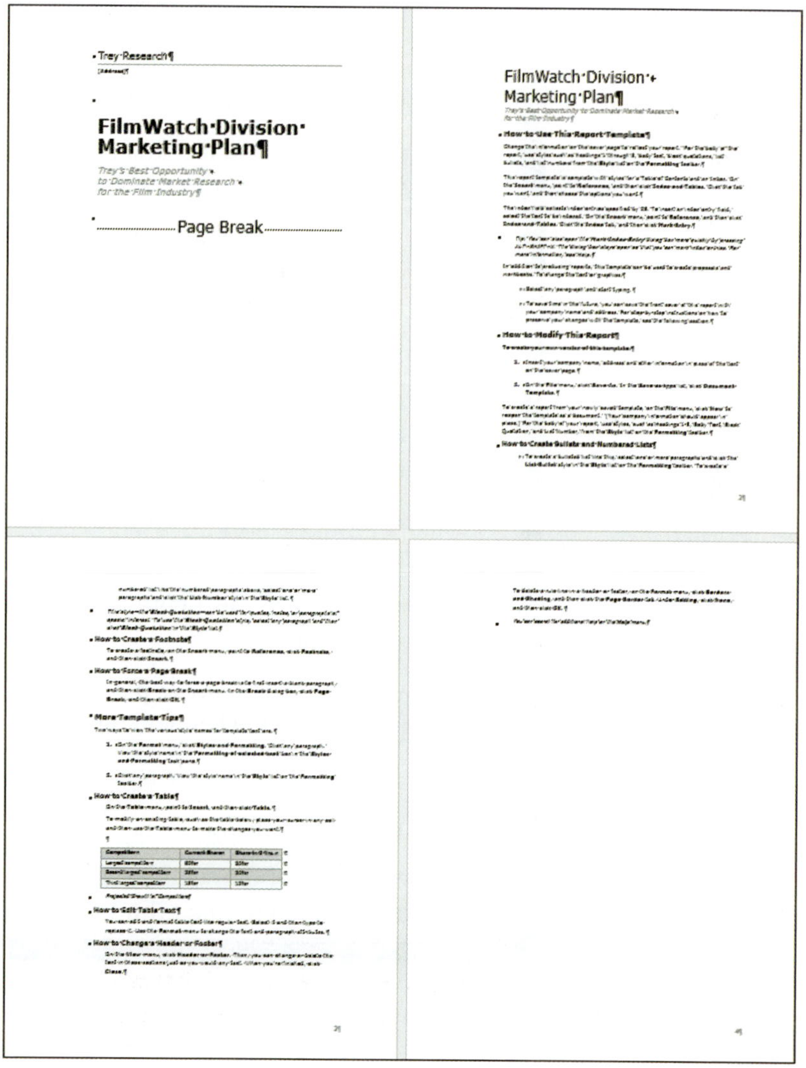
Trey·Research¶

FilmWatch·Division·
Marketing·Plan¶

Trey's·Best·Opportunity
to·Dominate·Market·Research
for·the·Film·Industry¶

Page Break

FilmWatch·Division·
Marketing·Plan¶

PRACTICE 102 (1 of 1)

1. Note that the multipage report template shown in the previous illustration opens automatically, ready for input with an assigned name in the title bar. Turn on **Show/Hide ¶** to see formatting marks.
2. On the first line of the first page, select the company name "Trey Research."
3. With the name still selected, type this new company name:

   `Digital Media Associates`

   In this step or those that follow, do <u>not</u> use DELETE to delete selected text! If you delete the selected text rather than typing the replacement text while the original text is still selected, the embedded paragraph styles will also be deleted. If you make this mistake, click Undo to reverse your actions, and try again.

4. On the second line of the first page, click over the *Address* placeholder to select it as shown in the illustration:

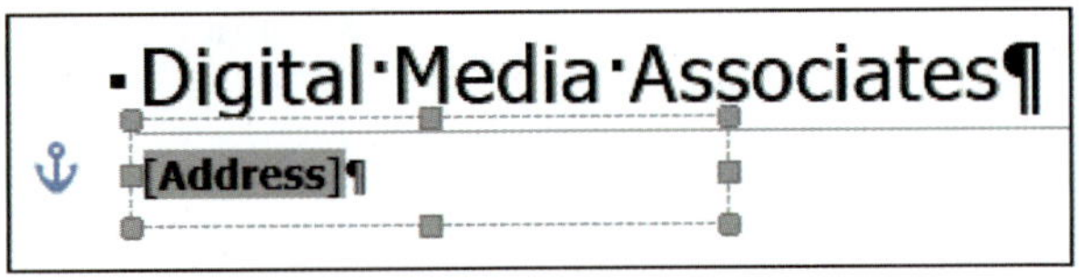

5. With the placeholder still selected, type these lines—press **ENTER** after the street address; type the city, state, and ZIP; then click outside of the text box when you are finished.

   ```
   4066 Main Avenue
   Orlando, Florida 32806
   ```

6. On the first page, select both lines of the title "FilmWatch Division Marketing Plan."

   Although the *Address* placeholder also appears highlighted, it will not be deleted when you type the new title.

7. With both lines of the title still selected, type this new title:

   `Business Solutions`

8. Select all lines of the subtitle "Trey's Best Opportunity to Dominate Market Research for the Film Industry."

PRACTICE (continued)

9. With the subtitle lines still selected, type this new subtitle:

   `Digital Media Products`

   The first page of your unfinished report should look similar to this:

10. Move to the top of the second page of the template, select both lines of the title "FilmWatch Division Marketing Plan," and type this new title:

    `Business Solutions`

11. Select the subtitle "Trey's Best Opportunity to Dominate Market Research for the Film Industry," and type this new subtitle:

    `Digital Media Products`

12. Click in front of the first word in the second paragraph under the heading "How to Use This Report Template"; hold down **CTRL+SHIFT+END** to select all remaining text in the template; press **DELETE**. The second page of the template should look like this:

PRACTICE (continued)

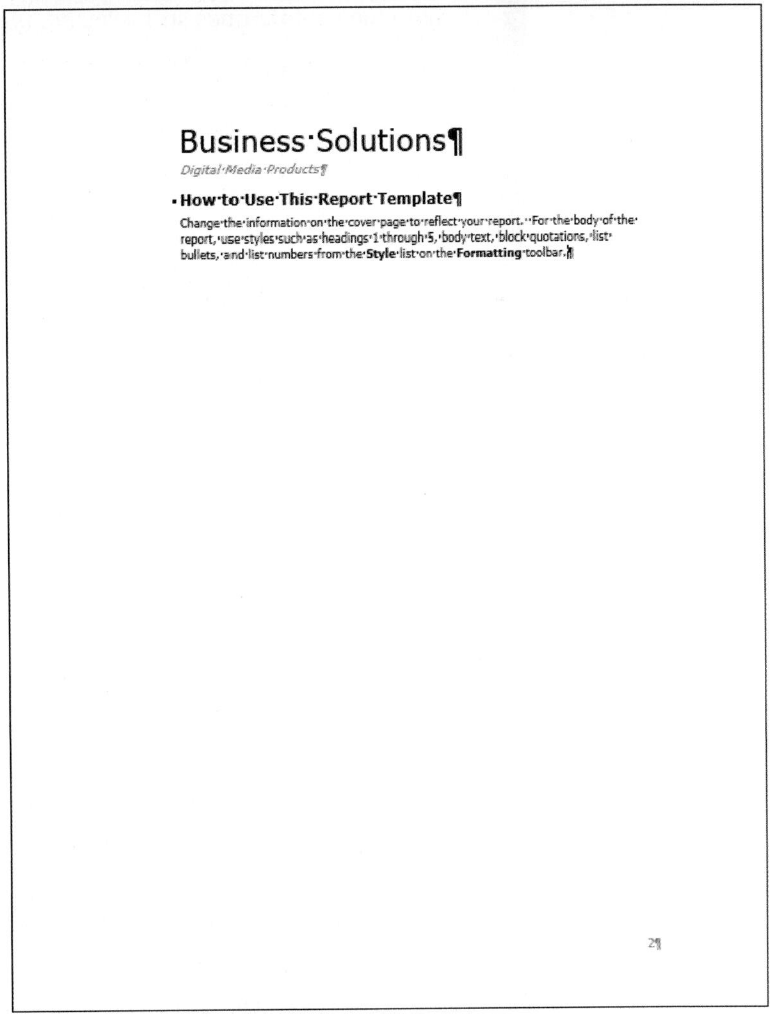
Business·Solutions¶

Digital·Media·Products¶

• **How·to·Use·This·Report·Template¶**

Change·the·information·on·the·cover·page·to·reflect·your·report.··For·the·body·of·the·report,·use·styles·such·as·headings·1·through·5,·body·text,·block·quotations,·list·bullets,·and·list·numbers·from·the·**Style**·list·on·the·**Formatting**·toolbar.¶

2¶

13. Triple click inside the remaining paragraph under the heading to select it; press **CTRL+C** to copy it; click immediately to the left of the side heading "How to Use This Report Template," and press **CTRL+V** to paste the paragraph.
14. Triple-click inside the newly pasted paragraph to select it; with the paragraph still selected, type this:

    Digital Media Associates specializes in e-commerce and e-learning solutions. We are committed to designing, developing, and marketing the world's best digital media products.

PRACTICE (continued)

15. Select the side heading "How to Use This Report Template"; with the heading still selected, type `E-Commerce Solutions` as the new side heading.
16. Triple-click inside the paragraph below the new side heading; with the paragraph still selected, type this:

    `Our e-commerce solutions make buying and selling of goods and services on the Internet simple and cost effective. We deliver integrated, customizable online shopping cart solutions for companies of all sizes.`

17. The last page of your finished report should look similar to this:

Business·Solutions¶

Digital·Media·Products¶

Digital·Media·Associates·specializes·in·e-commerce·and·e-learning·solutions.·We·are· committed·to·designing,·developing,·and·marketing·the·world's·best·digital·media· products.¶

E-Commerce·Solutions¶

Our·e-commerce·solutions·make·buying·and·selling·of·goods·and·services·on·the· Internet·simple·and·cost·effective.·We·deliver·integrated,·customizable·online·shopping· cart·solutions·for·companies·of·all·sizes.¶

If you need to add additional paragraphs and headings to the report, follow the same select/copy/paste/edit process you followed in steps 13 through 16.

18. Save changes to *practice-102*, and return to GDP.

GO TO Textbook

Designing Letterheads

LESSON 103

COMPATIBILITY MODE

If *[Compatibility Mode]* displays in the title bar of a document, the Word version in use is newer than the version used to create the file. Converting such files updates certain features to the newer Word version in use and removes the title bar notice. For most jobs, Compatibility Mode is acceptable. However, jobs with text boxes (text boxes are introduced in Lesson 103) and WordArt (WordArt is introduced in Lesson 106) should always be converted before beginning work—watch for GDP screen notes that alert you to jobs that must be converted.

To convert a file from Compatibility Mode:

1. From the **File** tab, click **Convert**, **OK**.

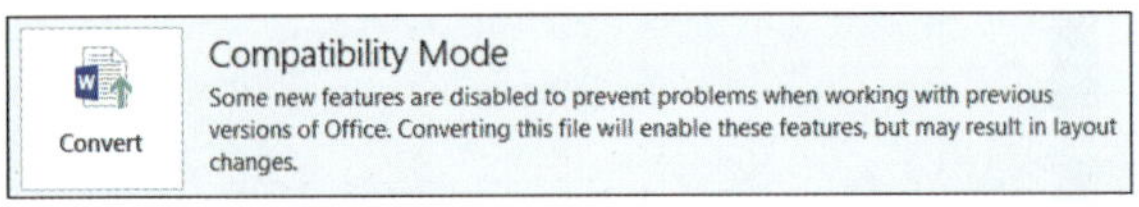

2. If a dialog box appears prompting you about the upgrade, click **OK**.
3. Note that *[Compatibility Mode]* no longer appears in the title bar of the Word file because the file has now been upgraded to Word 2016.

If at any point you are prompted to upgrade your document when you go to save it and you don't want to convert it, click **Cancel**. From the **Save As** dialog box, check **Maintain compatibility with previous versions of Word** on the bottom left of the dialog box; verify that the file name in the **File name** box is correct; click **Save**.

Font—Small Caps

To change the font to Small caps: From the **Home** tab, **Font** group, click the **Dialog Box Launcher**; from the **Font** dialog box, **Font** tab, under **Effects**, check **Small caps**, **OK**.

Text Boxes

Use text boxes to float (freely move) text and images. You can draw a text box manually, or you can select a built-in preformatted text box from a gallery. Text inside a text box can be formatted, the borders and fill can be changed, and the text box is resizable.

To insert and draw a text box:

1. Change the zoom to **Page Width**.
2. From the **Insert** tab, **Text** group, click the **Text Box** button; then click the **Draw Text Box** button at the bottom of the list.

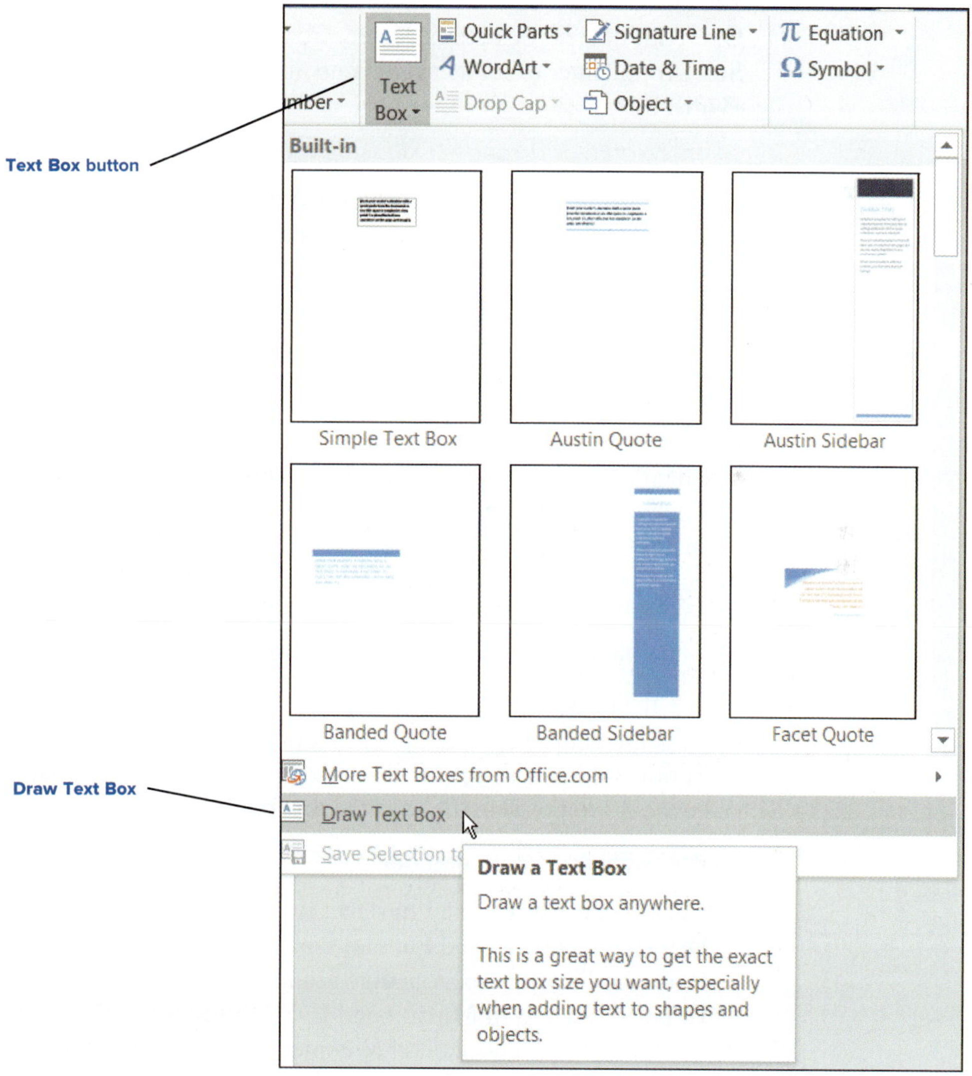

Cross hair pointer

3. Position the cross hair pointer where you want the text box to appear; then drag to insert the text box.
4. Note that an on-demand **Drawing Tools** tab with a **Format** tab below it appears when you insert or select a text box.

To size a text box:

1. Display the **Ruler**, and click on the outside border of the text box to select it—the text box outline should appear solid.
2. Position the mouse pointer on a sizing handle until the pointer changes to a 2-headed resize pointer; then drag to size the box using the rulers to help you visually size the text box.
3. Repeat this step for all sides of the box.

Or: With the text box still selected, from the **Drawing Tools**, **Format** tab, **Size** group, enter exact measurements in the **Shape Height** and **Shape Width** boxes.

To enter, edit, or arrange text inside a text box:

1. Click inside the text box to enter text.
2. Type and format the desired text inside the box, and drag on the bottom border to display any hidden text.
3. To align the text at the top, middle, or bottom of the text box, from the **Drawing Tools**, **Format** tab, **Text** group, **Align Text** button, click **Top**, **Middle**, or **Bottom** as desired.

To visually position a text box:

1. Change the **Zoom** level to see the entire page.
2. Click on the outside border of the text box to select it—the text box outline should appear solid.
3. Position the mouse pointer on any text box edge until 4-headed **Move** pointer appears; drag the text box to position it.
4. Note that an outline of the box appears as you drag the text box.

Move pointer

If you lose sight of the desired text box, change the Zoom level to view the entire page or click the Zoom Out or Zoom In button or drag the Zoom slider. Or select the text box, and use the directional arrows on the keyboard to position the selected text box.

To precisely position a text box relative to the document margins:

1. Click the text box border to select it and to activate the on-demand **Drawing Tools** tab and **Format** tab.
2. From the **Format** tab, **Arrange** group, click the **Align Objects** button; verify that **Align to Margin** and **Use Alignment Guides** are checked.
3. Click the desired horizontal alignment—**Align Left**, **Align Center**, or **Align Right**; or click the desired vertical alignment—**Align Top**, **Align Middle**, or **Align Bottom**.

Or: Drag the text box up, down, left, or right until a green **Alignment Guide** line appears at a margin, at the center of the page, or at a page edge; then release the text box. With the text box selected, nudge it into place with the keyboard directional arrows.

REFER TO
WM L. 88, Clip Art—Insert (Online Pictures—Insert)

If you are using an image, insert it first, and then format the text box. Thus, you can coordinate text box style described next with the image to create a unified, attractive design.

Shape Fill button

To change the text box fill and shape outline in a selected text box:

1. Select the text box or click inside it.
2. From the **Drawing Tools**, **Format** tab, **Shape Styles** group, click the **Shape Fill** button.

   Make sure you change the Shape Fill under the Drawing Tools, Format tab, Shape Styles group, and not under the Home tab, Paragraph group, Shading button.

3. Click the desired fill color (**Theme Colors** or **Standard Colors**), **No Fill**, **More Fill Colors**, **Picture**, **Gradient**, or **Texture**. Experiment freely with all these choices—the results can be dramatic and interesting.
4. Under the **Drawing Tools**, **Format** tab, **Shape Styles** group, click the **Shape Outline** button; then click the desired color, weight, dashes, and so forth. Experiment freely with all choices.
5. Under the **Drawing Tools**, **Format** tab **Shape Styles** group, click the **Edit Shapes** button, **Change Shapes**; click the desired shape. Experiment freely with all choices.

To make the text box fill transparent: From the **Drawing Tools**, **Format** tab, **Shape Styles** group, **Shape Fill**, click **No Fill**.

To change the overall visual text box style in a selected text box: From the **Drawing Tools**, **Format** tab, **Shape Styles** group, click the **More** list arrow at the right of the style gallery. Point to any predefined style, note the **Live Preview**, and click the desired style. Use **Undo** to reverse any choices.

To change the overall design of the document: From the **Design** tab, **Document Formatting** group, click the **Colors**, **Fonts**, or **Effects** button as desired; point to the various choices, and watch the **Live Preview**. Click any desired choices.

To change the text box shape in a selected text box: Under the **Drawing Tools**, **Format** tab, **Insert Shapes** group, click the **Edit Shape** button; click **Change Shape**, and click the desired shape from the gallery.

To remove the shape outline in a selected text box: Under the **Drawing Tools**, **Format** tab, **Shape Styles** group, click **Shape Outline**, **No Outline**.

PRACTICE 103 (1 of 1)

Note: In this exercise, you will create a letterhead similar to this:

1. As soon as the Word file is open, note that *[Compatibility Mode]* appears in the title bar of the Word file; convert this file. (*Hint:* From the **File** tab, click **Convert**, **OK**; click **OK** in the pop-up dialog box; note that the compatibility notice is gone from the title bar.)
2. Activate **Show/Hide ¶**, display the **Ruler**, and begin this job in **Whole Page** view (also known as **One Page** view from the **View** tab, **Zoom** group); adjust the zoom setting as needed as you follow each step.
3. Change the top, left, and right margins to 0.3".

   If a prompt appears about margins being outside the printable area of the page, click Fix, OK, to accept the new margins. Your finished job dimensions will looks slightly different from the illustration, but this is not cause for concern.

4. Draw a text box at the top of the page 1.1" high and 7.8" wide—enter the exact measurements in the **Shape Height** and **Shape Width** boxes as shown in the illustration; drag the text box into position using green **Alignment Guide** lines to help position it at the top margin centered horizontally.

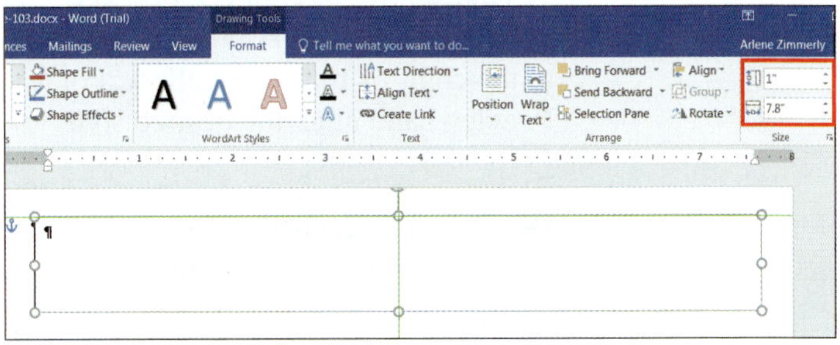

   You might need to increase the height slightly to accommodate the text you will type later. You might need to drag the text box around the top margin and right margin to make the green alignment guide lines appear.

REFER TO

WM L. 24, Zoom
WM L. 45, Tab Set—Ruler Tabs
WM L. 88, Clip Art—Insert (Online Pictures—Insert)

PRACTICE (continued)

5. Click inside the text box—change the text alignment to center; change to Calibri 24 pt., bold, italic, Small Caps; then type this:

   California Aqua Sports

6. Press **ENTER** 1 time, and change to Calibri 12 pt. bold (release italic and Small Caps); and type this:

   759 Wilshire Boulevard

7. Type 2 spaces, and insert a black square bullet Wingding symbol. (*Hint:* From the **Insert** tab, **Symbols** group, click **Symbol**, **More Symbols**; from the **Symbols** tab, **Font** box, select **Wingdings**; scroll down a few rows until you see the first black square shaped symbol numbered as **Wingdings: 110**; click it, and click **Insert**.)

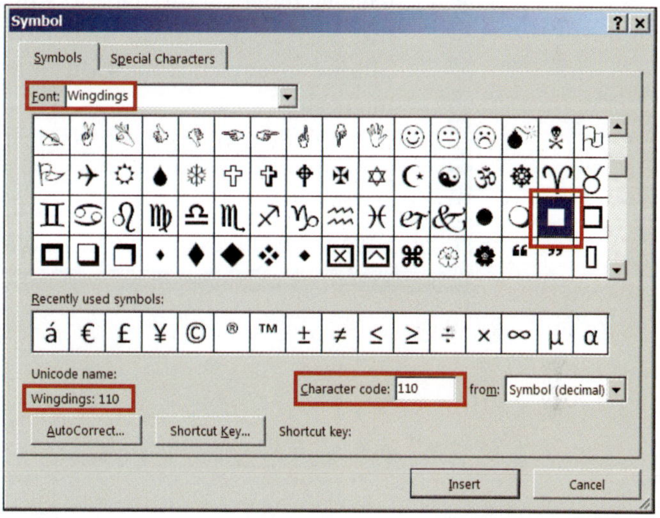

8. In the text box, type 2 spaces after the Wingdings symbol, type the address below, type 2 spaces, and insert another black square bullet Wingdings symbol:

   Los Angeles, CA 90017 ■

9. Type 2 spaces, and type this phone number:

   323-555-1721

10. Press **ENTER** 1 time; change the font to Calibri 12 pt. bold, italic; type the text below, and click outside the text box to close it.

    www.CalAquaSports.com

PRACTICE (continued)

11. Insert an image related to sailing or water sports, set the width to about 1", and change the wrap style to **In Front of Text**; drag the image and position it as shown in the illustration; select the image, hold down **CTRL**, and drag the copied image to the right side of the text box. Your text box should look similar to this:

Make sure the insertion point is outside of the text box before inserting the image or you will not be able to set the wrap style.

12. Change the text box shape to **Rounded Rectangle**. (*Hint:* With the text box selected, under the **Drawing Tools**, **Format** tab, **Insert Shapes** group, click the **Edit Shape** button, **Change Shape**; click the desired shape.)
13. Change the text box style (shape outline, shape fill, etc.) and font color to coordinate with the clip art. Your finished job should look similar to the one at the start of this exercise.
14. Save the changes and close *practice-103*; return to GDP.

GO TO Textbook

Designing Notepads

104

LESSON

Print Options

To print: From the **File** tab, click **Print** to view the **Print** pane with print options.

Or: Press **CTRL+P** to go directly to the **Print** pane.

The Print pane allows you to set the desired number of copies, select a printer, and adjust other settings. Clicking the File tab, Print, Print, button sends all pages of the document directly to the default printer. The document preview in the right pane allows you to see how your document will look when printed.

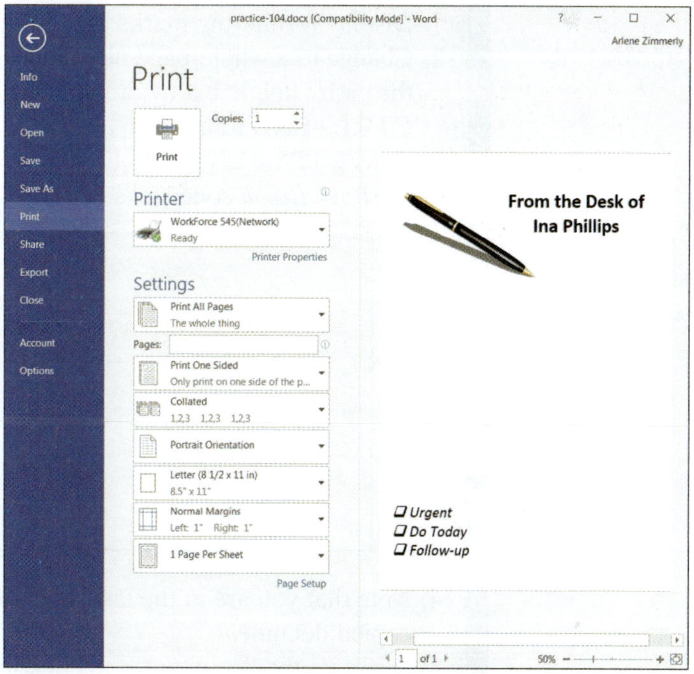

You can print specific pages, print all pages, or use a specific paper size. For example, if you have created a 4-page document, such as the notepad illustrated on page 177, and you wanted all 4 pages to print on one sheet of paper, under Settings (the last option), select 4 Pages Per Sheet, and click Print. The 4 pages will be automatically scaled down and reduced to fit on the selected paper size.

You can add Preview and Print buttons to the Quick Access Toolbar. Click the list arrow to the right of the Quick Access Toolbar, and click any relevant print choices.

To print 4 Pages Per Sheet: From the **File** tab, click **Print**. Under **Settings**, click the list arrow on the last button (**1 Page Per Sheet**); (the last option), click **4 Pages Per Sheet**; click the **Print** button.

If your pictures or text boxes won't print, you may need to adjust your print settings. From the File tab, Options, click the Display tab on the left; under Printing options, check Print drawings created in Word; click OK.

PRACTICE 104 (1 of 1)

Always check with your instructor before printing.

1. Display formatting marks by turning on **Show/Hide ¶**.
2. Change to a whole-page view, click outside any objects, and select the entire document by pressing **CTRL+A**, **CTRL+C** to copy, and **CTRL+END** to move to the end of the document.
3. Press **CTRL+ENTER** 3 times to create 3 additional blank pages—the *Page Break* code looks like this:

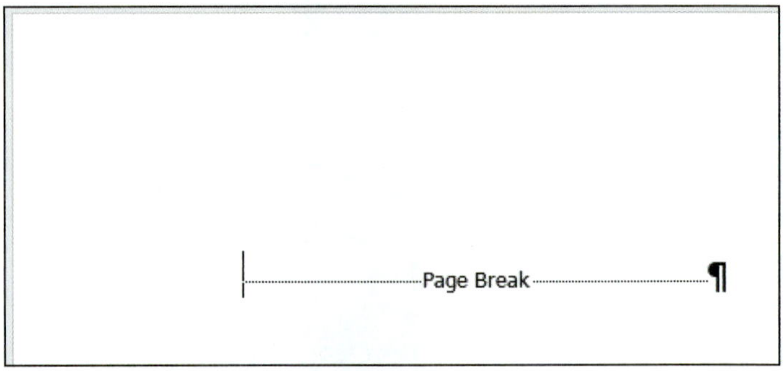

4. Note that you are in the last page; press **CTRL+V** to paste the copied document.
5. Scroll up the document, and click just before the **Page Break** formatting code on the third page, and paste; click just before the **Page Break** formatting code on the second page, and paste.
6. Change the zoom level to view all 4 pages; note that all 4 pages are identical.

PRACTICE (continued)

7. Use the print option to print 4 pages per sheet—this illustration represents *practice-104* after using that option.

8. Save changes and close *practice-104*; return to GDP.

GO TO Textbook

Designing Cover Pages

106

WordArt

REFER TO
WM L. 103, Compatibility Mode

Use WordArt to create a text box with special effects. WordArt can be formatted, rotated, realigned, and shaped. Jobs with WordArt must be converted from Compatibility Mode before beginning work. See Lesson 103 for details.

To insert a WordArt object:

1. From the **Insert** tab, **Text** group, click the **WordArt** button; then click the desired style from the **WordArt** gallery.

   Pause over each style to read the ScreenTip name.

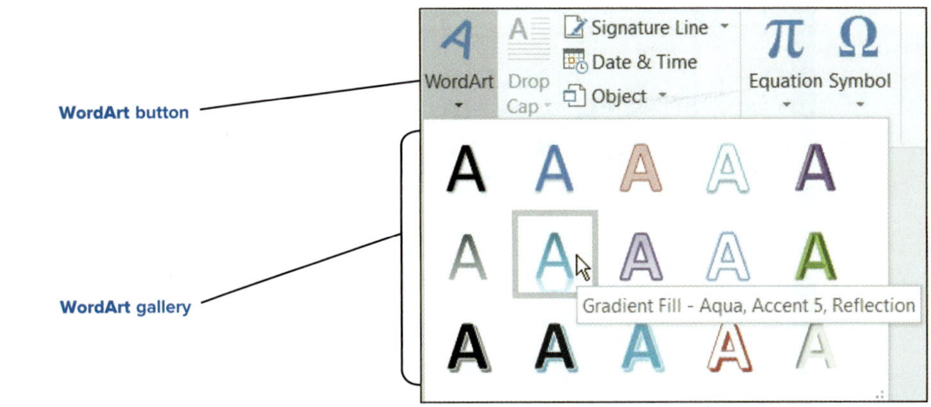

2. Note that a **WordArt** object appears in the document with sample text, and an on-demand **Drawing Tools** tab appears with a **Format** tab below it.

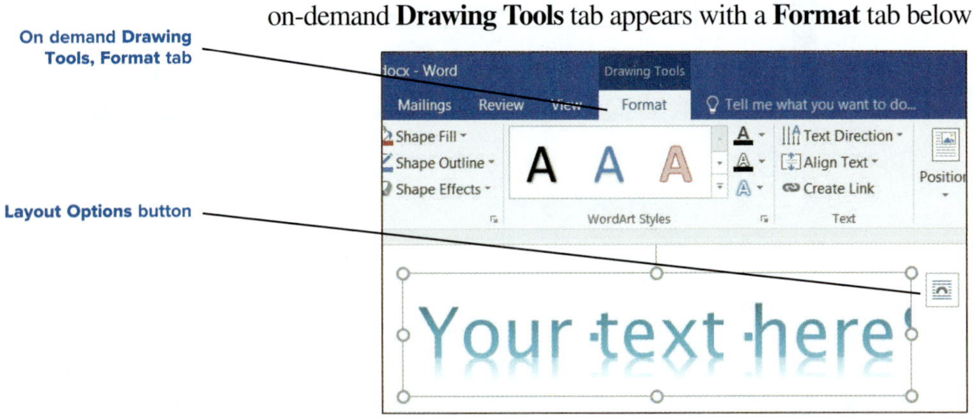

3. From the **Drawing Tools**, **Format** tab, click on the various features in the **Shape Styles**, **WordArt Styles**, and **Text** groups and experiment freely.
4. From the **Drawing Tools**, **Format** tab, **WordArt Styles** group, click the list arrow to view other gallery styles; point to each style, look at the **Live Preview**, then click the desired style to change it.

WordArt styles with "Outline" in the name are bolder and easier to read; a specific color in the style name varies with the theme in use and can be easily changed; focus on the overall style as you make your choice.

5. From the **Drawing Tools**, **Format** tab, **Shape Styles** group, click the **Shape Fill**, **Shape Outline**, and **Change Shape** buttons to change fills, outlines, and shapes. Look at the **Live Preview** as you point; then click the desired choice.
6. From the **Drawing Tools**, **Format** tab, **Shape Styles** group, click the **Shape Effects** button list arrow; from the drop-down gallery, click the different effects buttons, and note the effect on your **WordArt** object.
7. From the **Drawing Tools**, **Format** tab, **Size** group, experiment with the arrows next to the boxes to change sizes, or drag on the size handles on the **WordArt** object.

To transform the WordArt shape: Select the **WordArt** object; from the **Drawing Tools**, **Format** tab, **WordArt Styles** group, click the **Text Effects** button, **Transform**; click the desired text effects shape.

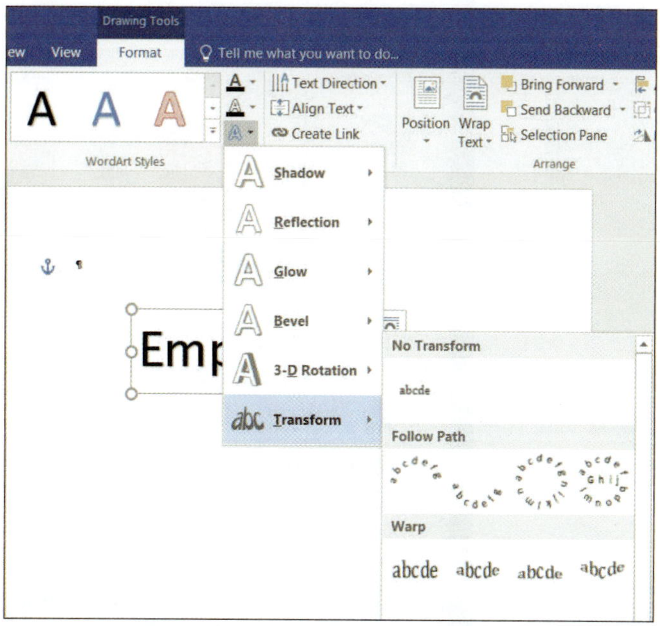

To edit text in your WordArt: Click inside the **WordArt** object and edit text as desired.

To align the WordArt horizontally:

1. Click over the **WordArt** border to select the object.
2. From the **Drawing Tools**, **Format** tab, **Arrange** group, click the **Align** button list arrow; click the desired horizontal alignment (**Align Left**, **Align Center**, or **Align Right**).

PRACTICE 106 (1 of 1)

Note: In this exercise, you will add WordArt to an existing cover page. Your finished job will look similar to this:

1. As soon as the Word file is open, note that *[Compatibility Mode]* appears in the title bar of the Word file; convert this file. (*Hint:* From the **File** tab, click **Convert**, **OK**; click **OK** in the pop-up dialog box; note that the compatibility notice is gone from the title bar.)
2. Activate **Show/Hide ¶**, display the **Ruler**, and begin this job in **Whole Page** view (also known as **One Page** view from the **View** tab, **Zoom** group); adjust the zoom setting as needed as you follow each step.

REFER TO
WM L. 24, Zoom
WM L. 45, Tab Set—Ruler Tabs
WM L. 103, Compatibility Mode

PRACTICE (continued)

3. Insert the first WordArt object—select a WordArt style that complements the overall design of the page.

   You will be creating two WordArt objects—the first will contain "Employee" as the text and the second will contain "Benefit Plan" as the text.

4. Replace the default WordArt text ("Your text here") with this word:

   `Employee`

5. Make any desired font changes in the WordArt object.
6. With the WordArt selected, experiment with all features from the **Drawing Tools**, **Format** tab until you are satisfied with your choices—color choices should coordinate with the colors in the art and text box at the bottom of the document.
7. Drag the WordArt object until it is positioned toward the top of the page and centered similar to the illustration.
8. Transform the selected WordArt shape similar to the illustration. (*Hint:* From the **Drawing Tools**, **Format** tab, **WordArt Styles** group, click the **Text Effects** button, **Transform**; click the desired text effects shape. **Inflate Top** and **Inflate Bottom** were used in the illustrated job.)
9. Select the WordArt object; point to the bottom border until you see a move pointer; hold down **CTRL** while dragging down on the object to create a duplicate; edit the text to read as follows, and transform the shape as desired:

   `Benefit Plan`

10. Position your finished WordArt similar to this illustration using the green **Alignment Guides** to center each object.

11. Save changes to *practice-106*, and return to GDP.

GO TO Textbook

Designing Announcements and Flyers

LESSON **107**

Table—Move

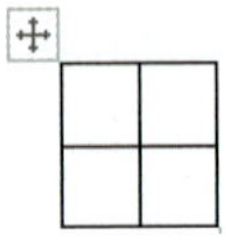

Table Move handle

The easiest way to move a table is to point to the Table Move handle just above the top left-hand corner of Cell A1 and drag the table into position. To add overall style and design to your table, use the Table Tools Design tab groups.

? You must be inside a table cell for the dynamic Table Tools tab to display.

On-demand **Table Tools** tab with **Design** and **Layout** tab

The insertion point must be inside the table for the on-demand tabs to appear.

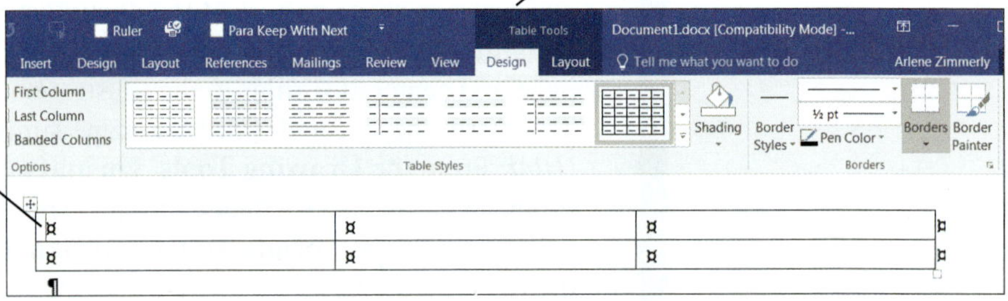

To move a table: Point to the 4-headed arrow **Table Move** handle at the top left corner of the table. Drag and drop the table to the new location.

Page Color

To add a background page color: From the **Design** tab, **Page Background** group, click the **Page Color** button; click the desired color from the color palette.

Or: Click the **Page Color** button, **More Colors**, to display the **Colors** dialog box; experiment with settings in the **Standard** and **Custom** tabs.

Or: Click the **Page Color** button, **Fill Effects**, to display the **Fill Effects** dialog box; experiment with settings in the **Gradient**, **Texture**, **Pattern**, and **Picture** tabs.

PRACTICE 107 (1 of 1)

Note: In this exercise, you will add formatting effects to create an announcement similar to this:

REFER TO
WM L. 24, Zoom
WM L. 45, Tab Set—Ruler Tabs
WM L. 46, Margins
WM L. 103, Compatibility Mode

1. As soon as the Word file is open, note that *[Compatibility Mode]* appears in the title bar of the Word file; convert this file. (*Hint:* From the **File** tab, click **Convert**, **OK**; click **OK** in the pop-up dialog box; note that the compatibility notice is gone from the title bar.)
2. If your document opens distorted on two pages, change all page margins to 0.5"; drag the WordArt, image, and table into position similar to the illustration. If a prompt appears regarding margins, click **Fix**, **OK**.
3. Activate **Show/Hide ¶**, display the **Ruler**, and begin this job in **Whole Page** view. Adjust the zoom setting as needed as you follow each step.

PRACTICE (continued)

4. Add a page background color with a textured fill effect; for example:

5. Experiment with table styles, borders, shading, fonts, spacing, and **WordArt** as desired.
6. In **One Page** view, verify the final arrangement of your document; make any changes as desired.
7. Save changes to *practice-107*, and return to GDP.

GO TO Textbook

Designing an Online Resume

111 LESSON

Table—Borders and Shading, Custom

An online resume uses advanced formatting features, such as customized borders, customized shading, and themes.

REFER TO

WM L. 37, Table—Borders
WM L. 68, Table—Shading

To apply the same border with customized colors and widths to a selected row, column, or cell:

1. Select the desired row, column, or cell.
2. From the **Table Tools**, **Design** tab, **Borders** group, click the list arrow next to the **Line Style** button.
3. Click the desired **Line Style**—the first choice is the solid line style.
4. From the **Table Tools**, **Design** tab, **Borders** group, click the list arrow next to the **Line Weight** button.
5. Click the desired weight from the drop-down list.
6. From the **Table Tools**, **Design** tab, **Borders** group, click the list arrow next to the **Pen Color** button.
7. Point to a color from the drop-down color palette, and pause until the **ScreenTip** with the color name appears.
8. From the **Table Tools**, **Design** tab, **Table Styles** group, click the list arrow on the **Borders** button, and click the desired border. (Do not click the **Borders** button itself or you will apply a border.)

To apply the same customized border to a deselected cell immediately after following the preceding steps:

1. Click in the desired cell.
2. Click the desired **Line Style**, **Line Weight**, and **Pen Color** as explained in the previous section.
3. When you click the desired **Pen Color**, the mouse pointer should change to a **Pen Color** tool; if necessary, click the **Border Painter** button to activate the **Pen Color** tool; point to any desired border with the **Pen Color** tool, and click exactly on the border or just below it to apply the new border.

Border Painter button

Experiment with selecting a group of desired cells to apply borders more efficiently for large areas.

4. If necessary, press **ESC** to drop the **Pen Color** tool.

   If the mouse pointer does not change to a Pen Color tool or if border choices are not behaving as expected, do this: From the Table Tools, Design tab, Table Styles group, click the list arrow below the Borders button. Then click the desired border to apply the border choices to the selection. Click and release the border button until the desired border appears.

5. If desired, change to a different **Line Style**, **Line Weight**, or **Line Color**, and repeat the preceding steps until all desired borders have been applied.

To apply shading with a customized color:

1. Select the desired row, column, or cell.
2. From the **Table Tools**, **Design** tab, **Table Styles** group, click the list arrow under the **Shading** button. (Do not click the **Shading** button itself or you will apply a shading.)
3. Point to a color from the drop-down color palette, pause until the **ScreenTip** with the color name appears, and note the **Live Preview**.
4. Click the desired color to apply the shading to the selection.

THEME

After you have applied customized borders and shading, you can apply a theme color palette to change border and shading colors and/or a theme font selection to change font styles.

To apply a theme color or change theme colors:

1. From the **Design** tab, **Document Formatting** group, click the **Themes** button.
2. Point to any theme, note the **Live Preview**, and click the desired theme.
3. Click the **Colors** button, point to any color group, note the **Live Preview**, and click the desired color.

To apply a theme font:

1. From the **Design** tab, **Document Formatting** group, click the list arrow under the **Fonts** button.
2. Point to any theme name noting the font changes in the **Live Preview**.
3. Click on the desired selection.

PRACTICE 111 (1 of 1)

Note: In this exercise, you will format an online resume similar to this:

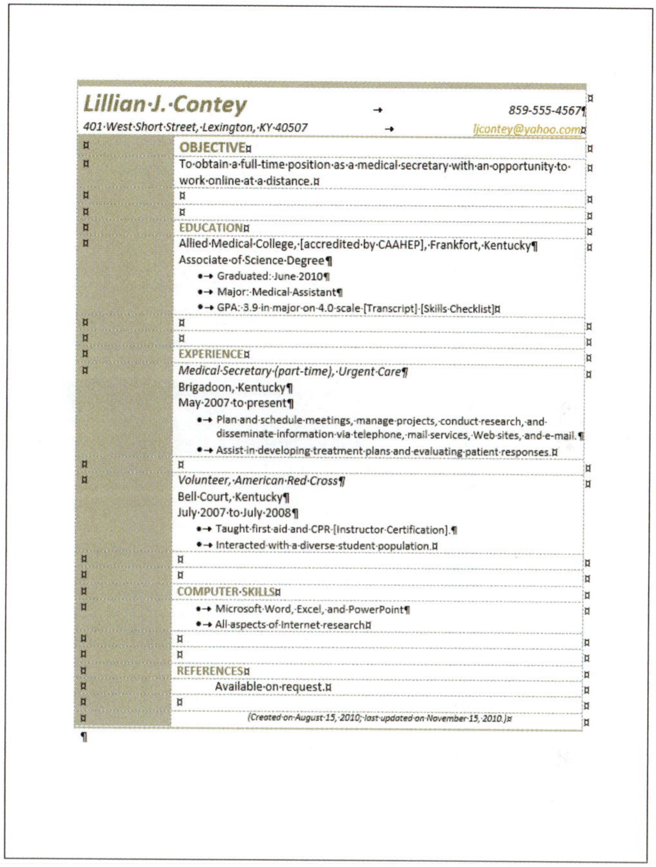

Lillian J. Contey — 859-555-4567
401 West Short Street, Lexington, KY 40507 — ljcontey@yahoo.com

OBJECTIVE
To obtain a full-time position as a medical secretary with an opportunity to work online at a distance.

EDUCATION
Allied Medical College, [accredited by CAAHEP], Frankfort, Kentucky
Associate of Science Degree
- Graduated: June 2010
- Major: Medical Assistant
- GPA: 3.9 in major on 4.0 scale [Transcript] [Skills Checklist]

EXPERIENCE
Medical Secretary (part-time), Urgent Care
Brigadoon, Kentucky
May 2007 to present
- Plan and schedule meetings, manage projects, conduct research, and disseminate information via telephone, mail services, Web sites, and e-mail.
- Assist in developing treatment plans and evaluating patient responses.

Volunteer, American Red Cross
Bell Court, Kentucky
July 2007 to July 2008
- Taught first aid and CPR [Instructor Certification].
- Interacted with a diverse student population.

COMPUTER SKILLS
- Microsoft Word, Excel, and PowerPoint
- All aspects of Internet research

REFERENCES
Available on request.

(Created on August 15, 2010; last updated on November 15, 2010.)

1. Remove all table borders, and turn on **View Gridlines**.
2. In Row 1, select "Lillian J. Contey," and change the font to Calibri 24 pt. bold.
3. Select Row 1 and apply italic.
4. In Row 1, carefully drag across both lines of the text to select only the text (do not select the entire row), and set a right tab at the right margin to align text at the right margin. (*Hint:* From the **Home** tab, **Paragraph** group, click the **Dialog Box Launcher**; from the **Paragraph** dialog box, **Indents and Spacing** tab, click the **Tabs** button; in the **Tab stop position** box, type 6.5; in the **Alignment** section, click **Right**; click **OK**.) Note that the phone number and e-mail address are now positioned at the right margin of the row.

REFER TO

WM L. 45, Tab Set—Ruler Tabs
WM L. 50, Tab Set—Dot Leaders

PRACTICE (continued)

5. Select each heading, and change the font to Calibri 14 pt. bold.
6. Select each bulleted list, and change the font to Calibri 11 pt.
7. In the EXPERIENCE section, capitalize the job title and business name for both listed jobs; do not italicize the comma between them.
8. Click in the line under the REFERENCES section; from the **Home** tab, **Paragraph** group, click the **Increase Indent** button 1 time.
9. Select the last line of text in the resume, center it, and change the font to Calibri 9 pt. italic.
10. Select Row 1; select a solid **Line Style** with a 6-pt. width and this **Pen Color**: **Tan**, **Background 2**, **Darker 25%**; apply this border across the top of Row 1 using the **Top Border** button or draw one using the **Border Painter** pen.

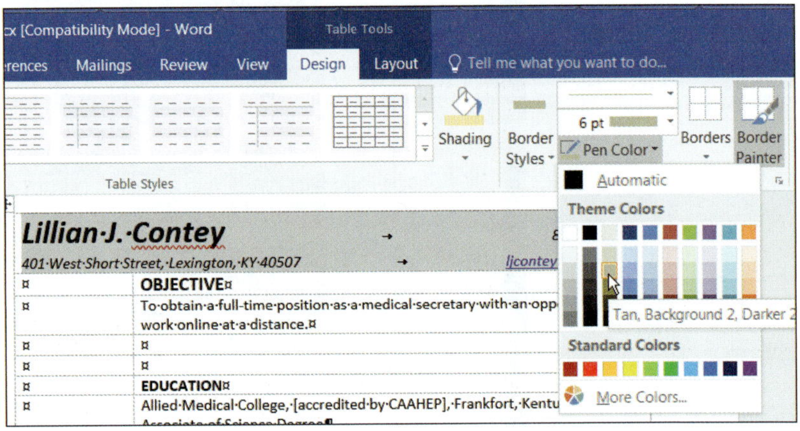

11. Press **ESC** to release the pen tool.
12. To apply a bottom border to Row 1, change the **Line Weight** to 2¼-pt.; leave all other border settings the same.
13. When the **Pen Color** tool appears, point to the bottom border of Row 1 (Cell A1 and Cell B1); release the pen tool when finished.
14. In the last row in the table, use the **Border** button to apply a **Bottom Border** with a 2¼-pt. width to the bottom border of both cells. Release the pen tool.
15. Click in Cell A2, scroll down, hold down **SHIFT**, and click in the last cell of Column A to select the range of cells.
16. From **Table Tools**, **Design** tab, **Table Styles** group, click the list arrow below the **Shading** button.

PRACTICE (continued)

17. Point to **Tan**, **Background 2**, **Darker 25%**, from the drop-down color palette; then click that color square to apply shading to the selection.
18. Change the font color of "Lillian J. Contey" in Row 1 and the font color of each heading to **Tan**, **Background 2**, **Darker 50%**. (*Hint:* After you've applied the color in Row 1, click in the first heading; press **CTRL+Y** to repeat the action or use the **Format Painter**; continue in like manner for each heading.)
19. From the **Design** tab, **Document Formatting** group, **Colors** button, point to the various choices, and observe the changes in the **Live Preview**.
20. From the **Design** tab, **Document Formatting** group, click the **Themes** button located on the far left side of the screen. Scroll down to the bottom of the gallery and apply the **Wood Type** theme; note the changes in the colors and fonts. Apply the **Office** theme on the top of the gallery for a gray color palette. Apply the **Wood Type** theme again.
21. From the **Design** tab, **Document Formatting** group, click the list arrow under the **Fonts** button and point to various custom theme fonts; note the **Live Preview** and apply the **Calibri** font.
22. Turn off **View Gridlines**. Your resume should look similar to the illustration at the start of this exercise.

    Note: If you need to convert the e-mail address in Row 1 to a hyperlink, select the e-mail address; right-click and click Hyperlink, OK.

23. Save changes to *practice-111*, and return to GDP.

GO TO Textbook

Mail Merge—A

112 LESSON

REFER TO

WM L. 115, Mail Merge—Envelopes | Mail Merge—Labels
GDP—Help (merged documents)

In this lesson, you'll use mail merge to create a *main document* file (a form letter with inserted placeholder merge fields) and to create a corresponding *data source* file (a database with variable information, such as an address list for multiple recipients).

Follow these important recommendations for all merge projects—this information will not be repeated in subsequent lessons.

- Close all Word files before beginning any merge project to avoid unexpected results.
- Because an electronic link is created between the two merge files (the main document and the data source), you should complete all steps of a merge project uninterrupted in one location. If you begin a merge project in one location (in the classroom) and then move to another location (your home computer), you will need to access both files, and you will have to reestablish links between them at the second location when you open the main document.
- If you must work between two locations, save the main document and the data source to removable media (a flash drive), and be prepared to follow the steps in a later section, under MERGE—MISCELLANEOUS, "To reestablish a broken link from a main document to the data source" at the second location.

To execute a mail merge, follow four basic steps:

1. Create the main document with unchanging content and with space to insert variable information via merge fields; for example, in this lesson, the main document is a letter; in Lesson 113, a memo; and in Lesson 115, an envelope and a label.
2. Create a data source file with variable information; for example, addresses and greetings for merged letters; addressees for envelopes and labels; and heading block information in memos.
3. Insert placeholder merge fields (codes that will be replaced with actual text upon merging) in the main document in order to link variable content from the data source file to the main document.
4. Merge the main document and data source to create a multipage document, which is a collection of all merged documents.

Mail Merge—Letters

LETTERS—MAIN DOCUMENT

Before beginning any merge project, close any open Word files to avoid linking data sources to an open file by mistake and to avoid other unexpected behavior! Carefully study all information under the MERGE—MISCELLANEOUS section in this lesson on pages 196–197 before completing the Practice exercise. That information applies to all merge projects in Unit 23 and will not be repeated.

To create the main document for a letter:

1. Open a blank document.
2. Press **ENTER** 5 times, type the date, and press **ENTER** 8 times after the date to allow space for the placeholders, which will automatically insert the variable information for the **Address Block** and **Greeting Line** placeholder fields later in the merge.

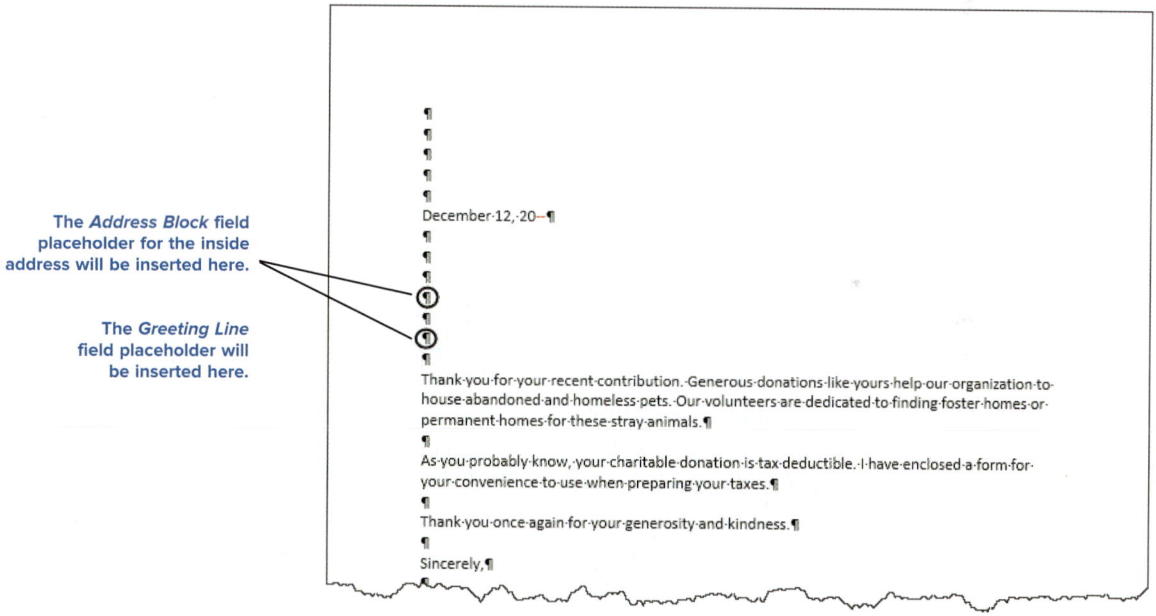

December·12,·20--¶

Thank·you·for·your·recent·contribution.·Generous·donations·like·yours·help·our·organization·to·house·abandoned·and·homeless·pets.·Our·volunteers·are·dedicated·to·finding·foster·homes·or·permanent·homes·for·these·stray·animals.¶

As·you·probably·know,·your·charitable·donation·is·tax·deductible.·I·have·enclosed·a·form·for·your·convenience·to·use·when·preparing·your·taxes.¶

Thank·you·once·again·for·your·generosity·and·kindness.¶

Sincerely,¶

3. Type the rest of the letter (the body, closing, and so forth), save the main document, and name it descriptively—for example, *practice-112-main-letter*.

LETTERS—DATA SOURCE FILE

To create the data source file:

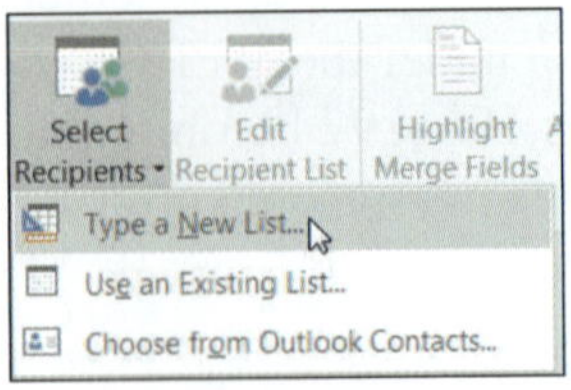

Select Recipients button

1. Open the main document for the letter. Click **Yes** if you see a warning that opening the document will run an SQL command, or just continue working in the main document if it is already open.
2. From the **Mailings** tab, **Start Mail Merge** group, click the **Select Recipients** button; then click **Type a New List**.
3. In the **New Address List** dialog box, type the information for the first recipient in each of the desired fields, press **TAB** to move from field to field, and skip any fields that are not applicable (for example, skip *Address Line 2*). Do <u>not</u> add any extra spaces after the last typed character in each field.

The insertion point is in the *Title* field ready for input.

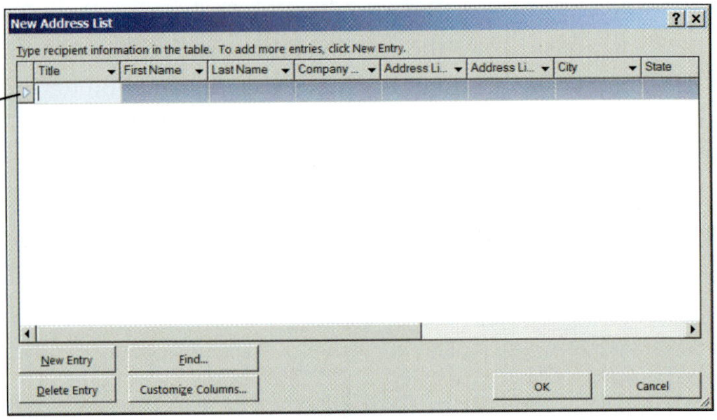

4. When you finish with one entry, click **New Entry** to begin the next one until all entries are completed; click **OK**.
5. Note that the **Mailings** tab, **Write & Insert Fields** group, is dimmed behind the open dialog box. This group will become active when you save the address list in the next step.
6. From the **Save Address List** dialog box, in the **File name** box, type a name that will be easy to recognize later (use "data" in the file name)—for example, *practice-112-data-letter*. The "mdb" file name extension is added automatically.
7. Click **Save** to save the file in the **My Data Sources** folder.

LETTERS—PLACEHOLDERS

To add the AddressBlock and Greeting Line placeholder merge fields in the main document:

1. Open the main document; click **Yes** if you see a warning that opening the document will run an SQL command.

2. Click where the inside address would normally be typed—in front of the fourth blank line below the date as shown in the illustration.

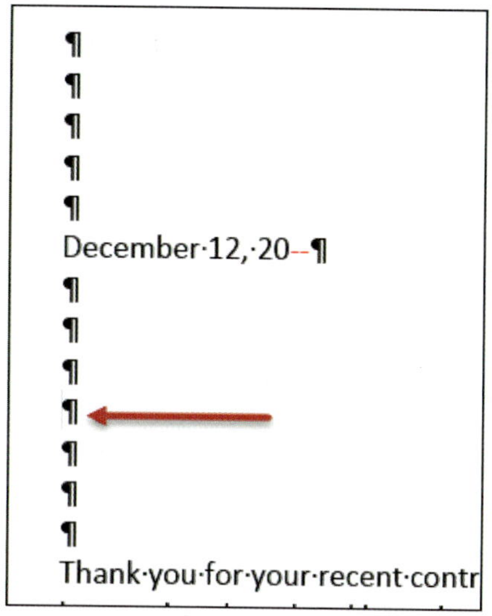

3. From the **Mailings** tab, **Write & Insert Fields** group, click **Address Block**, edit any choices as directed or as needed, and click **OK**.

You must already have recipients selected (step 2 in the previous section), or this button will be dimmed.

Click the **Address Block** button to insert an *≪Address Block≫* field where the inside address would normally be typed.

The *≪Address Block≫* field will be inserted here.

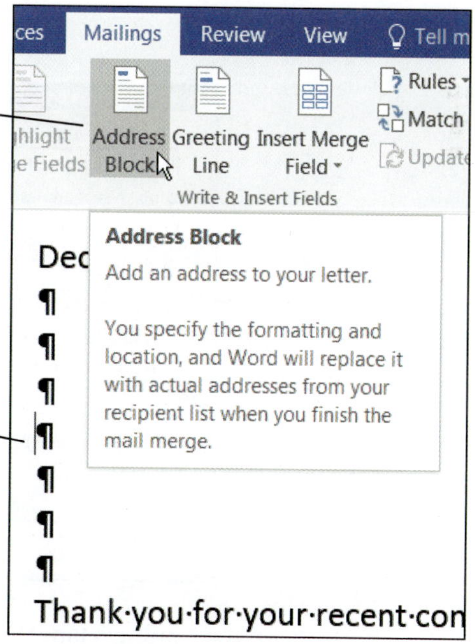

4. Note that the ≪*AddressBlock*≫ field has been inserted.

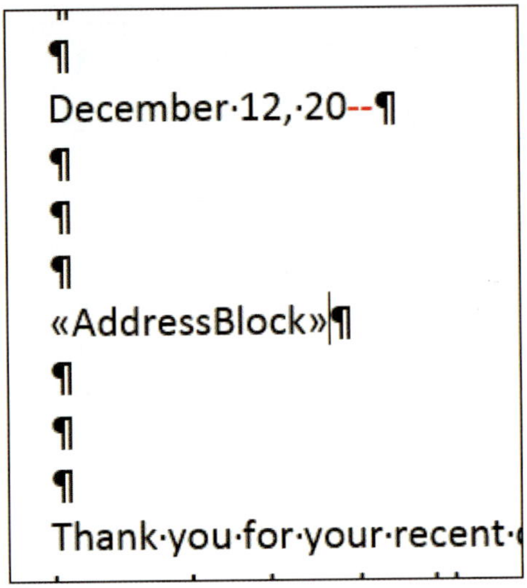

5. Click where the salutation would normally be typed—in front of the second blank line below the ≪*AddressBlock*≫ field.
6. Insert a greeting line merge field placeholder: From the **Mailings** tab, **Write & Insert Fields** group, click the **Greeting Line** button.
7. From the **Insert Greeting Line** dialog box, under **Greeting line format**, click the list arrow in the third box and click **:** (colon) for the salutation; click **OK**.

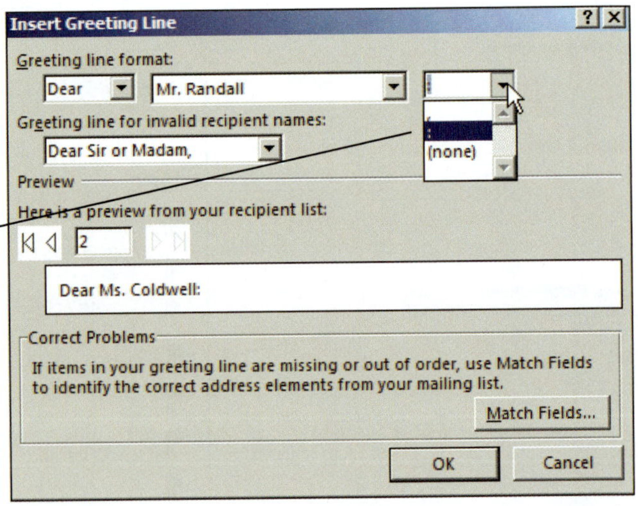

Change the punctuation from a comma (,) to a colon (:) for the salutation.

8. From the **Mailings** tab, **Write & Insert Fields** group, click **Highlight Merge Fields** to highlight the inserted placeholder merge fields.

9. Review each field and the field's position, and edit as needed. Your merge field placeholders should be positioned like this:

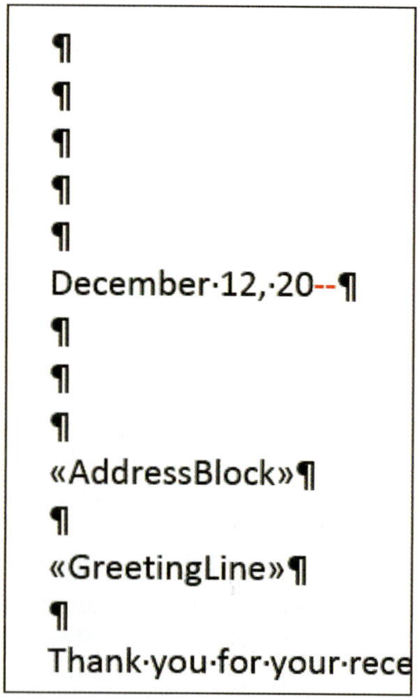
¶
¶
¶
¶
¶
December·12,·20--¶
¶
¶
¶
«AddressBlock»¶
¶
«GreetingLine»¶
¶
Thank·you·for·your·rece

LETTERS—MERGE

To begin the merge process, preview, and save merge results:

1. From the **Mailings** tab, **Write & Insert Fields** group, verify that **Highlight Merge Fields** is active to highlight the inserted placeholder fields.
2. Review the position of each field and edit as needed.
3. From the **Mailings** tab, **Preview Results** group, click **Preview Results**.
4. Click the **Next Record** (>) and **Previous Record** (<) buttons to page through your finalized merge documents.
5. From the **Mailings** tab, **Preview Results** group, click **Preview Results** to toggle it off and to view the placeholders in the main document again.
6. Edit the main document or data source as needed; preview your results again.
7. When you're satisfied with the merge results, from the **Mailings** tab, **Finish** group, click **Finish & Merge**, **Edit Individual Documents**, **All**, **OK**.
8. Note that a new multipage document containing all the merged letters on separate pages opens with a generic file name, such as *Letters1*.
9. Save the merged letters file—name it descriptively so it will be easy to find later—for example, *practice-112-letter*.
10. Save and close the main document.

REFER TO

WM L. 112, Mail Merge—Letters, Merge—Miscellaneous, "To edit the recipient list information in the data source file"

MERGE—MISCELLANEOUS

This information applies to all merge projects and will not be repeated.

To delete a merge field: Select the field and delete it—**CTRL+X** or **DEL** or **BACKSPACE.**

To edit the recipient list information in the data source file: If the main document is closed, open the main document; click **Yes** to the warning that opening the document will run an SQL command.

1. From the **Mailings** tab, **Start Mail Merge** group, click the **Edit Recipient List** button.
2. From the **Mail Merge Recipients** dialog box, under **Data Source**, click the desired data source file to edit; click **Edit**.
3. The **Edit Data Source** dialog box opens; in the **Edit Data Source** dialog box, click a box under any desired field; edit the information as needed. (Click **New Entry** and **Delete Entry** if you need to add a new entry or delete one.)
4. Click **OK** when you're finished; click **Yes** to the prompt "Do you want to update your recipient list and save these changes . . ." Click **OK** to close the **Mail Merge Recipients** dialog box.
5. Preview your merge results again; repeat this process as needed.

To open a main document with an SQL warning: Click **Yes** to the prompt "Opening the document will run the following SQL command." This SQL warning is expected behavior and occurs after the main document and data source files are created and linked to each other. When a main document is created and an existing data source file is associated with it, each time you open the main document thereafter, you will see this prompt.

To reestablish a broken link from a main document to the data source: After creating a main document with selected recipients in an associated data source file, if you save the data source *.mdb file to a location other than Word's default Data Source Directory or if you move the data source file, the link between the two files will be broken. Multiple prompts will appear when you try to open the main document. You must reestablish the link between the two files as follows:

1. Open the main document file. Click **Yes** to the prompt "Opening the document will run the following SQL command."
2. Click **OK** to the prompt "An error has occurred: Could not find file . . ."
3. A **Data Link Properties** window will appear; click **Cancel**.
4. Click **OK** to the prompt "An operation cannot be completed because of database engine errors."

5. The next prompt will identify the name of the main document and state "Word cannot find its data source . . ." and will display the path to the *.mdb data source file. Make a note of the path because you will browse to it in the next step! Click the **Find Data Source** button.
6. In the **Select Data Source** dialog box, Word's default *My Data Source* directory opens; browse to the location of the *.mdb file that you noted in step 5; click the *.mdb data source file, and click **Open**.
7. You have now reestablished a link between the main document and the data source, and you can continue working.

To locate the My Data Sources folder and *.mdb data source file: Microsoft Office Address List files are stored as Access database files with the file extension of "mdb" in a default location set by Microsoft. To see the location, from the **Mailings** tab, **Start Mail Merge** group, click **Select Recipients**, **Use an Existing List**, or note the location when you save a new list. See Word Help for further details.

To detach (unlink) a main document from the data source: From the **Mailings** tab, **Start Mail Merge** group, click the **Start Mail Merge** button, and click **Normal Word Document**.

PRACTICE 112 (1 of 1)

Close any other Word files before beginning! You will now create a new data source file, insert merge fields, and finish creating the main document.

1. Note that *practice-112-main-letter* opens partially completed and ready for input.
2. Turn on **Show/Hide ¶**; then create a new data source file by typing the information shown next. (*Hint:* From the **Mailings** tab, **Start Mail Merge** group, click **Select Recipients**, **Type a New List**. Type the first entry. Click **New Entry** to begin the second entry. Click **OK** to end the list.)

Title	First...	Last Name	Address Line 1	City	S.	ZIP Code
Dr.	Karen	Simpson	4309 Pine Bouquet Road	Lake Tahoe	CA	96150
Ms.	Gloria	Freeman	4135 Zephyr Road	Lake Tahoe	CA	96150

Do not add trailing spaces after the last typed character in each field! Be sure you are typing information in the correct field—remember to skip the *Company Name* field and the *Address Line 2* field.

PRACTICE (continued)

3. From the **Save Address List** dialog box, save the data source file as *practice-112-data-letter*. The extension "mdb" will be added to the file name automatically.

   Make a note of this location in case you need to browse to it later to reestablish a link to it from the main document.

4. Click **Save** to save the file in the **My Data Sources** folder.
5. In the main letter document, click in the fourth blank line below the date.
6. Insert an **Address Block** merge field. (*Hint:* From the **Mailings** tab, **Write & Insert Fields** group, click **Address Block**, edit any choices as directed or as needed, and click **OK**.)
7. Press the directional down arrow on the keyboard 2 times to position the insertion point where the salutation will be inserted.
8. Insert a greeting line merge field placeholder. (*Hint:* From the **Mailings** tab, **Write & Insert Fields** group, click the **Greeting Line** button.)
9. From the **Insert Greeting Line** dialog box, under **Greeting line format**, click the list arrow in the third box and click **:** (colon) for the salutation; click **OK**.
10. From the **Mailings** tab, **Write & Insert Fields** group, click **Highlight Merge Fields** to highlight the inserted placeholder merge fields.
11. Review each field and the field's position, and edit as needed.

Note: Now you will begin the merge process and preview your merge results.

1. From the **Mailings** tab, **Write & Insert Fields** group, verify that **Highlight Merge Fields** is active to highlight the inserted placeholder fields.
2. Review the position of each field, and edit as needed.
3. To begin the merge process, from the **Mailings** tab, **Preview Results** group, click **Preview Results**.
4. Click the **Next Record** (>) and **Previous Record** (<) buttons to page through your finalized merge files; edit the main document or data source as needed.

PRACTICE (continued)

5. When you're satisfied with the merge results, from the **Mailings** tab, **Finish** group, click **Finish & Merge**, **Edit Individual Documents**, **All**, **OK**. Your first merged letter should look similar to this:

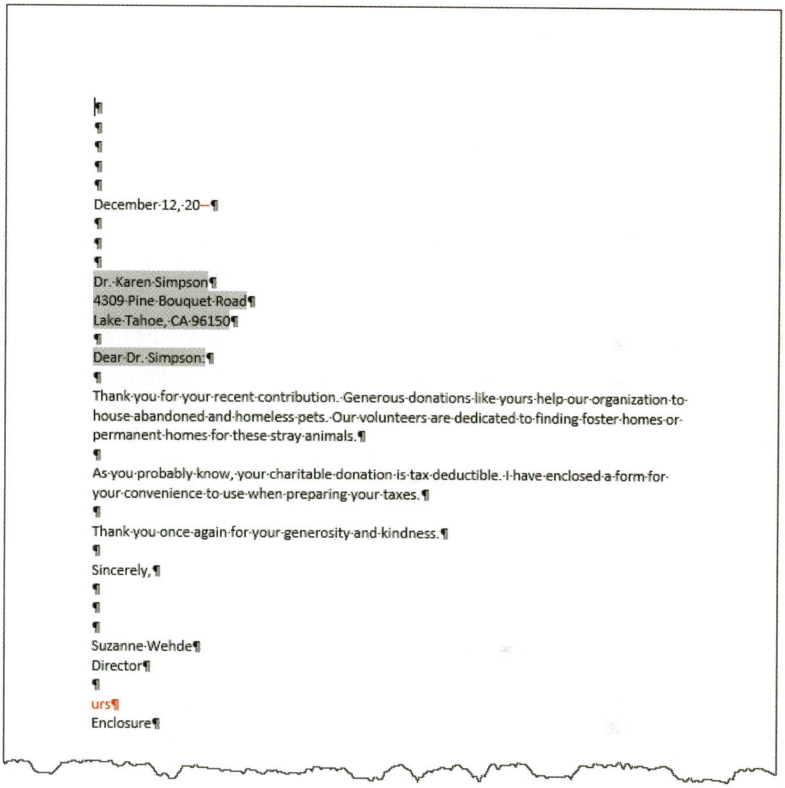

December 12, 20--

Dr. Karen Simpson
4309 Pine Bouquet Road
Lake Tahoe, CA 96150

Dear Dr. Simpson:

Thank you for your recent contribution. Generous donations like yours help our organization to house abandoned and homeless pets. Our volunteers are dedicated to finding foster homes or permanent homes for these stray animals.

As you probably know, your charitable donation is tax deductible. I have enclosed a form for your convenience to use when preparing your taxes.

Thank you once again for your generosity and kindness.

Sincerely,

Suzanne Wehde
Director

urs
Enclosure

6. Note that a new multipage document containing all the merged letters on separate pages opens with a generic file name, such as *Letters1*.
7. Save the merged letters file as *practice-112-letter*, and return to GDP.

GO TO Textbook

Mail Merge—D

LESSON 115

REFER TO
WM L. 112: Mail Merge—Letters
GDP—Help (merged documents):
WM L. 28, Envelopes

In Lesson 112, you used mail merge to create a main document file (a letter with inserted placeholder merge fields) and its corresponding data source file (an address list database). That same data source file could be used again to create merged envelopes and mailing labels. However, in this lesson, you will create an envelope and a label as main documents, and you will create new data source files to practice your mail merge skills.

Envelopes may be typed individually or inserted automatically into a business letter via Word's envelope feature. In Lesson 28, you created No. 10 envelopes. Now you will learn to create multiple envelopes with different delivery addresses automatically by creating a single envelope as a main document and linking it to a data source with multiple recipients.

Mail Merge—Envelopes

ENVELOPES—MAIN DOCUMENT

Before creating a main document and its linked data source file, always close any other Word files to avoid linking data sources to an open file by mistake!

To create the main document for an envelope:

1. Open a blank document; from the **Mailings** tab, **Start Mail Merge** group, **Start Mail Merge** button, click **Envelopes**.

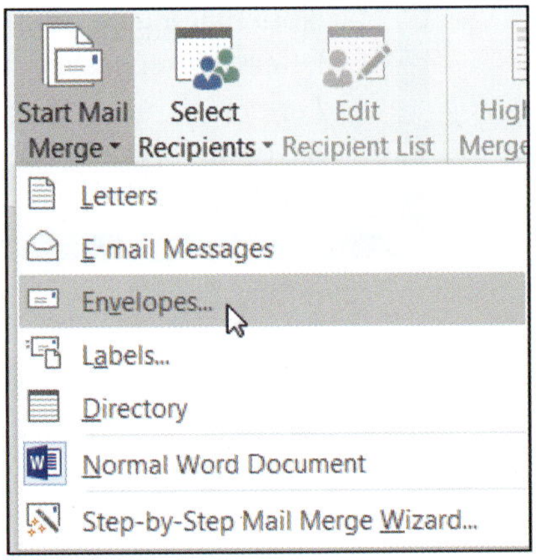

2. From the **Envelope Options** window, **Envelope Options** tab, make any desired changes (for example, choose an envelope size—the standard envelope size is **Size 10**); click **OK**.
3. Note that the original blank document is converted to a blank envelope in landscape orientation and is ready for input—you will insert merge fields later.

A return address to be used on all merged envelopes could be typed here, or merge field codes for varying return addresses could be inserted here.

Address Block merge field codes will be inserted here.

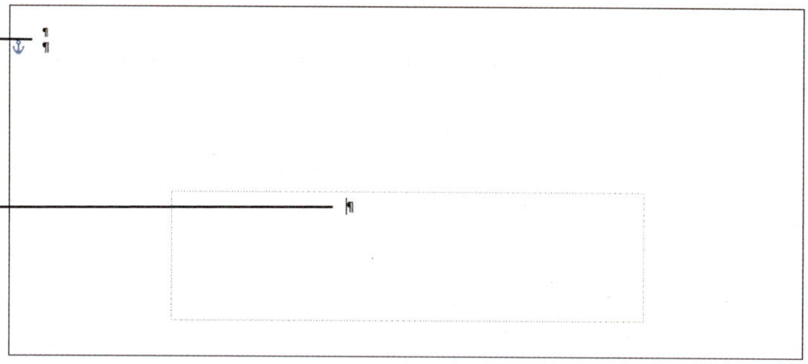

4. Save the main document for the envelope, and name it descriptively (use "main" in the file name) so it will be easy to recognize later—for example, *practice-115-main-envelope*.

ENVELOPES—DATA SOURCE FILE

To create the data source file:

REFER TO

WM L. 112, Mail Merge—Letters, Merge—Miscellaneous, "To open a main document with an SQL warning"

1. Open the main document for the envelope. Click **Yes** if you see a warning that opening the document will run an SQL command. Or begin with step 2 if the main document is already open.
2. From the **Mailings** tab, **Start Mail Merge** group, click the **Select Recipients** button, **Type a New List**.
3. In the **New Address List** dialog box, type the information for the first recipient in each of the desired fields, press **TAB** to move from field to field, and skip any fields that are not applicable (for example, skip *Company Name* and *Address Line 2*). Do <u>not</u> add any trailing spaces after the last typed character in each field.
4. When you finish with one entry, click **New Entry** to begin the next entry until all entries are completed; click **OK**.
5. Note that the **Mailings** tab, **Write & Insert Fields** group, is dimmed behind the open dialog box. This group will become active when you save the address list in the next step.

REFER TO

WM L. 112, Mail Merge—Letters, Merge—Miscellaneous, "To locate the My Data Sources folder and *.mdb data source file"

6. From the **Save Address List** dialog box, in the **File name** box, type a name that will be easy to recognize later; for example, use "data" in the file name—*practice-115-data-envelope*. The "mdb" file name extension is added automatically.
7. Click **Save** to save the file in the default **My Data Sources** folder.
8. Note that the **Write & Insert Fields** group on the **Mailings** tab is now active; therefore, you can now insert merge placeholder fields.

ENVELOPES—PLACEHOLDERS

To add the AddressBlock field in the main document:

1. Open the main document; click **Yes** if you see a warning that opening the document will run an SQL command.
2. Click at the point in the document where the **Address Block** field should be inserted.
3. From the **Mailings** tab, **Write & Insert Fields** group, click the **Address Block** button.

   You must already have recipients selected (step 2 in the previous section), or this button will be dimmed.

4. From the **Insert Address Block** dialog box, review the choices, make any desired changes, and click **OK**.
5. From the **Mailings** tab, **Write & Insert Fields** group, click the **Highlight Merge Field** button. Your *≪AddressBlock≫* merge field placeholder should be positioned like this (a return address might not be present):

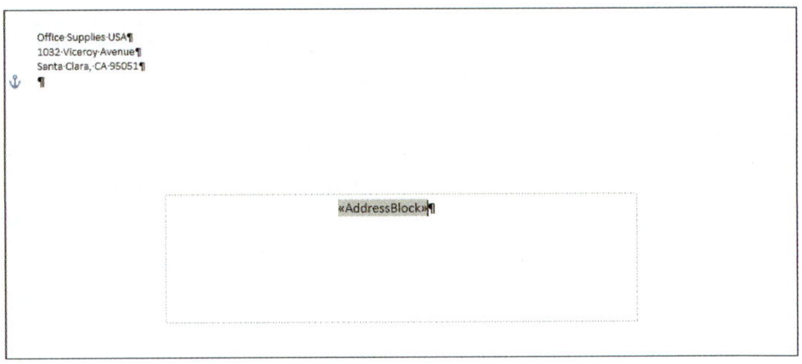

ENVELOPES—MERGE

To begin the merge process, preview, and save merge results:

1. From the **Mailings** tab, **Write & Insert Fields** group, click **Highlight Merge Fields**, to highlight the merge fields in the main document clearly.
2. Adjust any spacing around the merge fields as needed.
3. From the **Mailings** tab, **Preview Results** group, click **Preview Results**.
4. Click the **Next Record** (>) and **Previous Record** (<) buttons to page through your finalized merge documents.
5. From the **Mailings** tab, **Preview Results** group, click **Preview Results** to toggle it off and to view the placeholders in the main document again.
6. Edit the main document or data source as needed (right-click the *≪Address Block≫* field, click **Edit Address Block**); preview your results again.

REFER TO

WM L. 112, Mail Merge—Letters, Merge—Miscellaneous, "To edit the recipient list information in the data source file"

7. When you're satisfied with the merge results, from the **Mailings** tab, **Finish** group, click **Finish & Merge**, **Edit Individual Documents**, **All**, **OK**.
8. Save this file of merged results, and name it descriptively so it will be easy to find later—for example, *practice-115-envelope*.
9. Save and close the main document.

PRACTICE 115 (1 of 2)

Note: In the first part of this Practice exercise, you will create merged envelopes from a blank start file; in the second half, you will create merged labels from a blank start file.

Close any other Word files before beginning! You will now create a new data source file, insert merge fields, and finish creating the main document.

1. From the **Mailings** tab, **Start Mail Merge** group, click the **Start Mail Merge** button; click **Envelopes**.
2. From the **Envelope Options** window, **Envelope Options** tab, **Envelope size** box, verify that **Size 10** is selected; click **OK**.
3. Note that an envelope is created and is ready for input.
4. Click in the first blank line in the top left-hand corner of the envelope to enter the return address—if necessary, delete any existing return address that might be present; type the return address in the main document envelope as shown here:

Office·Supplies·USA¶
1032·Viceroy·Avenue¶
Santa·Clara,·CA·95051¶
¶

5. Save the main document as *practice-115-main-envelope*.
6. Create a new data source file with the information as shown in the next illustration. (*Hint:* From the **Mailings** tab, **Start Mail Merge** group, click **Select Recipients**, **Type a New List**. Type the first entry. Click **New Entry** to begin the second entry. Click **OK** to end the list.)

Title	First Name	Last Name	Company Name	Address Line 1	Ad...	City	State	ZIP...
Mr.	Steven	Keller	ABC Interiors	155 Franklin Street		Juneau	AK	95801
Mrs.	Maude	Golden	Sports Galore	200 Chopin Plaza		Maimi	FL	33131

PRACTICE (continued)

Do not add trailing spaces after the last typed character in each field! Be sure you are typing information in the correct field—remember to skip the *Address Line 2* field.

7. From the **Save Address List** dialog box, save the data source file as *practice-115-data-envelope*. The extension "mdb" will be added to the file name automatically.
8. Click **Save** to save the file in the default **My Data Sources** folder.
9. In the main envelope document, click in the blank line where you would normally type the delivery address.
10. Insert an address block merge field and highlight it. (*Hint:* From the **Mailings** tab, **Write & Insert Fields** group, click **Address Block**, edit any choices as directed or as needed, and click **OK**. From the **Mailings** tab, **Write & Insert Fields** group, click **Highlight Merge Fields**.)

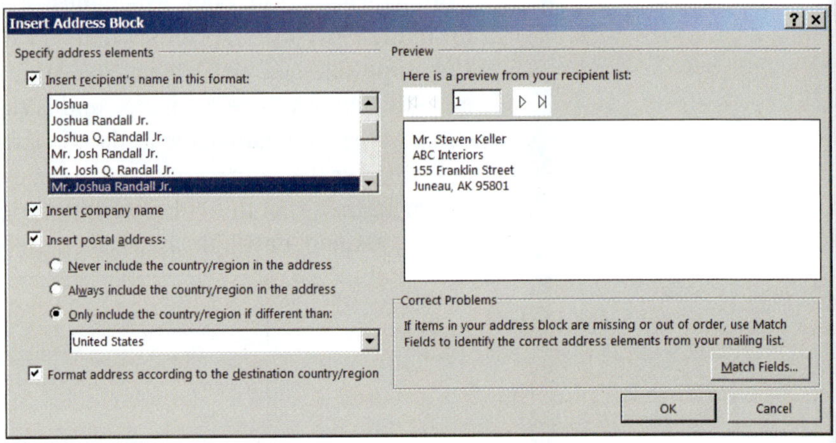

11. To begin the merge process, from the **Mailings** tab, **Preview Results** group, click **Preview Results**.
12. Click the **Next Record** (>) and **Previous Record** (<) buttons to page through your finalized merge files.
13. Edit the main document or data source as needed, and preview your results again.

PRACTICE (continued)

14. Your first merged envelope should look similar to this:

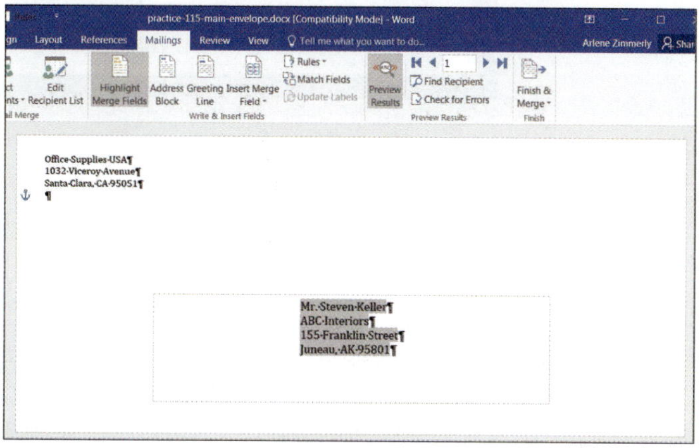

15. From the **Mailings** tab, **Finish** group, click **Finish & Merge**, **Edit Individual Documents**.
16. From the **Merge to New Document** dialog box, under **Merge Records**, click **All**, **OK**.
17. Note that a new document containing the merged envelopes opens with a generic file name (for example, *Envelopes1*).
18. Save the merged letters file as *practice-115-envelope*. Your merged envelopes should look similar to this:

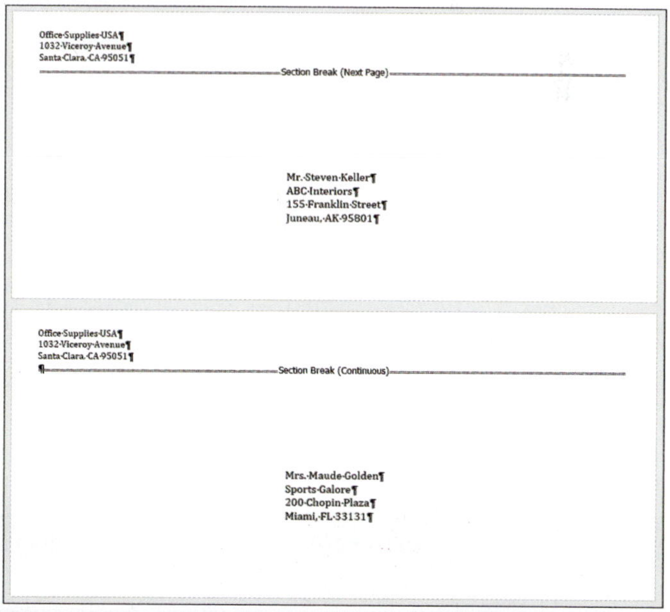

PRACTICE (continued)

19. Close all files (**CTRL+W**), but leave Word open.
20. Go to GDP's Lesson 115F screen to download another blank, unnamed file; then return here to continue.

Mail Merge—Labels

REFER TO
WM L. 28, Labels

In Lesson 28, you learned that labels may be typed individually or inserted automatically into a preset label or a label template via Word's Label feature. In this lesson, you will learn to create labels with different delivery addresses automatically by creating a single label as a main document and linking it to a data source with variable label information.

LABELS—MAIN DOCUMENT

To create the main document for a label:

1. Open a blank document.
2. From the **Mailings** tab, **Start Mail Merge** group, **Start Mail Merge** button, click **Labels**.

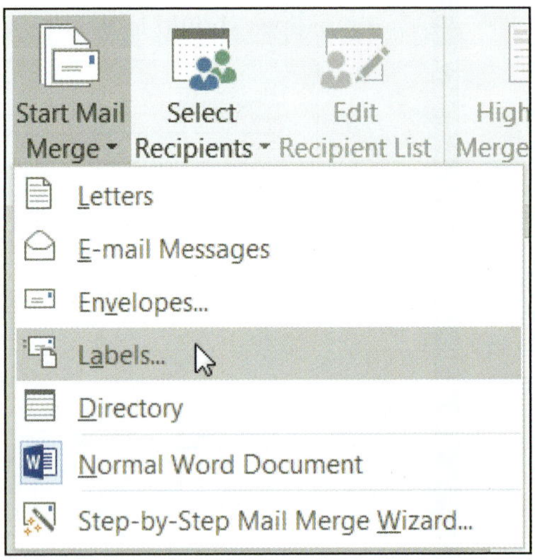

3. From the **Label Options** window, under **Label vendors**, click **Avery US Letter** (or the desired label vendor).

4. Under **Product number**, scroll down and click **5160 Easy Peel Address Labels** (or the desired product number).

Click the list arrow to select the desired label vendor.

Click the desired product number.

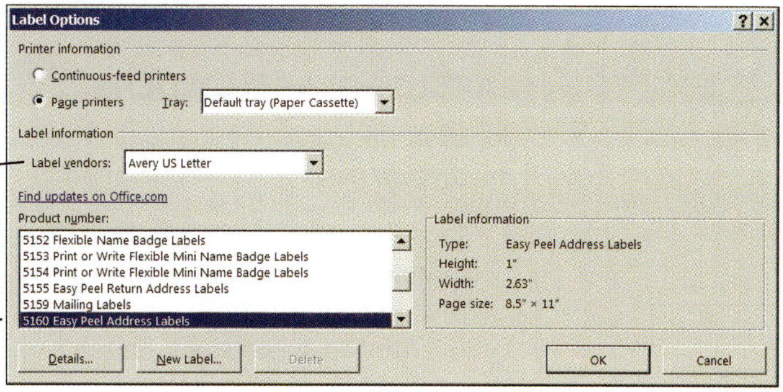

5. Click **OK** to create a page of blank labels. (Turn on **View Gridlines** if necessary.)

The **Address Block** merge field will be inserted here and in all remaining cells.

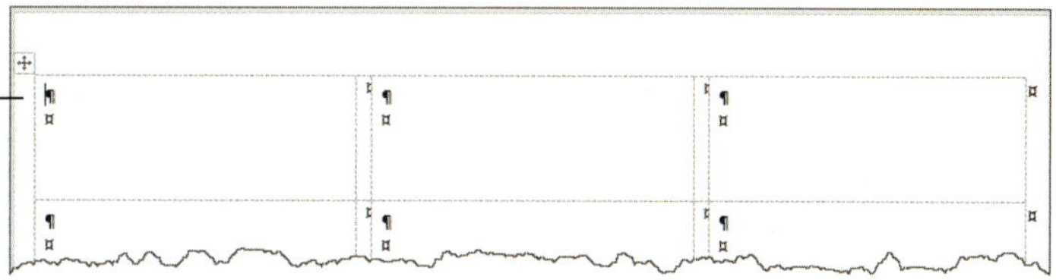

6. Save the main document for the envelope, and name it descriptively (use "main" in the file name) so it will be easy to recognize later—for example, *practice-115-main-label*.

LABELS—DATA SOURCE FILE

To create the data source file:

REFER TO

WM L. 112, Mail Merge—Letters, Merge—Miscellaneous, "To open a main document with an SQL warning"

1. Open the main document for the envelope. Click **Yes** if you see a warning that opening the document will run an SQL command.
2. From the **Mailings** tab, **Start Mail Merge** group, click the **Select Recipients** button, **Type a New List**.
3. In the **New Address List** dialog box, type the information for the first recipient in each of the desired fields, press **TAB** to move from field to field, and skip any fields that are not applicable (for example, skip *Company Name* and *Address Line 2*). Don't add any trailing spaces after the last typed character in each field.
4. When you finish with one entry, click **New Entry** to begin the next entry until all entries are completed; click **OK**.
5. Note that the **Mailings** tab, **Write & Insert Fields** group, is dimmed behind the open dialog box. This group will become active when you save the address list in the next step.
6. From the **Save Address List** dialog box, in the **File name** box, type a name that will be easy to recognize later (for example, use "data" in the file name: *practice-115-data-label.mdb*).

REFER TO

WM L. 112, Mail Merge—Letters, Merge—Miscellaneous, "To locate the My Data Sources folder and *.mdb data source file"

7. Click **Save** to save the file in the default **My Data Sources** folder.
8. Note that the **Write & Insert Fields** group on the **Mailings** tab is now active; therefore, you can now insert merge placeholder fields.

LABELS—PLACEHOLDERS

To add the ≪AddressBlock≫ placeholder merge field in the main document:

1. Open the main document; click **Yes** if you see a warning that opening the document will run an SQL command.
2. Click in Cell A1; from the **Mailings** tab, **Write & Insert Fields** group, click the **Address Block** button.

   You must already have a recipients selected (step 2 in the previous section) or this button will be dimmed.

3. From the **Insert Address Block** dialog box, review the choices, make any desired changes, and click **OK**.
4. Note that Cell A1 now contains an *≪Address Block≫* merge field placeholder and the remaining cells contain a *≪Next Record≫* code.

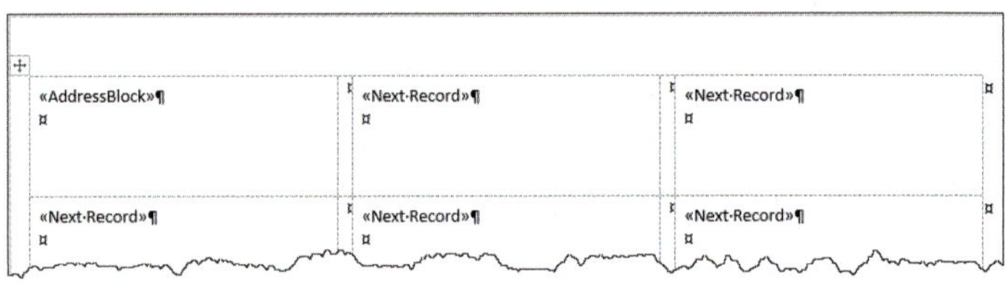

5. To insert the same *≪Address Block≫* merge field placeholder in each label, from the **Mailings** tab, **Write & Insert Fields** group, click **Update Labels**.

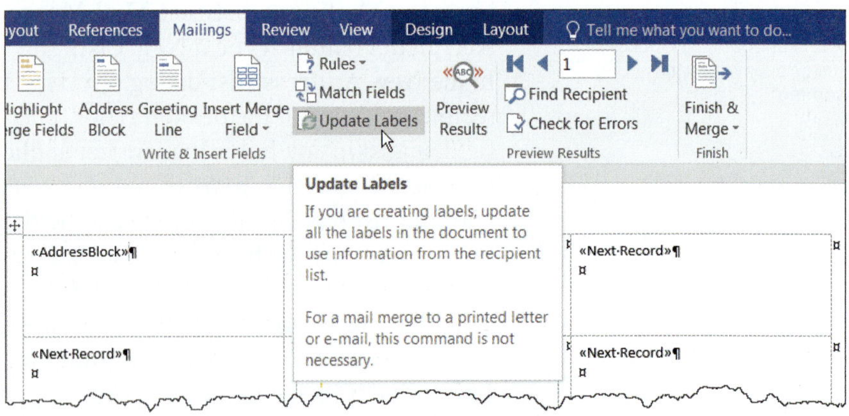

6. Note that the *≪Address Block≫* merge field placeholder now appears in each label.

To create a full page of the same label (no merge fields): From the **Mailings** tab, **Create** group, click **Labels**. From the **Envelopes and Labels** dialog box, **Labels** tab, type the address in the **Address** box. Click **New Document**.

LABELS—MERGE

To begin the merge process, preview, and save merge results:

1. From the **Mailings** tab, **Write & Insert Fields** group, click **Highlight Merge Fields** to highlight the merge fields in the main document.
2. Adjust any spacing around the merge fields as needed.
3. From the **Mailings** tab, **Preview Results** group, click **Preview Results**.
4. Edit the main document or data source as needed (right-click the *≪Address Block≫* field, click **Edit Address Block**, etc.).
5. Preview your results again. When you're satisfied with the merge results, from the **Mailings** tab, **Finish** group, click **Finish & Merge**, **Edit Individual Documents**, **All**, **OK**.
6. Save this file of merged results, and name it descriptively so it will be easy to find later—for example, *practice-115-label*. (See the illustration at the end of the next exercise for an example of finished labels.)
7. Save and close the main document.

REFER TO

WM L. 112, Mail Merge—Letters, Merge—Miscellaneous, "To edit the recipient list information in the data source file"

PRACTICE 115 (2 of 2)

Note: In the first part of this Practice exercise, you created merged envelopes; now you will create merged labels.

Close any other Word files before beginning!

1. From GDP's Lesson 115F screen, click the **Start Work** button again; and follow your browser's prompts to download and open a blank, unnamed Word file ready for input.
2. Turn on **Show/Hide ¶**, and then create a new main document. (*Hint:* From the **Mailings** tab, **Start Mail Merge** group, click the **Start Mail Merge** button; click **Labels**.)
3. From the **Label Options** window, under **Label vendors**, scroll down and click **Avery US Letter**.
4. Under **Product number**, click **5160 Easy Peel Address Labels**; click **OK**.
5. Save the main document as *practice-115-main-label*.

PRACTICE (continued)

6. Create a new data source file with this information—be careful not to add trailing spaces after the last typed character in each field. (*Hint:* From the **Mailings** tab, **Start Mail Merge** group, click **Select Recipients**, **Type a New List**. Type the first entry. Click **New Entry** to begin the second entry. Click **OK** to end the list.)

Title	First Name	Last Name	Co...	Address Line 1	Ad...	City	State	ZIP Code
Mr.	Derek	Lohman		1212 Champa Road		Denver	CO	80202
Dr.	Denise	Garcia		420 Sixth Street		Topeka	KS	66607

Do not add trailing spaces after the last typed character in each field! Be sure you are typing information in the correct field—remember to skip the *Company Name* field and the *Address Line 2* field.

7. From the **Save Address List** dialog box, save the data source file as *practice-115-data-label*. The extension "mdb" will be added to the file name automatically.
8. Click **Save** to save the file in the **My Data Sources** folder.
9. In the main label document, click in Cell A1.
10. Insert an address block merge field and highlight it. (*Hint:* From the **Mailings** tab, **Write & Insert Fields** group, click **Address Block**, edit any choices as directed or as needed, and click **OK**; from the **Mailings** tab, **Write & Insert Fields** group, click **Highlight Merge Fields**.)
11. To insert the same ≪*Address Block*≫ placeholder in other cells, do this: From the **Mailings** tab, **Write & Insert Fields** group, click **Update Labels**.

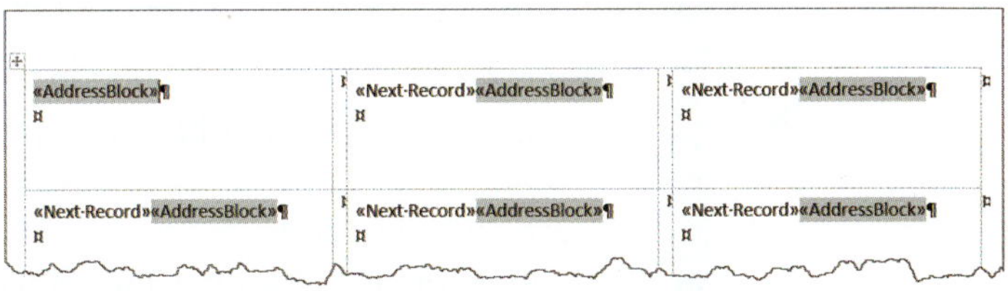

12. To begin the merge process, from the **Mailings** tab, **Preview Results** group, click **Preview Results**; with merge fields highlighted, your labels should look similar to this:

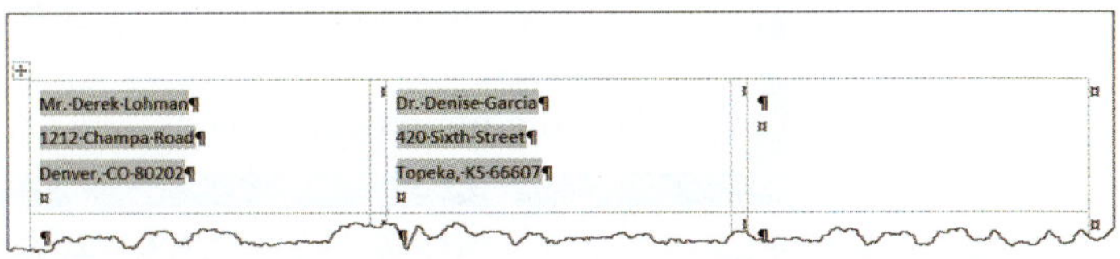

PRACTICE (continued)

13. From the **Mailings** tab, **Finish** group, click **Finish & Merge**, **Edit Individual Documents**.
14. From the **Merge to New Document** dialog box, under **Merge Records**, click **All**, **OK**.
15. Note that a new document containing both merged labels opens with a generic file name, such as *Labels1*.
16. Save the merged labels file as *practice-115-label*. Your merged labels should look similar to this:

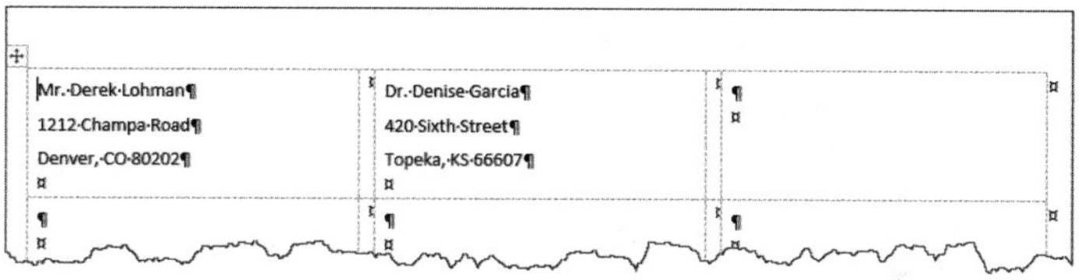

17. Save changes and close all documents; return to GDP.

GO TO Textbook

Using Microsoft Word in the Workplace

APPENDIX **A**

GDP—Word Settings

REFER TO
WM L. 21, Choosing Commands, From the Quick Access Toolbar.

Because you will display and hide the Ruler frequently during this course, consider adding a Ruler checkbox to the Quick Access Toolbar. See Lesson 21 for steps.

NORMAL STYLE

Word 2016's *Normal* style includes a font size of 11, multiple line spacing, and spacing after paragraphs of 8 pt. Word documents in GDP use these formatting defaults:

Font Name and Size	Calibri 12
Line Spacing	Single
Spacing After Paragraphs	0 pt.

Before opening Word documents via GDP, you must set or verify the Word settings outlined in the next few sections. After doing so, Word will behave as expected as you follow steps in this manual to complete Practice exercises and document processing jobs.

STATUS BAR

Page 1 of 1   At: 1"   0 words

Status bar
Vertical Page Position active

In the status bar illustrated on the left, *At: 1"* informs you that the insertion point is positioned 1" from the top of the page.

To display the Vertical Page Position button on the status bar: Point to Word's **Status bar** and right-click; from the **Customize Status Bar** pane, check **Vertical Page Position**.

AUTOCORRECT OPTIONS

Capitalization

REFER TO
L. 26D, Basic Parts of a Business Letter
WM Appendix B, Using GDP for Document Processing, GDP—Reference Initials

Disable the setting for the automatic capitalization of the first letter of a new line to avoid undesired capitalization; for example; if you press ENTER and the first letter of the reference initials in a business letter is automatically capitalized, you need to disable automatic capitalization. (See Appendix B for an example.)

To disable the automatic capitalization of the first letter of a new line:

1. From the **File** tab, click **Options** at the bottom of the pane.
2. From the **Proofing** tab in the left pane, **AutoCorrect options** group, click the **AutoCorrect Options** button.
3. From the **AutoCorrect** dialog box, **AutoCorrect** tab, uncheck **Capitalize first letter of sentences**—your **AutoCorrect** tab settings should look like this. Click **OK** twice to close.

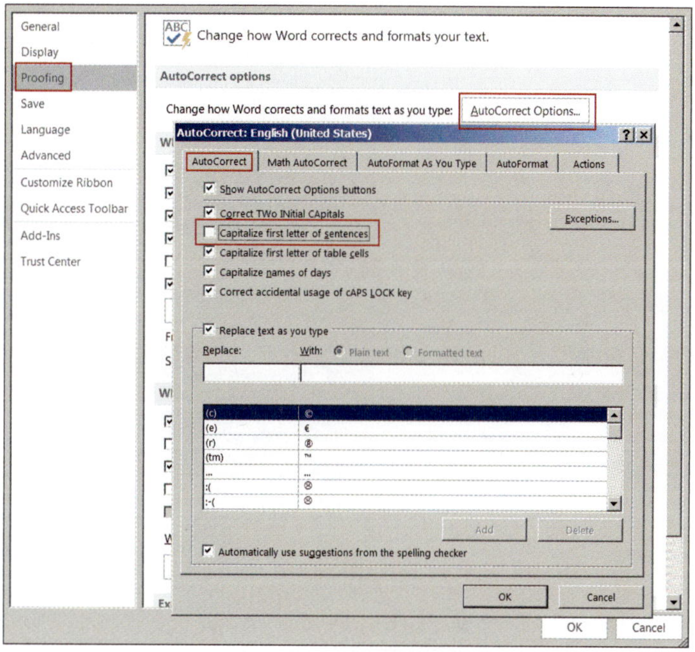

To undo the capitalization of the first letter of a new line immediately after it happens: Press **CTRL+Z**; or from the **Quick Access Toolbar**, click **Undo**.

AUTOFORMAT AS YOU TYPE OPTIONS

To change the **AutoFormat As You Type** options in this section, open the **AutoFormat As You Type** tab as explained next in steps 1–3; then complete the steps that correspond to each option in these sections: Quotes, Hyperlinks, Superscripts, Dashes, and Tabs and Indents.

To open the AutoFormat As You Type tab:

1. From the **File** tab, click **Options** at the bottom of the pane.
2. From the **Proofing** tab in the left pane, **AutoCorrect options** group, click the **AutoCorrect Options** button.
3. From the **AutoCorrect** dialog box, **AutoFormat As You Type** tab, set the options exactly as shown in the next illustration.

When you're finished setting all AutoFormat As You Type options, click OK twice to return to the document. Your AutoFormat As You Type tab should look like this:

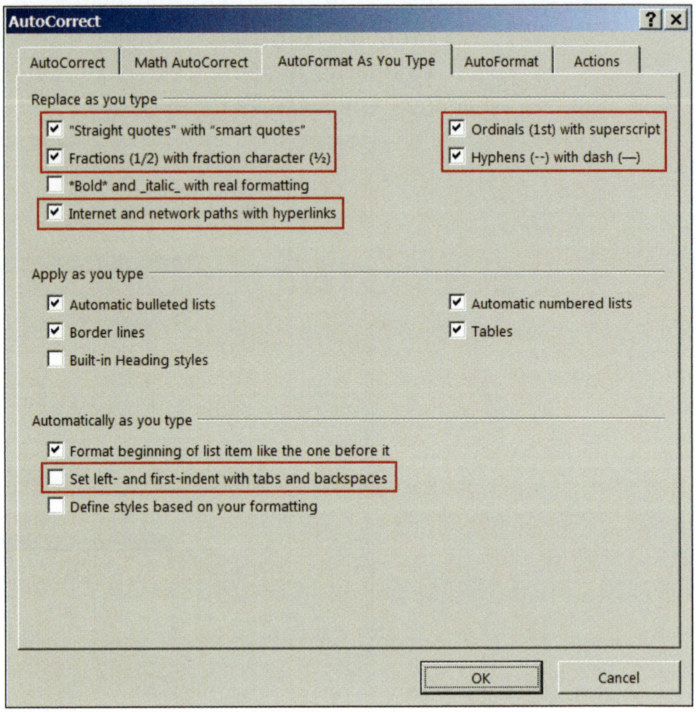

Quotes

Verify that single quotes or double quotes are inserted as *smart quotes* ("curved") automatically. If quotes are inserted as *straight quotes* ("straight"), change this setting:

To replace "straight quotes" with "smart quotes" as you type: Check **"Straight quotes" with "smart quotes."**

Sometimes you need to change a smart quote to a straight quote to type a measurement, such as 1"; to do so, press **CTRL+Z**, or click **Undo** on the **Quick Access Toolbar** immediately after typing the curved quotes.

Hyperlinks

REFER TO
WM L. 49, AutoCorrect—Hyperlink

Internet and network paths will be converted to hyperlinks automatically under certain conditions. If you type an e-mail or Internet address, press the SPACE BAR or press ENTER, an automatic hyperlink should appear. If an automatic hyperlink is not created, change this setting:

To activate automatic hyperlinks as you type: Check **Internet and network paths with hyperlinks**.

To create a manual hyperlink, select the desired text, right-click, click Hyperlink, type the address to be hyperlinked in the address box, and click OK.

It's more convenient to be able to click an active hyperlink than it is to hold done CTRL as you click. If you have to hold down CTRL to follow a hyperlink, change this setting:

To follow a hyperlink with a mouse click:

1. From the **File** tab, click **Options** at the bottom of the pane.
2. From the **Advanced** tab in the left pane, **Editing options** group, uncheck **Use CTRL+Click to follow hyperlink**; click **OK** twice.

Superscripts

If you type an ordinal number such as "1st" or "2nd" and press the SPACE BAR, the ordinals should appear as "1st" and "2nd." If superscripts do *not* appear, follow either of these steps:

To activate automatic hyperlinks as you type: Check **Ordinals (1st) with superscript**.

To create a superscript manually: Select the desired text. Then press **CTRL+SHIFT+=**.

Dashes

If you type text followed by two hyphens (--) followed by more text and then press the SPACE BAR, a solid em dash (—) should appear. If a solid dash does *not* appear, change this setting:

To activate automatic solid em dashes as you type: Check **Hyphens** (--) **with dash** (—).

If two hyphens rather than a solid dash appear between two words you have already typed, click immediately after the second word and press the SPACE BAR 1 time to create a solid dash; delete the extra space.

Tabs and Indents

If you press TAB to indent the first line of the paragraph and then press ENTER and the second paragraph is indented automatically, change this setting:

To stop automatic left- and first indents: Uncheck **Set left- and first-indent with tabs and backspaces**.

REFER TO

WM L. 24, Spelling and Grammar Check

SPELLING AND GRAMMAR CHECK

Word's automatic spelling checker marks typographical errors based on comparisons with a built-in dictionary. A red wavy underline under words flags words that are not in the dictionary and might be misspelled.

Word's automatic grammar checker marks frequently confused words. A blue wavy underline below words flags words that might be used in the wrong context. Only certain options in Word's spelling and grammar checker should be active due to inconsistencies and inaccuracies in some grammar alerts.

To change settings for spelling and grammar checking:

1. From the **File** tab, click **Options** at the bottom of the pane.
2. From the **Proofing** tab in the left pane, **When correcting spelling and grammar in Word** group, check these boxes: **Check spelling as you type** and **Frequently confused words**.
3. Verify that these options are not checked: **Mark grammar errors as you type** and **Check grammar with spelling**; settings should look like this:

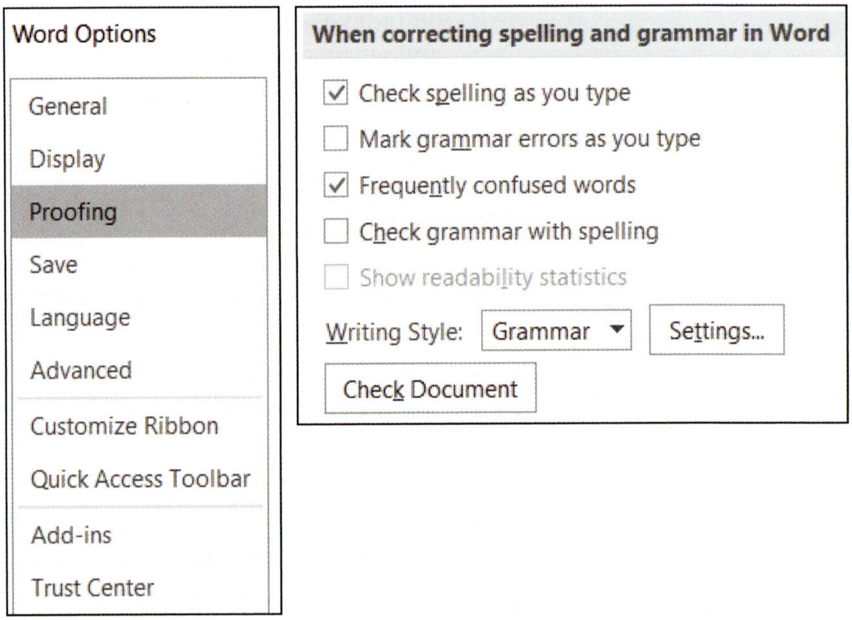

4. Click **OK** twice.

Using GDP for Document Processing

APPENDIX B

GDP features relevant to document processing are introduced on a "need-to-know" basis. Refer to the index below for their order of introduction.

GDP—Feature Index

GDP—Reference Initials

REFER TO
GDP—Help (reference initials)

In Lesson 26, reference initials in business letters are introduced. Because reference initials are unique for each student, GDP must compare the initials the student specifies against the ones typed in the document for scoring purposes. The lowercase initials must match exactly, including capitalization, to avoid a scoring error. See GDP Help for details on entering your unique reference initials.

REFER TO
WM Appendix A, Using Microsoft Word in the Workplace, GDP—Word Settings, AutoCorrect Options, Capitalization

If you press the SPACE BAR or press ENTER after typing your reference initials, and the first letter of your reference initials is automatically capitalized (see "Urs" in the illustration), change the AutoCorrect option to disable automatic capitalization. See Appendix A for steps.

```
Nicole·Hensen↵
Administrative·Assistant¶
¶
Urs¶
¶
Enclosure¶
```

Saving a Word File in PDF Format

Saving a Word file such as a resume or newsletter in a format that doesn't require Word to view and is hard to modify is a good idea. You can convert Word files to PDF format directly from Word without installing a program add in.

To save a Word file in PDF format:

1. From the **File** tab, and click **Export**, **Create PDF/XPS Document**; click the **Create PDF/XPS** button.
2. From the **Publish as PDF or XPS** dialog box, click the list arrow next to the **Save as type** box, and click **PDF** or **PDF (*.pdf)**.
3. Type the desired name in the **File name** box.
4. If you wish to view the PDF file after publishing, check **Open file after publishing**.
5. If the print quality is less important than the file size, under **Optimize for**, click either **Standard (publishing online and printing)** or **Minimum size (publishing online)**.
6. Click **Publish**. (If you checked **Open file after publishing** in step 4, the file should open in a PDF reader.)
7. Close the reader when finished.

Or: From the **File** tab, **Save As**, browse to the desired folder; then follow steps 2–7, starting with "click the list arrow next to the **Save as type** box"; in step 6, click **Save** instead of **Publish**.

Index

Feature	Shortcut
Align, center	CTRL+E
Align, justify	CTRL+J
Align, left	CTRL+L
Align, right	CTRL+R
Bold	CTRL+B
Column break	CTRL+SHIFT+ENTER
Copy	CTRL+C
Cut	CTRL+X
Find and replace—replace	CTRL+H
File, save	CTRL+S
Document, close	CTRL+W
Document, new	CTRL+N
Document, open	CTRL+O
Font, decrease size	CTRL+SHIFT+<
Font, dialog box	CTRL+D
Font, increase size	CTRL+SHIFT+>
Font, italic	CTRL+I
Font, small caps	CTRL+SHIFT+K
Font, underline	CTRL+U
Footnote, insert	CTRL+ALT+F
Formatting, reveal	SHIFT+F1
Formatting, show/hide	CTRL+SHIFT+8
Indent, decrease	CTRL+SHIFT+M
Indent, hanging (begin indent)	CTRL+T
Indent, hanging (end indent)	CTRL+SHIFT+T
Indent, increase	CTRL+M
Line spacing, 1 (single)	CTRL+1

Feature	Shortcut
Line spacing, 1.5 (one and a half)	CTRL+5
Line spacing, 2 (double)	CTRL+2
List, move an item up or down	ALT+SHIFT+↑ ALT+SHIFT+↓
Navigate, beginning of document	CTRL+HOME
Navigate, beginning of line	HOME
Navigate, end of document	CTRL+END
Navigate, end of line	END
Page break (manual)	CTRL+ENTER
Paragraph/line break	SHIFT+ENTER
Paste	CTRL+V
Print	CTRL+P
Print preview	CTRL+P
Redo	CTRL+Y
Select, all	CTRL+A
Superscript	CTRL+SHIFT+
Symbol, í (i acute)	ALT+161
Symbol, ñ (n tilde)	ALT+164
Symbol, ó (o acute)	ALT+162
Table, indent text	CTRL+TAB
Table, move a row up or down	ALT+SHIFT+↑ or ALT+SHIFT+↓
Table, move to next cell	TAB
Table, move to previous cell	SHIFT+TAB
Spelling and grammar check	F7
Undo	CTRL+Z
Windows, switch	ALT+TAB
Word, close	ALT+F4
Word, close file	CTRL+F4